WORKSHOP MANUAL No. II

FOR

Motorcycles

SPEED TWIN 1945-1955

TIGER 100 1945-1955

THUNDERBIRD 1950-1955

TIGER 110 1954-1955

TROPHY 1949-1955

3T DE LUXE 1945-1951

MODELS

1945 — 1955

A Floyd Clymer Publication
This edition published in 2024 by
www.VelocePress.com

All rights reserved. This work may not be reproduced
or transmitted in any form without the express written
consent of the publisher

INTRODUCTION

Welcome to the world of digital publishing ~ the book you now hold in your hand was printed using the latest state of the art digital technology. The advent of print-on-demand has forever changed the publishing process, never has information been so accessible and it is our hope that this book serves your informational needs for years to come. If this is your first exposure to digital publishing, we hope that you are pleased with the results. Many more titles of interest to the classic automobile and motorcycle enthusiast, collector and restorer are available via our website at www.VelocePress.com. We hope that you find this title as interesting as we do.

NOTE FROM THE PUBLISHER

The information presented is true and complete to the best of our knowledge. All recommendations are made without any guarantees on the part of the author or the publisher, who also disclaim all liability incurred with the use of this information.

TRADEMARKS

We recognize that some words, model names and designations, for example, mentioned herein are the property of the trademark holder. We use them for identification purposes only. This is not an official publication.

INFORMATION ON THE USE OF THIS PUBLICATION

This manual is an invaluable resource for those interested in performing their own maintenance. However, in today's information age we are constantly subject to changes in common practice, new technology, availability of improved materials and increased awareness of chemical toxicity. As such, it is advised that the user consult with an experienced professional prior to undertaking any procedure described herein. While every care has been taken to ensure correctness of information, it is obviously not possible to guarantee complete freedom from errors or omissions or to accept liability arising from such errors or omissions. Therefore, any individual that uses the information contained within, or elects to perform or participate in do-it-yourself repairs or modifications acknowledges that there is a risk factor involved and that the publisher or its associates cannot be held responsible for personal injury or property damage resulting from the use of the information or the outcome of such procedures.

WARNING!

One final word of advice, this publication is intended to be used as a reference guide, and when in doubt the reader should consult with a qualified technician.

INTRODUCTION

This Workshop Manual has been compiled to enable the owner to service his motorcycle and thoroughly to understand its mechanism. The book is written on a practical basis and no attempt has been made to introduce the theoretical side.

Although the book is comprehensive in its instruction regarding major overhauls, we strongly advise the uninitiated to entrust such work as the repair of engines, spring wheel, telescopic forks and gearboxes, to a recognised Triumph Dealer who will have the necessary facilities and special workshop tools available. Remember that the purchase of special tools can be very expensive when only required for limited use.

Each section of the book is headed by a general description. It is then followed by a complete account of the dismantling, inspection and re-assembly of units and final assembly. This has been compiled in the most simple form to obviate any difficulties on the part of the operator, who may be a newcomer to motorcycling or not fully conversant with repair procedure. Each chapter deals with a specific operation (i.e. Dismantling the Engine) which is then broken down into sub-paragraphs. The sequence in which they are broken down is the correct dismantling and assembly procedure. To avoid confusing the operator during this procedure, the sub-assemblies (i.e. Cylinder Head or Crankshaft Assembly) are dealt with as separate units under the heading "Dismantling, Preparation and Assembly of Units".

The book is well illustrated with exploded and assembled illustrations of the main units, which will give the operator a comprehensive view of the internal parts before commencing an operation and will also assist during assembly.

Finally, remember that if the essential adjustments are neglected and only casual attention is paid to the lubrication and periodical maintenance, reliability will be affected and in time the servicing costs will be very high.

A supplement is included at the back of this Workshop Manual and should always be referred to before any operations are carried out on the machine.

If additional information is required, please consult a Triumph Distributor or Dealer who will always be pleased to assist. Should any difficulty then arise, write to the Triumph Service Department quoting the model and full engine number. The latter is stamped on the left hand crankcase just below the cylinder base flange as shown in the example below.

EXAMPLE — 6T-93264

SERVICE ARRANGEMENTS

CORRESPONDENCE

Technical Advice, Guarantee Claims and Repairs

Communications dealing with any of these subjects should be addressed to the **SERVICE MANAGER.**

Replacement Parts

Orders for replacement parts should be addressed to the **SPARES MANAGER.**

> In all communications the full engine number complete with all prefix letters and figures should be stated. This number will be found on the L.H. side of the crankcase just below the cylinder flange.

ORDERS

Orders should always be sent to us in the form of a list and not in letter form. Owners are strongly advised to purchase a Spare Parts List so that the correct part numbers can be quoted. These lists contain numerous exploded drawings and cross references which make it very easy to recognise the various parts and are also of great assistance in servicing the model. The specimen order which is printed in the Spare Parts List should be used as a guide.

TECHNICAL ADVICE

Owners will appreciate how very difficult it is to diagnose trouble by correspondence and this is made impossible in many cases because the information sent to us is so scanty. Every possible point which may have some bearing on the matter should be stated so that we can send a useful and detailed reply.

REPAIRS

Before a motorcycle is sent to our Works an appointment must be made. This can be done by letter or telephone. When an owner wishes to return his machine for guarantee repairs, he should first consult his dealer as we do not normally accept machines in our Repair Shop until the Dealer has inspected them. Frequently the Dealer can overcome the trouble without the delay and expense of sending the machine to the Works. This avoids the machine being out of use for some days when it could be on the road. Where parts such as cylinders, petrol tanks, etc., are forwarded for repair, they should be packed securely so as to avoid damage in transit. The owner's name and address should be enclosed together with full instructions. In the case of complete motorcycles, a label showing the owner's name and address should always be attached and all accessories such as tools, inflator, handlebar mirrors and other parts removed.

PROPRIETARY FITTINGS

Ancillary equipment which is fitted to our motorcycles is of the highest quality and is guaranteed by the manufacturers and not by ourselves. Any repairs or claims should be sent to the actual maker, or one of their accredited agents who will always give owners every possible assistance. The following are the addresses of the various manufacturers.

Carburetters ... ... Amal Ltd.,
Holdford Road, Witton,
Birmingham, 6.

S.U. Carburetter Co. Ltd.,
Wood Lane, Erdington.
Birmingham, 24.

Chains ... ... Renold Chains Ltd.,
Wythenshawe, Manchester.

Electrical Equipment ... ... J. Lucas Ltd.,
Great Hampton Street,
Birmingham, 18.

Rear Suspension ... ... Girling Ltd.,
King's Road, Tyseley,
Birmingham, 11.

Sparking Plugs ... ... Champion Sparking Plugs Co. Ltd.,
Feltham, Middlesex.

K.L.G. Sparking Plugs Ltd.,
Cricklewood Works,
London, N.W.2.

Lodge Plugs Ltd.,
Rugby,
Warwickshire.

Speedometers ... ... Smith's Motor Accessories Ltd.,
Cricklewood Works,
London, N.W.2.

Tyres ... ... Dunlop Rubber Company Ltd.,
Fort Dunlop,
Birmingham, 24.

Technical Data

SPEED TWIN (5T) TECHNICAL DATA

ENGINE
Type	O.H.V. Twin
B.H.P. and R.P.M.	27 at 6,300
Bore	2.48 ins. (63 mm.)
Stroke	3.15 ins. (80 mm.)
Capacity	30.5 cu. in. (498 c.c.)
Compression Ratio	7 : 1
Valve Clearance (Cold)	0.010 in. (0.26 mm.)

Valve Timing:—(with .020 in. Tappet clearance for checking)

Inlet Valve opens B.T.C.	$26\frac{1}{2}°$
Inlet Valve closes A.B.C.	$69\frac{1}{2}°$
Exhaust Valve opens B.B.C.	$61\frac{1}{2}°$
Exhaust Valve closes A.T.C.	$35\frac{1}{2}°$

IGNITION
Distributor Contact Point Gap	0.014″-0.016″ (0.36-0.40 mm.)
Sparking Plugs (Champion)	L10S
Distributor Range	15°
Sparking Plug Gap	0.020″ (0.50 mm.)

Ignition Timing (Fully Retarded):—

Crankshaft position	7° B.T.C.
Piston position	$\frac{1}{32}$″ (0.8 mm.) B.T.C.

CARBURETTER
Type	Amal Monobloc
Main Jet	200
Needle Jet	.1065
Needle Position	3
Throttle Valve	$376/3\frac{1}{2}$
Pilot Jet	30

Technical Data

TRANSMISSION
Gearbox—Type		Positive selection (Foot operated)
Speeds		Four
Gear Ratios	Solo	Sidecar
4th—Top	5.00	5.80
3rd—Third	5.95	6.90
2nd—Second	8.45	9.80
1st—Bottom	12.20	14.15

CLUTCH
Type ... Cork in Oil

SPROCKETS
	Solo	Sidecar
Engine	22 teeth	19 teeth
Gearbox	18 teeth	18 teeth
Clutch	43 teeth	43 teeth
Rear Wheel	46 teeth	46 teeth

CHAIN
Primary-Front-Pitch	½" × .335" × .305"
Links	70 Solo 69 Sidecar
Secondary-Rear-Pitch	⅝" × .400" × ⅜"
Links	100

CAPACITIES
Fuel Tank	4 galls. (18 litres)
Oil Tank	6 pints (3.4 litres)
Gearbox	1 pint (.6 litres)
Primary Chaincase	⅓ pint (.2 litres)

TYRE SIZES
Front	3.25 × 19 in.
Rear	3.50 × 19 in.

SUSPENSION
Front	Telescopic
Rear	Swinging Fork

BRAKES
Type	Internal expanding
Front and Rear Diameter	7 ins. (17.78 cm.)

OVERALL DIMENSIONS
Seat Height	30.5 ins. (77.5 cm.)
Wheel Base	55.75 ins. (141.6 cm.)
Length	85.5 ins. (217 cm.)
Width	28.5 ins. (72 cm.)
Ground Clearance	5 ins. (12.7 cm.)

WEIGHT
Unladen ... 380 lbs. (173 kilos)

Technical Data

THUNDERBIRD (6T) TECHNICAL DATA

ENGINE
Type	O.H.V. Twin
B.H.P. at R.P.M.	34 at 6300
Bore	2.79 ins. (71 mm.)
Stroke	3.23 ins. (82 mm.)
Capacity	40 cu. in. (649 c.c.)
Compression Ratio	7 : 1
Valve Clearance (Cold)	0.010 in. (0.26 mm.)

Valve Timing:—(with .020 in. Tappet clearance for checking)

Inlet Valve opens B.T.C.	$26\frac{1}{2}°$
Inlet Valve closes A.B.C.	$69\frac{1}{2}°$
Exhaust Valve opens B.B.C.	$61\frac{1}{2}°$
Exhaust Valve closes A.T.C.	$35\frac{1}{2}°$

IGNITION
Distributor Contact Point Gap	0.014″–0.016″ (0.36–0.40 mm.)
Distributor Range	15°
Sparking Plugs	Champion L10S
Sparking Plug Gap	0.020″ (0.50 mm.)

Ignition Timing (Fully Retarded):

Crankshaft position	6° B.T.C.
Piston position	$\frac{1}{32}″$ (0.8 mm.) B.T.C.

CARBURETTER
Type	S.U. M.C.2
Needle	M.9

TRANSMISSION
Gearbox—type	Positive selection (Foot operated)

Technical Data

	Solo	Sidecar
Speeds	Four	
Gear Ratios	Solo	Sidecar
4th—Top	4.57	5.24
3rd—Third	5.45	6.24
2nd—Second	7.75	8.85
1st—Bottom	11.20	12.80

CLUTCH
Type ... Cork in Oil

SPROCKETS

	Solo	Sidecar
Engine	24 teeth	21 teeth
Gearbox	18 teeth	18 teeth
Clutch	43 teeth	43 teeth
Rear Wheel	46 teeth	46 teeth

CHAIN

Primary-Front-Pitch	$\frac{1}{2}'' \times .335'' \times .305''$
Links	70
Secondary-Rear-Pitch	$\frac{5}{8}'' \times .400'' \times \frac{3}{8}''$
Links	101 Solo 100 Sidecar

CAPACITIES

Fuel Tank	4 galls.	(18 litres)
Oil Tank	6 pints	(3.4 litres)
Gearbox	1 pint	(.6 litres)
Primary Chaincase	$\frac{1}{3}$ pint	(.2 litres)

TYRE SIZE
Front ... 3.25 × 19 in.
Rear ... 3.50 × 19 in.

SUSPENSION
Front ... Telescopic
Rear ... Swinging Fork

BRAKES
Type ... Internal Expanding
Front and Rear Diameter ... 7 ins. (17.78 cm.)

OVERALL DIMENSIONS

Seat Height	30.5 ins.	(77.5 cm.)
Wheel Base	55.75 ins.	(141.6 cm.)
Length	85.5 ins.	(217 cm.)
Width	28.5 ins.	(72 cm.)
Ground Clearance	5 ins.	(12.7 cm.)

WEIGHT
Unladen ... 385 lbs. (175 kilos)

Technical Data

TROPHY (TR5) TECHNICAL DATA

ENGINE
Type	O.H.V. Twin
B.H.P. at R.P.M.	33 at 6500
Bore	2.48 ins. (63 mm.)
Stroke	3.15 ins. (80 mm.)
Capacity	3.05 cu. in. (498 c.c.)
Compression Ratio	8 : 1
Valve Clearance (Cold): Inlet	.002 in. (.05 mm.)
Exhaust	.004 in. (.10 mm.)

Valve Timing:—(with .020 in. Tappet clearance for checking)

Inlet Valve opens B.T.C.	27°
Inlet Valve closes A.B.C.	48°
Exhaust Valve opens B.B.C.	48°
Exhaust Valve closes A.T.C.	27°

IGNITION
Magneto Contact Point Gap	.012″ (.3 mm.)
Sparking Plugs (Champion)	NA10
Sparking Plug Gap	.015″-.018″ (.4 mm.-.5 mm.)

Timing (Fully Advanced):—

Crankshaft position	41° B.T.C.
Piston position	$\frac{15}{32}$″ (12 mm.) B.T.C.

CARBURETTER
Type	Amal Monobloc
Main Jet	220
Needle Jet	.1065
Needle Position	3
Throttle Valve	376/3½
Pilot Jet	25

TRANSMISSION
Gearbox—Type	Positive selection (Foot operated)

Technical Data

Speeds ...	Four
Gear Ratios:—	
4th—Top ...	5.24
3rd—Third ...	6.24
2nd—Second ...	8.85
1st—Bottom ...	12.80

CLUTCH
Type ...	Cork in Oil

SPROCKETS
Engine ...	21 teeth
Gearbox ...	18 teeth
Clutch ...	43 teeth
Rear Wheel ...	46 teeth

CHAIN
Primary-Front-Pitch ...	$\frac{1}{2}'' \times .335'' \times .305''$
Links ...	70
Secondary-Rear-Pitch ...	$\frac{5}{8}'' \times .400 \times \frac{3}{8}''$
Links ...	100

CAPACITIES
Fuel Tank ...	3 galls.	(13.68 litres)
Oil Tank ...	6 pints	(3.4 litres)
Gearbox ...	1 pint	(.6 litres)
Primary Chaincase ...	$\frac{1}{3}$ pint	(.2 litres)

TYRE SIZE
Front ...	3.00 × 20 in.
Rear ...	4.00 × 18 in.

SUSPENSION
Front ...	Telescopic
Rear ...	Swinging Fork

BRAKES
Type ...	Internal Expanding
Front and Rear Diameter ...	7 ins. (17.78 cm.)

OVERALL DIMENSIONS
Seat Height ...	30.5 ins.	(77.5 cm.)
Wheel Base ...	55.75 ins.	(141.6 cm.)
Length ...	85.5 ins.	(217 cm.)
Width ...	28.5 ins.	(72 cm.)
Ground Clearance ...	5.5 ins.	(14 cm.)

WEIGHT
Unladen ...	365 lbs.	(165 kilos)

Technical Data

TIGER 100 (T100) TECHNICAL DATA

ENGINE
Type	O.H.V. Twin
B.H.P. at R.P.M.	32 at 6500
Bore	2.48 ins. (63 mm.)
Stroke	3.15 ins. (80 mm.)
Capacity	30.5 cu. in. (498 c.c.)
Compression Ratio	8 : 1
Valve Clearance (Cold)	.010 in. (0.26 mm.)

Valve Timing:—(with .020 in. Tappet clearance for checking)
Inlet Valve opens B.T.C.	$26\frac{1}{2}°$
Inlet Valve closes A.B.C.	$69\frac{1}{2}°$
Exhaust Valve opens B.B.C.	$61\frac{1}{2}°$
Exhaust Valve closes A.T.C.	$35\frac{1}{2}°$

IGNITION
Magneto Contact Point Gap	.012″ (.3 mm.)
Sparking Plugs (Champion)	NA10
Sparking Plug Gap	.015″–.018″ (.4 mm.–.5 mm.)

Timing (Fully Advanced):—
Crankshaft position	37° B.T.C.
Piston position	$\frac{3}{8}″$ (9.5 mm.) B.T.C.

CARBURETTER
Type	Amal Monobloc
Main Jet	220
Needle Jet	.1065
Needle Position	3
Throttle Valve	$376/3\frac{1}{2}$
Pilot Jet	25

TRANSMISSION
Gearbox—Type	Positive selection (Foot operated)

	Solo	Sidecar
Speeds ...	Four	
Gear Ratios:—		
4th—Top ...	5.00	5.80
3rd—Third ...	5.95	6.90
2nd—Second ...	8.45	9.80
1st—Bottom ...	12.20	14.15

CLUTCH
Type ... Cork in Oil

SPROCKETS

	Solo	Sidecar
Engine ...	22 teeth	19 teeth
Gearbox ...	18 teeth	18 teeth
Clutch ...	43 teeth	43 teeth
Rear Wheel ...	46 teeth	46 teeth

CHAIN
Primary-Front-Pitch ... $\tfrac{1}{2}" \times .335" \times .305"$
Links ... 70 Solo 69 Sidecar
Secondary-Rear-Pitch ... $\tfrac{5}{8}" \times .400" \times \tfrac{3}{8}"$
Links ... 100

CAPACITIES
Fuel Tank ... 4 galls. (18 litres)
Oil Tank ... 6 pints (3.4 litres)
Gearbox ... 1 pint (.6 litres)
Primary Chaincase ... $\tfrac{1}{3}$ pint (.2 litres)

TYRE SIZES
Front ... 3.25 × 19 in.
Rear ... 3.50 × 19 in.

SUSPENSION
Front ... Telescopic
Rear ... Swinging Fork

BRAKES
Type ... Internal Expanding
Front Diameter ... 8 ins. (20.32 cm.)
Rear Diameter ... 7 ins. (17.78 cm.)

OVERALL DIMENSIONS
Seat Height ... 30.5 ins. (77.5 cm.)
Wheel Base ... 55.75 ins. (141.6 cm.)
Length ... 85.5 ins. (217 cm.)
Width ... 28.5 ins. (72 cm.)
Ground Clearance ... 5 ins. (12.7 cm.)

WEIGHT
Unladen ... 375 lbs. (170 kilos)

Technical Data

TIGER 110 (T110) TECHNICAL DATA

ENGINE
Type	O.H.V. Twin
B.H P. at R.P.M.	42 at 6500
Bore	2.79 ins. (71 mm.)
Stroke	3.23 ins. (82 mm.)
Capacity	40 cu. in. (649 c.c.)
Compression Ratio	8.5 : 1

Valve Clearance (Cold):—
Inlet	0.002 in. (.05 mm.)
Exhaust	0.004 in. (.10 mm.)

Valve Timing:—(with .020 in. Tappet clearance for checking)
Inlet Valve opens B.T.C.	27°
Inlet Valve closes A.B.C.	48°
Exhaust Valve opens B.B.C.	48°
Exhaust Valve closes A.T.C.	27°

IGNITION
Magneto Contact Point Gap	.012" (.3 mm.)
Sparking Plugs (Champion)	L11S
Sparking Plug Gap	.015"-.018"(.4 mm.-.5 mm.)

Timing (Fully Advanced):—
Crankshaft position	35° B.T.C.
Piston position	$\tfrac{23}{64}$" (9.2 mm.) B.T.C.

CARBURETTER
Type	Amal Monobloc
Main Jet	250*
Needle Jet	.1065
Needle Position	3
Throttle Valve	376/3½
Pilot Jet	25

* For maximum performance detach air cleaner rubber hose and fit 270 Main Jet and LA11 Plugs.

TRANSMISSION

	Solo	Sidecar
Gearbox—Type	Positive selection (Foot operated)	
Speeds	Four	
Gear Ratios:—		
4th—Top	4.57	5.24
3rd—Third	5.45	6.24
2nd—Bottom	7.75	8.85
1st—Bottom	11.20	12.80

CLUTCH

Type ... Cork in Oil

SPROCKETS

	Solo	Sidecar
Engine	24 teeth	21 teeth
Gearbox	18 teeth	18 teeth
Clutch	43 teeth	43 teeth
Rear Wheel	46 teeth	46 teeth

CHAIN

Primary-Front-Pitch	$\frac{1}{2}'' \times .335'' \times .305''$
Links	70
Secondary-Rear-Pitch	$\frac{5}{8}'' \times .400'' \times \frac{3}{8}''$
Links	101 solo 100 sidecar

CAPACITIES

Fuel Tank	4 galls.	(18 litres)
Oil Tank	6 pints	(3.4 litres)
Gearbox	1 pint	(.6 litres)
Primary Chaincase	$\frac{1}{3}$ pint	(.2 litres)

TYRE SIZES

Front	3.25 × 19 in.
Rear	3.50 × 19 in.

SUSPENSION

Front	Telescopic
Rear	Swinging Fork

BRAKES

Type	Internal Expanding
Front Diameter	8 ins. (20.32 cm.)
Rear Diameter	7 ins. (17.78 cm.)

OVERALL DIMENSIONS

Seat Height	30.5 ins. (77.5 cm.)
Wheel Base	55.75 ins. (141.6 cm.)
Length	85.5 ins. (217 cm.)
Width	28.5 ins. (72 cm.)
Ground Clearance	5 ins. (12.7 cm.)

WEIGHT

Unladen ... 395 lbs. (179 kilos)

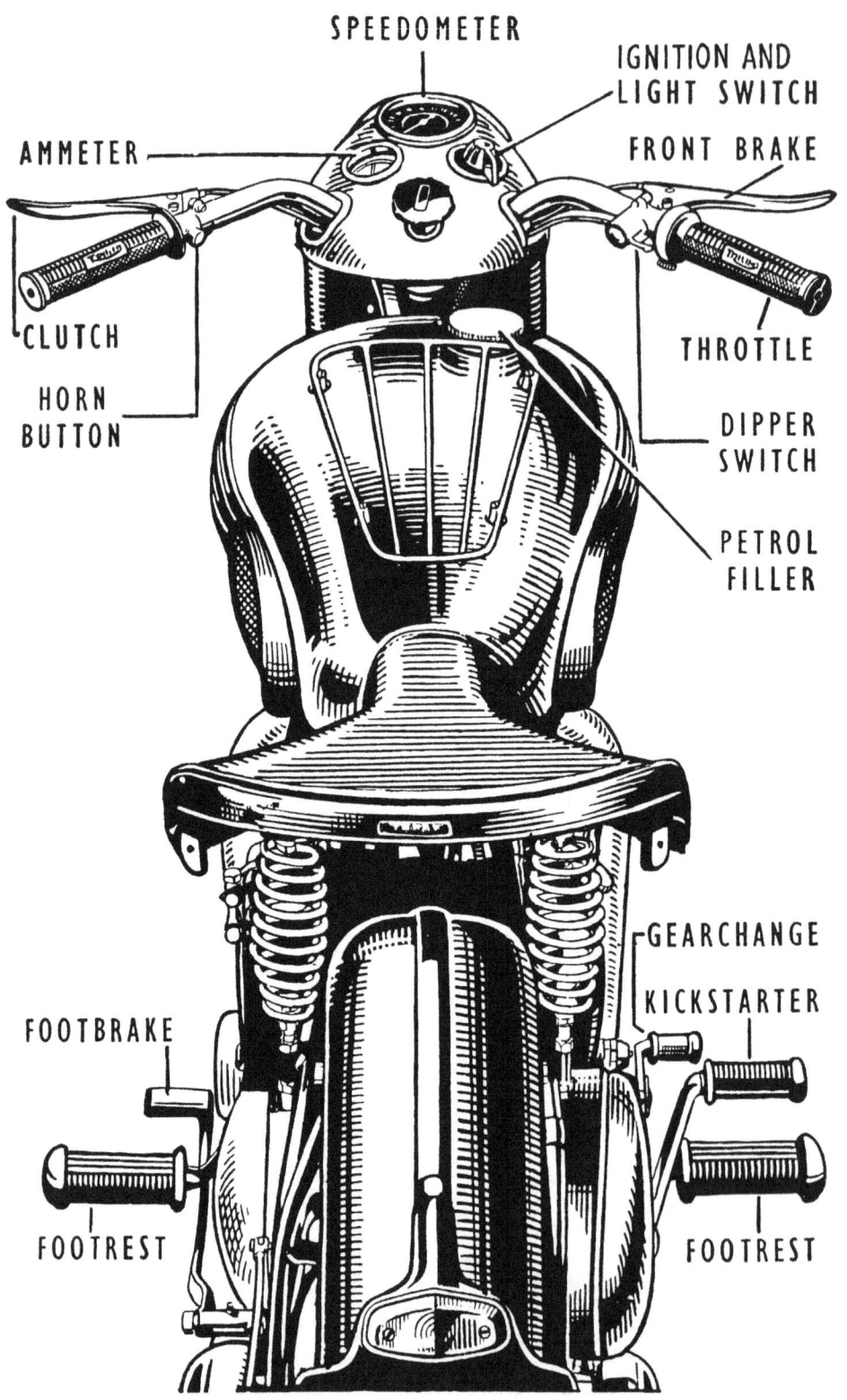

FIG. I. CONTROL LAYOUT

CONTROLS—INSTRUMENTS

The position and application of the controls is explained by assuming that the rider is sitting on the machine.

As the layout is not identical on all machines, differences will be shown by inserting the model type after the caption.

Clutch Lever. On the left portion of the handlebar. The clutch lever should not be operated when the machine is in motion except to change gear and when bringing the machine to a halt.

Front Brake Lever. On the right portion of the handlebar. Always apply gentle pressure to the lever and use in conjunction with the rear brake.

Throttle Control. This is a twistgrip operated by the right hand. Twist the grip towards you to open and away from you to close.

Magneto Control Lever (TR5, T100 & T110). On the left hand portion of the handlebar. Close the lever (anti-clockwise) to advance the magneto spark and open (clockwise) to retard.

Carburetter Air Control Lever (TR5). On the right hand portion of the handlebar. Pull (clockwise) to open air valve.

Horn Button. Fitted to the left portion of the handlebar. Push to operate.

Headlamp Dipper Switch. Fitted to the right portion of the handlebar. Depress or raise the switch lever to operate.

Ignition Cut-Out Button (TR5). Fitted to the left portion of the handlebar. Depress to stop engine running.

The Trophy (TR5) model is fitted with a detachable headlamp in lieu of the nacelle type to enable quick removal for sporting events.

Speedometer. Registers speed, trip and total mileage. Where a speedometer and revolution counter combined is fitted, the central figures indicate in hundreds the engine revolutions in 2nd, 3rd and top gears. Illumination of the speedometer for night riding is controlled by the main lighting switch.

Speedometer (TR5). This is mounted on the fork top lug and its operation is as that listed above.

Lighting Switch (T100 & T110). Turn the lever to operate. Switch positions:—
      OFF ... ... ALL LIGHTS OFF
      L ... ... TAIL AND PARKING LIGHT ON
      H ... ... TAIL AND HEADLIGHT ON

The TR5 lighting switch is fitted into the headlamp but the switch positions are identical.

Lighting and Ignition Switch (5T & 6T). Turn the lever to operate light. Switch positions:—

    O   ...   .   ALL LIGHTS OFF
    P   ...   .   TAIL AND PARKING LIGHT ON
    H   ...   .   TAIL AND HEADLIGHT ON

Ignition Switch:—
    CENTRAL   ... ... IGNITION OFF
    IGN ... ... IGNITION ON (NORMAL)
    *EMG ... ... IGNITION ON (EMERGENCY)

See page 167 before using this switch position.

Ammeter. This indicates the changing rate of either the dynamo or the alternator when the engine is running, and the amount of discharge when the lights are "ON" and engine stopped.

Ignition Cut-Out Button (T100 & T110). This button is centrally disposed in the nacelle and when depressed the ignition to the sparking plugs is "CUT-OUT". This is done by earthing the magneto primary circuit.

Steering Damper. Turn the damper knob clockwise to increase damping. The TR5 damper knob is in the same relative position, the operating rod passing through the head lug in all cases.

OIL PRESSURE INDICATOR

The indicator button operates through the oil pressure release valve, which is situated in the timing cover. When the engine is running the indicator button MUST protrude to ensure that oil is being fed to the crankshaft

CARBURETTER AIR CONTROL (AMAL)
(5T, T100 & T110)

The air control lever is located on the frame back stay (L.H.) immediately behind the saddle. Turn the lever away from the stop to open the air valve.

CARBURETTER MIXTURE CONTROL (S.U.)
(6T)

The mixture control lever is fitted to the base of the carburetter and connects to the jet. To enrich the fuel mixture raise the lever, and for normal running depress the lever to its lowest point (See page 155 for further information).

FOOT CONTROLS

Footbrake. A flat pedal in front of the left footrest. Depress to operate. The first application should be applied gently and then pressure increased as the road speed decreases.

Gearchange. A small foot lever in front of the right hand footrest. The lever is moved "DOWN" to select a low gear and "UP" to select a higher gear. The gear selected is indicated by a finger and indicator plate on the gearbox front. The neutral position is between 1st and 2nd gear and the marking "N" on the indicator plate denotes the selection position.

Kickstarter. This is behind the right hand footrest. All models have the fixed pedal type with the exception of the TR5; this model has the folding pedal type.

ADJUSTMENT OF CONTROLS AND RIDING POSITION

When first taking over the machine, the rider should re-adjust the various controls to suit his own individual requirements.

Footrests. The left footrest is located by two pegs and may be placed in three different positions. The right footrest is mounted on a taper, on the rigid frame models, and may be placed in any desired position. The right footrest is non-adjustable on the swinging arm frame models. After adjustment ensure that the nuts are tightened securely.

Gearchange Lever. This is fitted to a serrated shaft. To re-position, slacken off the setscrew and ease the lever off the serrations. Replace in a convenient position and tighten up the set-screw.

Footbrake Pedal. This pedal is adjustable on the Rigid Frame Models simply by adjusting the stop screw which is located on the brake pedal spindle lug. After making an adjustment, it may be necessary to re-adjust the rear brake (see page 108).

Handlebars. Adjustment is made by slackening off the four "U" bolt nuts and turning the handlebar to the desired position. The TR5 handlebar is clipped to the top lug by four set-screws and by releasing these the handlebar can be adjusted in a similar manner. Ensure that either set-screws or nuts are securely tightened to avoid handlebar slip.

Control Levers. If the clamping screws which secure the lever assemblies to the handlebar are slackened, the control can be moved to suit the rider's preference. (Air lever positioned on rear frame back stays below the saddle on Models 5T, T100 & T110).

Twinseat. This item cannot be adjusted for height, but has been so designed to suit the average rider.

When placing a machine with Swinging Arm rear springing on the prop stand, pull the rear of the machine upwards. If this is not done the rear suspension units will eventually extend against the damping and the movement may cause the machine to fall over.

CONTROL CABLES
ADJUSTMENT POSITIONS

Throttle Cable (5T, T100, TR5 & T110). The adjuster is located in the cable, approximately 12" from the twistgrip.

6T. Here the adjustment is made on the right side of the S.U. carburetter.

Starting

Air Cable (5T, T100 & T110). Adjust the cable abutment screw located in the carburetter top.

TR5	...	...	No adjustment
6T	...	...	Not fitted

Magneto Cable (TR5, T100 & T110). Raise the rubber sleeve where the cable enters the magneto when the adjuster can be turned after slackening off the locknut.

Clutch Cable. Adjustment is made at the lower portion of the cable immediately above the gearbox casing. (See page 91 for further details).

Front Brake Cable. An adjustable thumb nut is located on the anchor plate on all models.

TAKING OVER THE MACHINE

After taking delivery of the machine and before taking it on the road, carefully check that the oil tank, primary chaincase and gearbox levels are correct (See page 25). Ensure that the battery is in a charged condition, "topped up" to the correct level and the battery connections secured.

The tyres should be checked with a pressure gauge and if necessary adjusted in accordance with the instructions on page 139. Fill the petrol tank with a premium grade of fuel and the machine is ready for starting.

Although each machine is thoroughly checked before leaving the Works or Distributors for the security of all nuts, bolts, etc., it is advisable after the first 100 miles to re-check and again at 500 miles. This is a necessary precaution due to the bedding down of the engine and motorcycle parts.

STARTING THE ENGINE (COLD)

For machines fitted with the Amal Carburetter

Engage the gearbox in the neutral (N) position.

Turn the petrol tap ON.

Lift the clutch lever and depress the kickstarter two or three times to separate the clutch plates.

In very cold weather it may be necessary to close the air lever (move towards stop to close).

Partly retard the magneto spark by turning the control lever away from the closed position (clockwise).

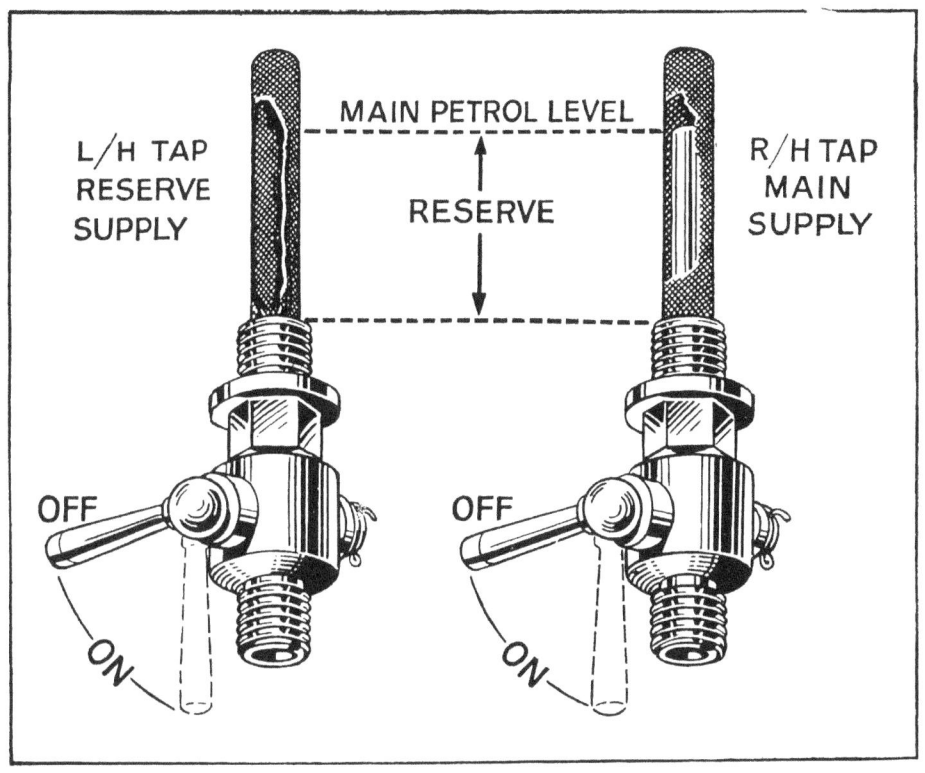

Fitted to Models TR5, T100 and T110—Turn on the L/H tap after the supply from the R/H tap is exhausted.

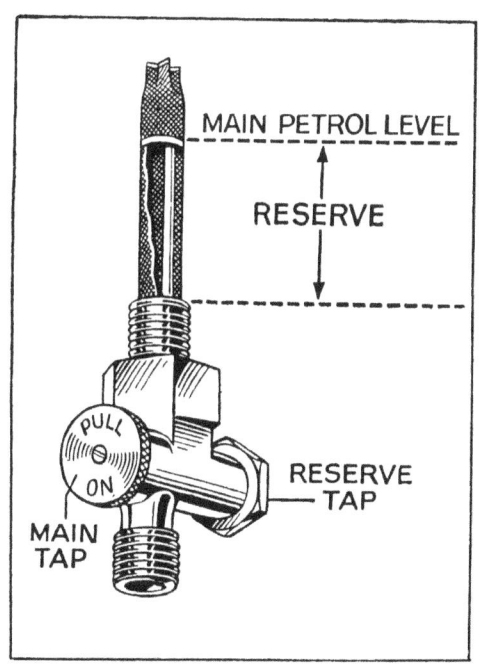

Fitted to 5T and 6T—Pull out the hexagon headed plunger for reserve supply. The main tap plunger **MUST** be left in **ON** position.

Fig. 2. PETROL TAP POSITIONS

Starting

Flood the carburetter by depressing the tickler on the lid of the float bowl until the base of the carburetter is just wet. Do not flood the carburetter until the petrol streams out of the air vent holes in the float bowl lid as this may cause difficult starting.

Turn the engine over until compression can be felt on one cylinder. Re-position the kickstarter pedal to almost the horizontal position by freeing the clutch.

On the 5T model, switch the ignition key to the "IGN" position (other Amal equipped machines are fitted with magneto ignition).

Open the throttle slightly by turning the twistgrip about $\frac{1}{8}$ turn and then depress the kickstarter pedal smartly when the engine should fire immediately. A second or third kick may be necessary if the controls are incorrectly set.

Failure to start the 5T model may be due to a flat battery, in this case turn the ignition key to "EMG" which is the emergency start position. Depress the kickstarter when the engine will fire. Once the engine is running the ignition key MUST be returned to the "IGN" position, as the engine should not be run longer than is absolutely necessary in the "EMG" position. (For special running conditions on the "EMG" circuit see page 167).

When the engine starts the air lever can be fully opened as it warms up. It is particularly important to open the air lever as soon as possible, otherwise the mixture strength may be too rich and the oil on the cylinder walls will be washed off, causing harmful results.

Under no circumstances allow the engine to "idle" when cold. The throttle should be adjusted to a fast "tickover" in order to warm the oil rapidly and ensure good circulation. This precaution will reduce cylinder wear.

Finally, attention must be paid to the oil pressure indicator immediately the engine starts. The indicator button MUST protrude from the release valve cap. If the button does not protrude, stop the engine at once and investigate the failure (See page 28).

Always turn the petrol taps "OFF" when parking the machine.

STARTING THE ENGINE (COLD)

For machines fitted with the S.U. Carburetter

Select the neutral (N) position in the Gearbox.

Turn the main petrol tap ON; when not in use turn it OFF.

Lift the clutch lever and depress the kickstarter two or three times to separate the clutch plates.

On the left side of the carburetter is the jet lever and to increase the mixture strength for a COLD start raise the lever. No predetermined position can be stated owing to the different starting characteristics of the various engines, but the rider will soon find the most suitable lever position. The lever should be put in the lowest position when the engine is warm.

Turn the engine over by the kickstarter until compression can be felt on one cylinder. Re-position the kickstarter pedal to almost the horizontal position by freeing the clutch.

Switch on the ignition by turning the key in the centre of the lighting switch to the position "IGN", open the throttle about $\frac{1}{8}$ turn and then depress the kickstarter pedal smartly when the engine should fire immediately, if not, re-position the throttle and jet lever.

Failure to start the engine after the controls have been re-set may be due to a flat battery; in this case turn the ignition key to "EMG" which is the emergency start position. Depress the kickstarter when the engine will fire. Once the engine is running the ignition key MUST be returned to the "IGN" position as the engine should not be run longer than is absolutely necessary in the "EMG" position. (For special running conditions on the "EMG" circuit see page 167).

When the engine starts, close the twistgrip to a brisk tickover. While the engine is COLD the jet lever should be raised sufficiently to keep the engine running fast and evenly and should remain in that position until it is warm enough to run with the lever fully depressed. It will be noted that the lever is friction loaded and can, therefore, be set in any position for any length of time according to climatic conditions. For this reason, no specific time for the RICH running conditions can be stated.

Always turn the petrol taps "OFF" when parking the machine.

RUNNING-IN

For many years, motor cyclists were advised to ride their new machines at a speed not in excess of 30 m.p.h. for the first thousand miles. With a modern machine of high, or comparatively high performance, this type of running-in is entirely useless, and at the end of the one thousand miles only very little improvement will have been effected in the bearing surfaces of the engine.

Running-in should be carried out progressively, and it is necessary for the rider to make what may be termed a very definite arrangement with himself before he starts riding the new machine. He should make up his mind never to be bustled during the running-in period and to ride at his own speed entirely irrespective of the speed of other traffic. It is, naturally, annoying when one owns a high performance machine

Running-in

to be passed on the open road by a lightweight, but the rider of a new model must control his impulses, happy in the thought that the treatment he is giving his engine will mean considerably improved performance at the end of the running-in period.

When a machine is intelligently and carefully run-in, it will be faster, mechanically quieter, and will wear longer than the mount of a rider who pays no attention to the finer points of running-in. With a new machine, speed, within reason, does not greatly come into the question; the main idea to keep in one's mind is that the engine must never be stressed. By far the best indication is the amount of throttle opening, and during the initial stages more than about a quarter throttle should not be used.

The engine must not be allowed to slog in the higher gear ratios; it is far better to change down to a lower gear when the engine will be revving faster, but much more easily. It is a good plan to put a little spot of white paint cn the twistgrip rubber and a spot of black paint on the chromium plated twistgrip body, in such a position that these coincide when the throttle is closed. It is then easy to estimate the throttle opening during the running-in period and the "spots" can easily be removed, or the position of the white one altered.

After about 250 miles have been covered, the throttle opening can be increased to say a third, and this means that the speed will gradually increase. A further amount of throttle can be used as the running-in progresses, until the full throttle opening has been worked up to at about 1,200 miles.

Following the principle throughout that the engine must never be unduly stressed, speed bursts will be carried out progressively. With experience it may be found that at a certain throttle opening the machine will easily reach 50 miles per hour. When the speedometer needle touches that speed for the first time, the engine should immediately be throttled down. After a period of slower running, the 50 m.p.h. mark can be worked up to again, and this time held for a little longer. By gradually working up in this way, the time will come when the first of a few miles at 50 m.p.h. has been arrived at progressively. The same care should be taken when higher speeds are reached. With the higher performance machines in the Triumph range, similar care should be taken to see that the maximum speed is worked up to very carefully and is only held for a very short period initially. At really high speeds, it is advantageous to close the throttle momentarily at regular intervals, as this enables an increased amount of oil to pass up the cylinder bore. When the engine is thoroughly run-in this precaution is, of course, unnecessary.

During the running-in period great care must be taken to follow the lubrication instructions which will be found on page 31.

Lastly, do not forget that you will have plenty of time to try the paces of your new mount during the many thousands of miles you will cover after the running-in period has been completed. Never be tempted to "see what she will do" in the early stages, and do not be persuaded by your friends to test the speed of the machine against theirs until you are quite satisfied that your engine is thoroughly run-in.

ENGINE LUBRICATION SYSTEM

The dry sump lubrication system is employed on all Triumph engines. The oil is fed by gravity from the oil tank via a filter and pipe to the pressure side of the oil pump. The pump is a double plunger type, fitted with two non-return valves. From this point the oil is forced through drilled passageways to the crankshaft, and from the big end the oil issues in the form of a fog to lubricate the pistons and the other internal engine parts.

The oil pressure is controlled by means of a release valve situated in the timing cover. This valve serves two purposes, first to release excessive oil pressure and secondly to indicate the pressure by visible means. The valve consists of a piston, main spring, secondary spring, oil seal and button indicator. When the engine is running the valve is forced back by oil pressure on the secondary spring, this being indicated by the button projecting through the cover nut. Excessive pressure will move the piston back still further on the main spring and allow oil to be by-passed through the release valve body to the crankcase, from there to be scavenged to the oil tank.

After lubricating the engine, oil falls to the bottom of the crankcase where it is filtered. The crankcase oil return pipe which can be seen protruding through the filter after the sump plate has been removed, then returns the oil to the suction side of the oil pump to be returned to the oil tank. The suction oil pump plunger has twice the capacity of the pressure side, in order to make certain that no surplus oil remains on the floor of the crankcase. To lubricate the valve rockers, oil is taken from the return scavenge pipe by tapping the supply just below the oil tank. The oil, after being forced through the rocker spindles, lubricates the valve stems and push rod cups. On all models, external drain pipes are fitted. These pipes collect the oil from the valve wells in the cylinder head and transfer it to the push rod cover tubes, where it then lubricates the tappets and finally drains into the sump.

LUBRICATION MAINTENANCE

ENGINE

The system employed is simple and will function over a long period of time without attention to the actual pumping mechanism. On the other hand, failure to observe the elementary precaution of changing the oil and cleaning the filters at regular intervals, may cause a complete breakdown due to foreign matter entering the system.

If the oil tank cap is removed after the engine has been started, it will be noted that the return of oil to the tank via the stack pipe (seen just inside the filler aperture) is intermittent. The reason for this is that the scavenge side of the oil pump has a greater capacity than the feed side. Therefore, the crankcase sump is kept free of oil under normal running conditions and the scavenge pump will draw air until the crankcase scavenge pipe is again submerged in oil. The air which is forced into the oil tank is vented out via an outlet pipe into the primary chaincase.

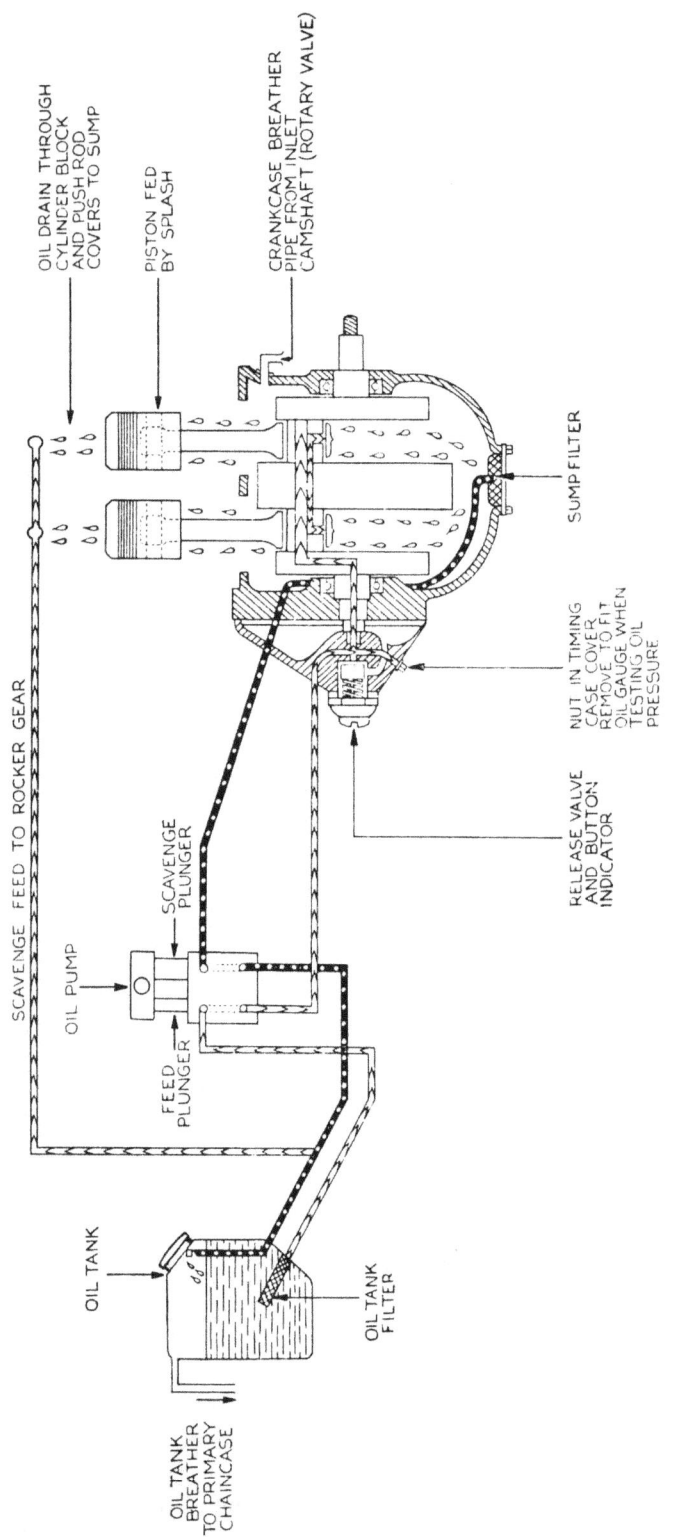

Fig. 3. LUBRICATION DIAGRAM

Lubrication System

In the event of a lubrication fault, the following causes have been listed to assist in diagnosing trouble:—

OIL TANK

The level in the oil tank should be 1½" (4 cms.) below the filler cap. Further addition of oil will cause excessive venting into the primary chaincase due to lack of air space. Always ensure that the vent pipe is clear as any obstruction will cause a back pressure in the oil tank, which in turn will prevent adequate scavenging by the oil pump, resulting in an oil flooded crankcase.

OIL PUMP

The only part likely to show wear after a considerable mileage is the oil pump block which can be replaced very cheaply. The plungers and the pump body being constantly immersed in oil, wear is negligible. It is unnecessary therefore, to suspect these parts if the lubrication is at fault. Should the non-return valve balls not be seating properly, the pump will not function satisfactorily. The remedy is to remove the oil pump and unscrew the two plugs situated under the oil pump body to remove the balls and springs. All parts should then be washed in petrol to remove any foreign matter, and when replacing the balls they should be given a sharp tap onto their seatings before re-assembly. Prime the pump with oil before fitting.

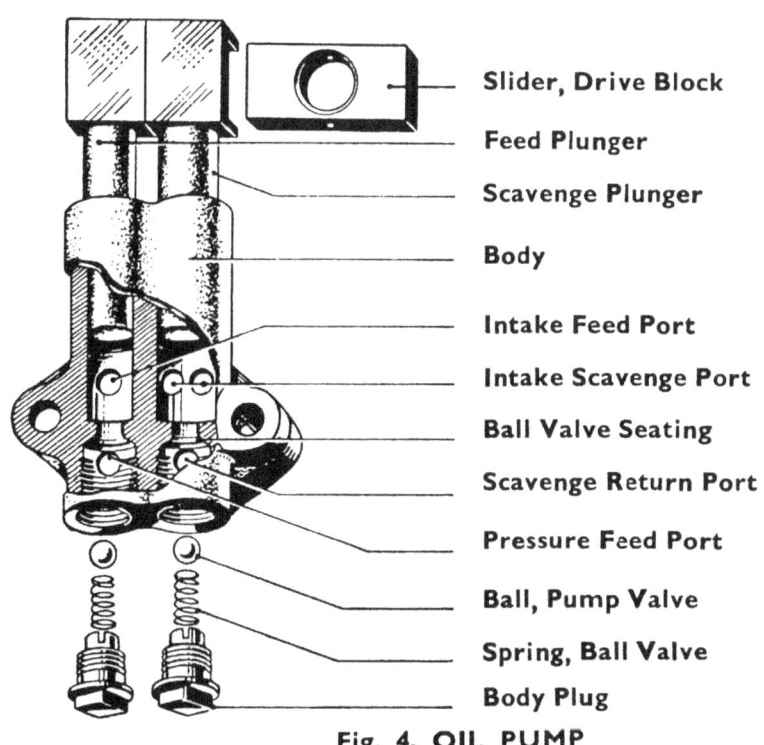

Fig. 4. OIL PUMP

Lubrication Maintenance

OIL RELEASE VALVE AND INDICATOR

This unit is very reliable and should require no maintenance other than cleaning. When the oil is changed it is advantageous to dismantle this unit and thoroughly wash it in petrol to ensure that the piston works freely in the release valve body. Under no circumstances should the release valve springs be tampered with as the spring poundage is set to give the correct oil pressure. Should it be necessary to replace these springs at any time, genuine Triumph spares should be obtained.

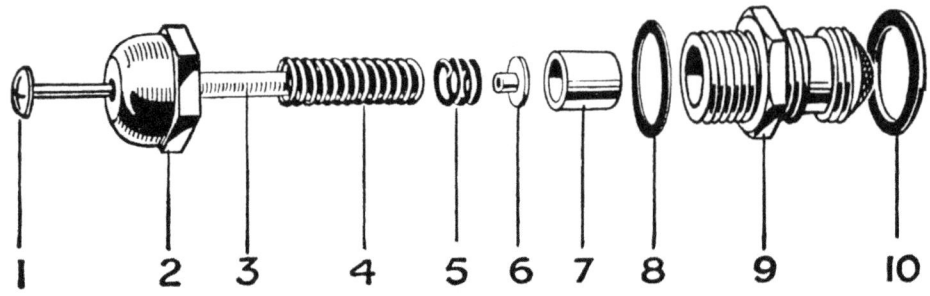

Fig. 5. INDEX

1 Indicator Shaft	5 Auxiliary Spring	8 Cap Washer
2 Valve Cap	6 Shaft Nut	9 Body
3 Rubber Seal	7 Piston	10 Body Washer
4 Main Spring		

OIL PIPES (TANK TO ENGINE)

When replacing the oil pipes to the rubber connections, care must be exercised to prevent chafing the inside of the rubber connection. Failure to observe this may result in a small piece of rubber entering the oil system, which, on reaching the oil pump would cause lack of pressure to the crankshaft. Foreign matter in the scavenge pipe line above the pump would be returned to the tank (in exceptional cases it may block the rocker oil feed) and is prevented from entering the oil system by the tank filter.

CRANKCASE SCAVENGE PIPE

In the unlikely event of this cracking or an air leak between the pipe and the crankcase, the oil will not scavenge from the crankcase. Trouble of this kind would only make itself known when the engine is hot. A simple method by which the tube can be tested is to first remove the crankcase sump plate and filter and then attach a length of rubber tubing over the scavenge pipe. Place the open end of the rubber tube in the mouth and suck. If the tubing collapses, this will prove the air tightness of the scavenge pipe. On the other hand if the tube does not collapse, a leak is evident. To rectify this fault, the engine must be removed from the frame and stripped.

VALVE ROCKERS, ROCKER SPINDLES AND PUSH RODS

The oil feed to the rocker spindles is supplied from the scavenge side of the main oil supply. Lack of lubricant to the rockers can only be caused by a stoppage in the oil pipe line. The obvious course is to remove the pipe and check by forcing air through it. To check the oil supply at the spindle; run the engine till it is warm to increase the oil temperature and then slacken off the two acorn nuts, which secure the oil pipe banjos to the rocker spindles, when a steady drip of oil should emerge. It is advantageous to flood the rocker mechanism if the machine has been "laid up" for an appreciable time, or even after de-carbonising etc. To do this, start the engine and then remove the oil tank filler cap, when a finger can be placed over the scavenge outlet pipe, thus forcing the oil through the rocker spindles, rockers and to the push rods. NOTE:—Always use the correct grade of oil as recommended on page 202. Cheap, inferior or the incorrect grade of oil will shorten the life of the engine.

GEARBOX
The gearbox is lubricated by oil and under no circumstances should a heavy viscous oil or grease be employed. Splash oil is fed to all parts including the enclosed gearchange and kickstarter mechanism to ensure complete lubrication. For oil changing and routine maintenance see pages 31 and 32.

PRIMARY CHAINCASE
The primary chaincase houses the clutch, primary drive chain, engine sprocket and for the Models 5T and 6T the alternator unit. Care should always be taken to ensure that the correct oil level is maintained; the lubricant qualities are not reduced by condensation if the correct grade oil (SAE 20) is employed. Failure to observe these elementary instructions may result in a burnt out clutch, chain failure and possibly damage to the alternator unit. If an oil of a higher viscosity than SAE 20 is used, the clutch plates will be difficult to separate thus causing extremely noisy gear changing. For oil changing and routine maintenance, see pages 31 and 32.

CYCLE PARTS
Component parts such as headraces, brakes and swinging fork mechanism are provided with grease nipples for lubrication purposes. Use only the recommended greases; heavier grades will not ensure correct lubrication, whereas lighter grades will have a tendency to pass the sealing points. It will be noted that no provision is made for greasing the wheels; on assembly the wheels are packed with grease and no further greasing is necessary until they are examined for general wear and tear (See Routine Maintenance, page 31).

CHAINS
The front chain is enclosed and positively lubricated (See Primary Chaincase, page 30). The rear chain however is lubricated by controlled oil splash from the primary chaincase. The method used is an oil trough in the rear of the inner chaincase and a hole drilled to atmosphere. In the outer cover a corresponding hole is drilled and tapped, into which a tapered needle valve is screwed, the taper entering the hole in the inner cover. By screwing the valve in or out the oil supply to the rear chain is decreased or increased accordingly.

CONTROLS
The control cables require lubricating at intervals, as, if they become dry, stiffness in operation will result. A good plan is to remove the cable at the handlebar end, wrap a piece of brown paper around the top end of the casing to form a funnel, securing it in position by a rubber band. If thin machine oil is then fed into the funnel and allowed to remain overnight, it will trickle down the casing and lubricate the inner wire.

CHANGING THE OIL

When the machine is new the oil should be changed frequently during the running-in period in order to make certain that any foreign matter which the oil picks up in the course of its circulation shall be eliminated.

ENGINE

The oil should be changed at 250, 500 and 1,000 miles (400, 800 and 1,600 kms.) during the running-in period and thereafter every 1,500 miles (2,500 kms.) regularly. When changing the oil it is essential that the oil filters are thoroughly cleaned in petrol.

Oil Tank Filter. To remove, unscrew the union nut attaching the feed pipe to the tank and then the large hexagonal nut to which the filter is fitted.

Crankcase Filter. This filter is located in the base of the crankcase, to remove, unscrew the four hexagon headed screws (on later models the sump plate is held by four nuts). Withdraw the filter carefully to avoid damage to the gauze.

It is advisable to flush out the oil tank with a flushing oil which is obtainable from most garages or accessory dealers. The flushing oil can be filtered through a piece of muslin and retained for further use. If the tank is very dirty it should be removed from the machine and thoroughly cleaned.

After the lubrication system has been drained and re-filled, all the joints which have been disconnected and the oil tank drain plug should be gone over again with a spanner to make certain that they are perfectly tight before the engine is started up. When the engine is again started, immediately check to see that the oil indicator is projecting and that the oil is returning to the tank. Inspect all joints for oil tightness.

PRIMARY CHAINCASE

The oil in the primary chaincase should be changed every 1,000 miles (1,600 kms.), or every month if a thousand miles has not been covered. The correct quantity is $\frac{1}{3}$ pint (200 c.c.). By carefully maintaining the oil level and changing the oil at regular intervals, the primary chain will be kept in excellent condition and will run for a long mileage without attention. If the oil is allowed to become dirty and partially broken down, wear will develop on the primary chain, which will require constant adjustment. (See Oil Chart, page 202).

GEARBOX

The oil in the gearbox should be drained and the gearbox flushed out after the machine has run 500 miles (800 kms.). Thereafter, the oil should be changed every 5,000 miles (8,000 kms.), but it is advisable to check the oil level at thousand mile intervals.

TELESCOPIC FORKS: See page 98.

ROUTINE MAINTENANCE AFTER RUNNING-IN PERIOD

APPROXIMATE MAINTENANCE PERIODS

	Miles.	Kilometres.
ENGINE		
Check oil and replenish if necessary	250	400
Drain oil tank when warm and re-fill	1,500	2,500
Clean oil filters	1,500	2,500
Check and adjust tappets	3,000-4,000	5,000-6,000
Clean and adjust sparking plugs	2,000-3,000	4,000-5,000
Decarbonise and top overhaul	10,000-12,000	15,000-18,000
GEARBOX		
Check oil and replenish	1,000	1,500
Drain oil (when warm) and re-fill	5,000	8,000
Check clamp bolts	1,000	1,500
PRIMARY CHAINCASE		
Drain oil and re-fill (if the mileage is not covered, change monthly)	1,000	1,500
Check over security screws	1,000	1,500
FORKS		
Drain oil and re-fill	5,000	8,000
Renew bushes, bearings and oil seals at least	20,000	30,000
Apply grease to lower headrace	1,000	1,500
Check play in headraces	5,000	8,000
Re-pack headraces with grease	10,000	15,000
SWINGING FORK		
Apply grease with gun	1,500	2,500
WHEELS (RIGID)		
Re-pack with grease	10,000	15,000
Check wheel bearings	2,000-3,000	4,000-5,000
WHEEL (SPRING)		
Re-pack with grease	20,000	30,000
Check wheel bearings	5,000	8,000

See pages 202 and 203 for recommended lubricants.

Routine Maintenance after Running-in Period

	APPROXIMATE MAINTENANCE PERIODS	
	Miles.	*Kilometres.*

CHAINS

Adjust tension if necessary	1,000	1,500
Lubricate rear chain (winter) ... ... (see page 95)		
Lubricate rear chain (summer)... ... (see page 95)		

BRAKES

Grease cable and rod mechanism	1,000	1,500
Adjust (normal running)	1,000	1,500

BATTERY

Check level of acid solution and add distilled water to bring level just above plates monthly. In very hot weather check more frequently.

TYRE PRESSURES

Check and correct weekly (see page 139)

CARBURETTER

Dismantle and clean	1,500	2,500

AIR FILTER

Clean and re-oil filter element	2,000	3,000

(Where machine is used in extremely dusty conditions the servicing period should be at more frequent intervals).

MAGNETO

Check and adjust contact points	2,000-3,000	4,000-5,000
Lubricate cam felt with thin oil	5,000	8,000
Grease (rocker shaft) with Petroleum Jelly	5,000	8,000

GENERAL

Lubricate all cables, check security of all nuts and bolts	1,000	1,500

See pages 202 and 203 for recommended lubricants.

THE ENGINE

CRANKCASE
The crankcase is cast in two halves from aluminium alloy and is designed to provide maximum rigidity. The crankshaft is supported by two heavy duty ball bearings in either crankcase half. The camshafts are housed fore and aft in the upper part of the crankcase and they operate in phosphor bronze bushes. The camshaft fitted to operate the inlet push rods (both camshafts are identical) is so designed, that crankcase pressure is released to atmosphere through a rotary disc valve. Located in the timing side crankcase are the timing gears, ancillary drive and the oil pump.

FLYWHEEL AND CRANKSHAFT
The balanced two throw crankshaft and flywheel are bolted together to make a complete unit. The "H" section connecting rods are forged from RR56 Hiduminium alloy and the bottom caps are steel stampings lined with white metal, the two parts being bolted together with two high-tensile bolts.

CYLINDER BLOCK
Two types of cylinder block are employed, one being cast from high grade cast-iron and the other die cast from aluminium alloy. The latter is fitted with steel liners which can be replaced when the existing liners are worn beyond their maximum re-bore limits. Each cylinder provides location for the tappet blocks and tappets.

PISTONS
The pistons are die-cast "LO-EX" aluminium alloy, each fitted with two compression and one scraper ring. The gudgeon pins are a tight push fit in the pistons and are held in position by spring steel circlips.

CYLINDER HEAD
The cylinder head houses the inlet and exhaust valves in separate combustion chambers. Two separate rocker boxes complete with the rockers are bolted to the head to operate the valves. As with the cylinder blocks, the heads are made from either cast-iron or die-cast aluminium alloy. The latter have cast-iron valve seats cast into the head during the manufacture.

LUBRICATION
Dry sump lubrication is employed. The system is operated by a twin plunger reciprocating oil pump. See page 27 for further information.

CARBURATION
Either by Amal or S.U. carburetter.

IGNITION
Either by Lucas magneto or Lucas RM14 alternator.

The Engine

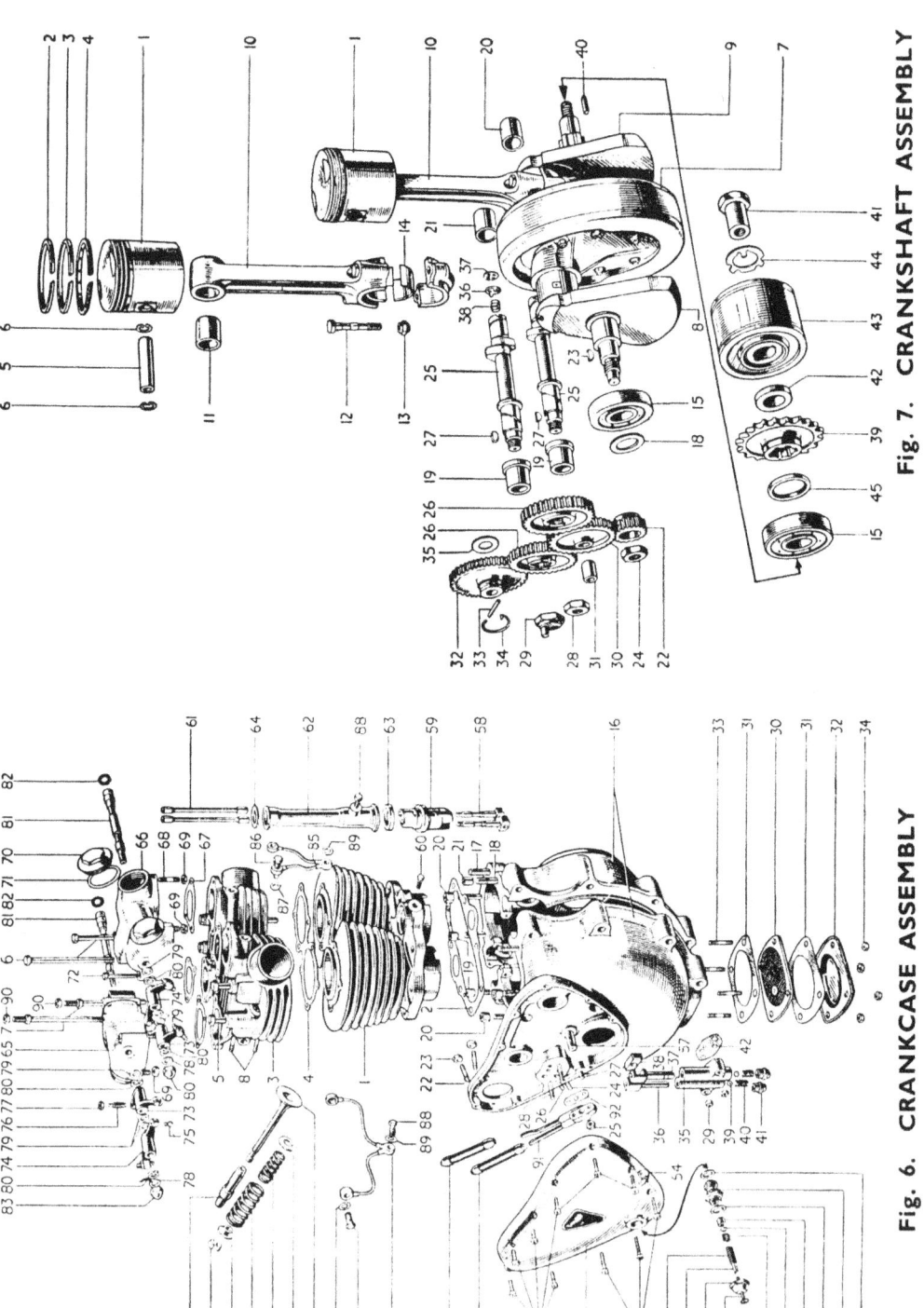

Fig. 7. CRANKSHAFT ASSEMBLY

Fig. 6. CRANKCASE ASSEMBLY

INDEX TO FIG. 6. CRANKCASE ASSEMBLY 6T

Index No.	Description.
1	Block, cylinder.
2	Washer, cylinder base.
3	Head, cylinder.
4	Gasket, cylinder head.
5	Bolt, short.
6	Bolt, medium.
7	Bolt, long.
8	Stud, inlet manifold.
9	Valve.
10	Guide, valve.
11	Spring, valve inner.
12	Spring, valve outer.
13	Collar, valve.
14	Cup, valve spring.
15	Cotter, valve split.
16	Crankcase.
17	Stud, cylinder base.
18	Stud, cylinder base (Dowel).
19	Nut, stud.
20	Nut, stud.
21	Dowel, cylinder base stud.
22	Stud, magneto to crankcase.
23	Nut, stud.
24	Stud, oil junction box.
25	Nut, stud.
26	Dowel, oil junction block.
27	Dowel, timing cover.
28	Stud, oil pump.
29	Nut, stud.
30	Filter, oil.
31	Washer, filter cover joint.
32	Cover, filter.
33	Stud, filter cover.
34	Nut, stud.
35	Body, oil pump.
36	Plunger, oil pump feed.
37	Plunger, oil pump scavenge.
38	Block, oil pump slider.
39	Ball, oil pump valve.
40	Spring, oil pump valve.
41	Plug, oil pump.
42	Washer, oil pump.
43	Body, oil release valve.
44	Piston, valve.
45	Cap, release valve.
46	Washer, body.
47	Washer, cap.
48	Spring, main.
49	Shaft, indicator.
50	Tube, rubber.
51	Spring, auxiliary.
52	Nut, shaft.
53	Cover, timing.
54	Plug, timing cover.
55	Screw, short.
56	Screw, long.
57	Spindle, intermediate wheel.
58	Tappet.
59	Block, guide.
60	Screw, lock.
61	Rod, push.
62	Tube, cover.
63	Washer, lower.
64	Washer, upper.
65	Box, inlet rocker.
66	Box, exhaust rocker.
67	Gasket, rocker box.
68	Stud, rocker box.
69	Nut, stud.
70	Cap, inspection.
71	Washer, cap.
72	Bolt, rocker box.
73	Rocker, valve R.H.
74	Rocker, valve L.H.
75	Ball pin, rocker.
76	Adjusting pin.
77	Locknut.
78	Washer, thrust.
79	Washer, thrust.
80	Washer, spring.
81	Spindle, rocker.
82	Seal, spindle.
83	Nut, dome.
84	Pipe, oil drain inlet rockers.
85	Pipe, oil drain exhaust rockers.
86	Adaptor, head to pipe.
87	Washer.
88	Adaptor, pipe to cover tube.
89	Washer.
90	Nut, torque stay.
91	Pipes and block, oil tank to engine.
92	Washer, oil pipe block.
93	Connection, oil pipe (rubber).

INDEX TO FIG. 7. CRANKSHAFT ASSEMBLY 6T

Index No.	Description
1	Piston.
2	Ring, top compression.
3	Ring, centre compression.
4	Ring, scraper.
5	Gudgeon pin.
6	Circlip.
7	Flywheel.
8	Crankshaft T/S.
9	Crankshaft D/S.
10	Rod, connecting.
11	Bush, small end.
12	Bolt, rod to cap.
13	Nut, rod to cap.
14	Bearing, T/S.
15	Bearing, D/S.
18	Clamping washer.
19	Bush, camshaft T/S.
20	Bush, camshaft D/S.
21	Bush, camshaft D/S (Breather).
22	Pinion timing.
23	Key, timing pinion.
24	Nut, timing pinion.
25	Camshaft.
26	Wheel, camshaft.
27	Key, camshaft wheel.
28	Nut, exhaust camshaft.
29	Nut, inlet camshaft (pump drive).
30	Wheel, intermediate gear.
31	Bush, intermediate wheel.
32	Pinion, distributor.
33	Pin, distributor pinion.
34	Circlip, distributor pinion.
35	Washer (Brass).
36	Valve, crankcase rotary.
37	Disc, rotary valve.
38	Spring, rotary valve.
39	Sprocket, engine.
40	Key, rotor.
41	Nut, sprocket and rotor.
42	Clamping washer.
43	Rotor.
44	Washer, locking.

TAPPET ADJUSTMENT (SEE SUPPLEMENT)
(Models 5T, 6T & T100)

These models are fitted with camshafts employing a Ramp-Cam form which makes it necessary to maintain a 0.010" (0.26 mm.) clearance (COLD), between the valve rocker adjusting pin and the valve tip in order to ensure silent operation and maximum efficiency. If the clearance is appreciably less the valve timing will be affected resulting in loss of power and the possibility of burnt valves.

Models T110 & TR5

These models have high-lift camshafts and no silencing ramps are incorporated in the cam form. The tappet adjustment, therefore, differs from the other models, the inlet being set at 0.002" (0.05 mm.) and the exhaust at 0.004" (0.10 mm.)

ADJUSTMENT (COLD)

Rocker Box Inspection Caps. Remove all four from the rocker boxes.

Positioning the Valves. This operation is made easier by first removing the sparking plugs. Turn the engine by the kickstarter until the timing side exhaust valve is fully open. This ensures that the other exhaust valve tappet is making contact with the base of the cam and no error can be made when checking or re-adjusting it.

Tools. In the toolkit, two spanners are provided for this adjustment. (See Fig. 8).

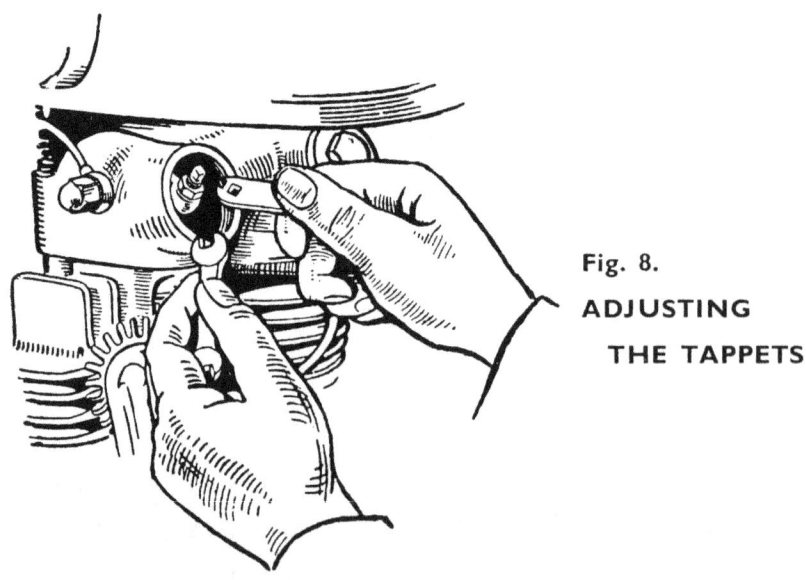

Fig. 8.

ADJUSTING THE TAPPETS

Rocker Adjuster Pin. Slacken off the adjuster pin locknut and screw down the adjuster until it just contacts the valve tip. For remaining details on models 5T, 6T, and T100 read (a) and (b) and for T110 & TR5 read (a) and (c).

(a) When the adjuster contacts the valve tip, hold the adjuster firmly with the spanner and tighten up the locknut with the other spanner. Grip the rocker adjuster between thumb and forefinger and move the rocker sideways to test for freedom of movement. Now test the up and down movement where the clearance between the adjuster and valve tip should be just perceptible.

(b) In order to obtain the 0.010" (0.26 mm.) clearance, first take particular note of the squared end of the adjuster and with both spanners in position, slacken the locknut slightly, taking care not to move the adjuster whilst doing so. Now slacken off the adjuster ONE FLAT ($\frac{1}{4}$ turn) and, maintaining it in the new position, re-tighten the locknut.
Carry out the same procedure with each tappet.

(c) The clearance on the exhaust valve can be estimated by first adjusting the tappet as in (a), paragraph (one). To obtain the 0.004" (0.10 mm.) clearance, slacken back the adjuster HALF A FLAT ($\frac{1}{8}$ turn). This may be slightly in excess of the clearance figure but the error is on the right side. For the inlet clearance, only slightly slacken off the adjuster so that when the rocker is held between thumb and forefinger and operated in an up and down movement, a distinct "click" can be heard when the adjuster strikes the valve tip.

DECARBONISING

The engine should be decarbonised only when it shows definite signs of requiring this attention. Falling off in power, loss of compression, noisy operation, and more difficult starting are all signs that the engine needs decarbonising. The engine will probably run at least ten thousand miles (15,000 kms.) between the decarbonising periods.

It should be noted that it is entirely unnecessary to remove the cylinder block when decarbonising the engine. We strongly recommend that this part is not taken off unless it is proposed to fit new piston rings or do some other work on the engine which necessitates the removal of the block. The engine will run more smoothly and give better service if the piston rings are left undisturbed.

Gasket sets are available for all models, and it is recommended that the correct set for the model is obtained before commencing the work.

Before commencing the operation, clean off any dirt, grease etc., with paraffin or a suitable degreasing agent. Secondly obtain two boxes; one for the cylinder head, etc., and the other for nuts, washers, etc. By doing this the operator will not have to search the four corners of the garage for the vital nut to complete the job.

Decarbonising

DISMANTLING

Saddle. Remove the front bolt and tie back the saddle clear of the petrol tank.

Twinseat. This must be removed.

Petrol Tank. Turn off the petrol tap or taps and disconnect the petrol pipes. Unscrew the four tank to bracket securing bolts when the tank can be removed. Take care not to lose the rubber tank pads.

Exhaust System. Slacken the exhaust pipe finned clip bolts, remove the pipe to bracket bolts, the silencer steady to frame nut and the silencer hanger bolts. Remove each pipe and silencer as an assembly. (On the TR5 the branch pipe clip bolt should also be slackened and the left pipe and silencer taken off first).

Torque Stays. Remove the nuts securing the stays to the cylinder head bolts and slacken off the stays to frame bolt when the stays can be disconnected.

Electrical Equipment. Disconnect the H.T. leads and remove the sparking plugs.

Carburetter—Amal. Remove the air cleaner connection and unscrew the two flange nuts. Withdraw the carburetter from the fixing studs and tie it to the frame. If it is desired to clean the unit, unscrew the knurled ring securing the throttle and air slides and take away the mixing chamber assembly. Carefully tie the slide assembly to the frame, out of harm's way.

Carburetter—S.U. Remove the air cleaner connection and vent pipe from the carburetter. Unscrew the flange nuts and disconnect the throttle cable at the carburetter body when the carburetter can be removed.

Rocker Feed Pipe. Unscrew the acorn nuts securing the rocker oil feed pipe banjos to the rocker spindles and then ease the pipe off the spindles.

Rocker Drain Pipes. Remove the adaptor bolts at the cylinder head only.

Rocker Boxes. First unscrew and remove the four centre bolts which secure the rocker boxes and cylinder head to the block. The next operation is to remove the FOUR NUTS holding the rocker boxes to cylinder head BEFORE removing the four small rocker box bolts. Failure to observe this WARNING may result in BROKEN CYLINDER HEAD LUGS. When all fixings have been unscrewed, remove the rocker boxes.

Exhaust Push Rods and Cover. Remove.

Cylinder Head. Unscrew the remaining four holding down bolts, when the head can be lifted off the block.

Inlet Push Rods and Cover. Remove.

INSPECTION AND PREPARATION

The method of decarbonising the parts and removing the valves and grinding-in etc. is fully explained under the above heading on page 46.

RE-ASSEMBLY

Inlet Push Rods and Cover. First fit the lower rubber oil seals over both tappet blocks. Now assemble the inlet push rods and cover to the tappets and block. Ensure that the drain pipes are fitted at this stage.

Cylinder Head. Fit the copper gasket to the cylinder block and then fit the head complete with manifold. Enter and screw down the four short bolts, but do not fully tighten.

Inlet Rocker Box. Grease the rocker box gaskets and upper push rod cover washer and assemble to the rocker box. Turn the engine over until both inlet push rods are nearly level and then assemble the rocker box to the cylinder head and push rod cover. Check that the gaskets have not been misplaced and then enter the two short rocker box holding down bolts and firmly screw down. Fit and tighten the two rocker box to cylinder head nuts. THE FITTING OF THE BOLTS MUST PRECEDE THE NUTS. If the valve seats have been re-cut and the valve faces re-ground, it is a good plan to slacken back the rocker adjuster before fitting the rocker box.

Exhaust Rocker Box. Fit the push rods and cover to the tappet and block (drain pipes fitted). Fit the exhaust rocker box in exactly the same manner as the inlet one.

Rocker Oil Drain Adaptors. Ensure that the oil drain adaptor bolts are clean and then fit a copper washer to each. Slide another copper washer between the oil drain banjo, and insert the adaptor and tighten. Care should be exercised when tightening into an alloy head (TR5 & T100).

Cylinder Head Holding Bolts. Position the remaining four bolts (the torque stay bolts to the rear, see supplement) and screw down until a grip is felt. All eight bolts should now be evenly tightened but do not use excessive force on the spanner. The actual force required, is 18 ft. pounds; if tightened beyond this figure distortion may take place.

Torque Stays. Replace the stays to the engine bolts and securely tighten the nuts and clip bolts.

Rocker Oil Feed Pipe. Place one copper washer on each rocker spindle; fit the oil pipe banjos over the spindles, followed by another copper washer and the two domed nuts. When tightening the nuts, steady the oil pipe at the spindles to prevent it turning, otherwise a broken joint may result.

Tappets. Re-set the tappets (see page 36) and replace the rocker inspection caps complete with new washers, to the rocker box.

Carburetter—Amal. If the carburetter slides have been removed, replace them at this stage and after screwing down the knurled fixing ring, test the slide operation by working the controls. Position the flange washer to the manifold (TR5 & T100 flange washer, tufnol block and flange washer) and then fit the carburetter to the studs. Connect up the filter connection; fit and tighten the flange nuts.

Carburetter—S.U. Fit the flange washer and assemble the carburetter to the manifold, connect the air filter connection and vent pipe. Fit and tighten the two flange nuts. Assemble the throttle cable to the carburetter body and test operation.

Removing the Engine from the Frame

Exhaust System. Replace the exhaust pipes and silencers as an assembly and ensure that all securing bolts are well tightened.

Petrol Tank. Replace the tank to the frame and ensure that a rubber pad is fitted at each side of the connection. Connect up the petrol pipes.

Saddle and Twinseat. Position to frame and tighten the fixing bolts.

Testing. Check that there is petrol in the tank, turn on the petrol tap, set the controls and start the engine. Run for a short time until the engine is warm and then set the slow running on the carburetter. Finally check over all engine nuts and bolts.

REMOVING THE ENGINE FROM THE FRAME
(RIGID FRAME MODELS)

Twinseat or Saddle. Remove the twinseat. If a saddle is fitted remove the front bolt and tie the saddle back.

Petrol Tank. Turn off petrol taps, disconnect the petrol pipes, unscrew the four tank bolts and remove the tank.

Exhaust System. Remove the exhaust pipe and silencer as an assembly on the models 5T & 6T by slackening the finned clip bolts and removing the silencer to frame bolts. On the TR5 the exhaust pipe to head is released by unscrewing the adaptors with a "C" spanner. Slacken off the branch clip bolt and remove the silencer bolt when the system can be removed.

Torque Stays (5T & 6T). Remove the nuts securing the stays to the cylinder head bolts and slacken off the stays to frame bolt, when the stays can be disconnected. The TR5 steady is made by utilising a front engine bolt through a clip which is fitted to the lower tank rail. To disengage, remove the bolt.

Control Cables. Disconnect the throttle, magneto (TR5 only) at the handlebar and the air cable (5T & TR5 only) at the rear stays. Neatly loop the cables as closely as possible to their respective engine fitting.

Footrests. Remove the L.H. footrest and detach the R.H. footrest and spindle by simply pulling out.

Footbrake Pedal. Unscrew the spindle nut and withdraw the pedal.

Primary Chaincase, Clutch, Alternator and Engine Sprocket. Remove these parts as described on page 83.

Air Filter, Battery Carrier and Battery. Disconnect the battery lead and remove the battery carrier clip bolt when the battery can be removed. Remove the carrier top nut and the two base bolts, when the carrier and air cleaner will be released.

Primary Chaincase Inner. Unscrew the rear chainguard to chaincase bolt and withdraw the chaincase from the shafts.

Oil Pipes. Place an oil drip tray under the engine and disconnect the engine oil pipes at the crankcase and the rocker feed pipe at the rocker box spindles.

Removing the Engine from the Frame

Dynamo. Remove the terminal wires and the domed nut on the timing cover. Slacken the clip screw and withdraw the dynamo.

Front Engine Plates. Place a box of suitable height under the crankcase so that the sump plate rests on it. Remove all the front engine plates, studs and nuts except the lower front.

Rear Engine Plates. Remove the two front top studs and nuts and slacken the remainder.

Engine. Tilt the engine towards the rear of the machine and swing forward the front engine plate. The engine can now be lifted out of the frame.

REMOVING THE ENGINE FROM THE FRAME
(SWINGING ARM FRAME MODELS)

Twinseat. Remove front and slacken the rear securing bolts; detach twinseat

Petrol Tank. Turn off the petrol taps, disconnect the petrol pipes, unscrew the four tank bolts and remove the tank.

Exhaust System. Remove the exhaust pipe and silencer assemblies by slackening the finned clip bolts and removing the bracket and silencer bolts.

Torque Stays. Slacken the frame lug bolt, unscrew the stay to engine bolt nuts when the stays can be removed from the engine.

Control Cables. Disconnect the magneto and throttle cable at handlebar and the air cable at rear stays (under twinseat). Neatly loop the cables as close as possible to their respective engine fitting.

Footrests. Remove both footrests but leave the spindle in position.

Footbrake Pedal. Take out the split-pin securing the operating rod to the pedal and then unscrew the pedal spindle nut when the pedal can be withdrawn after disengaging the stop lamp switch spring.

Primary Chaincase, Alternator, Clutch and Engine Sprocket. Remove these parts as described on page 83.

Oil Pipes. Place an oil drip tray under the engine and disconnect the engine oil pipes at the crankcase and the rocker feed pipe at the rocker box spindles.

Dynamo. Remove the terminal wires and the dome nut on the timing cover.

Front Engine Plates. Place a box of suitable height under the crankcase so that the sump plate rests on it. Remove the nuts from the two upper studs. The studs can then be driven out and the cover plate removed. Slacken the dynamo clip screw and withdraw the dynamo from the housing. Remove the remaining studs to release the front engine plates.

Rear Engine Plates. Here it is only necessary to deal with the engine plates to crankcase studs. Remove the two top studs and nuts and slacken off the nuts securing the lower stud.

Engine. Remove the box and tilt the engine towards the rear of the machine when the lower crankcase stud will disengage itself from the engine plates. Lift the engine out of the frame housing.

Dismantling the Engine

DISMANTLING THE ENGINE

Having removed the engine from the frame, it should be mounted on the bench in such a manner that the work can be conveniently carried out. The Fig. 9 shows a useful and simple method of holding the engine firmly to enable dismantling.

DISMANTLING

Oil Pressure Release Valve. Unscrew from the timing cover.

Timing Cover. Remove the securing screws and tap around the edge with a hide hammer to break the cover joint. Withdraw the cover.

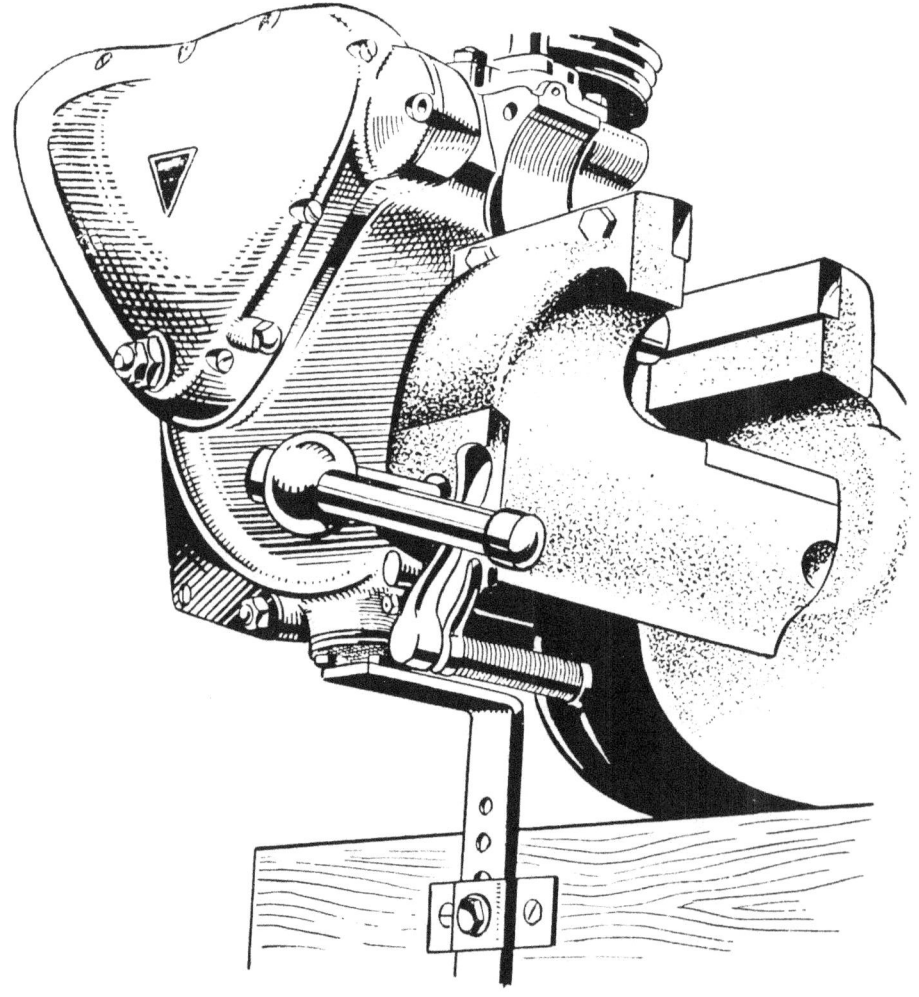

Fig. 9. ENGINE IN VICE

Dismantling the Engine

Oil Pump. Take off the two securing nuts and slide the pump off the studs.

Crankshaft and Camshaft Nuts. Remove these nuts. Note that the camshaft has a L.H. THREAD (turn clockwise to unscrew) and the crankshaft nut has a R.H. THREAD (turn anti-clockwise to unscrew).

Distributor Gear (Coil). Remove the circlip from the drive pinion boss groove, which retains the pin locking the drive gear on the shaft. Remove the pin when the gear and steel thrust washer can be withdrawn.

Magneto Gear. Unscrew the securing nut and screw into the gear centre the withdrawal tool (DA50/1) which is supplied with the tool kit. When the tool is in position, tighten the centre bolt when the gear will be withdrawn from the shaft.

Camwheels. If the bushes in the timing side crankcase are not worn, it is unnecessary to remove the camwheels as the crankcase can be split without detaching them. The removal of these gears necessitates the use of the special withdrawal tool Z89. Screw the body of the tool "C" on to the threaded portion of the camwheel (See Fig. 11), and by screwing the extractor bolt "A" in the camwheel is withdrawn from the shaft.

Intermediate Gear Wheel. Remove from the spindle.

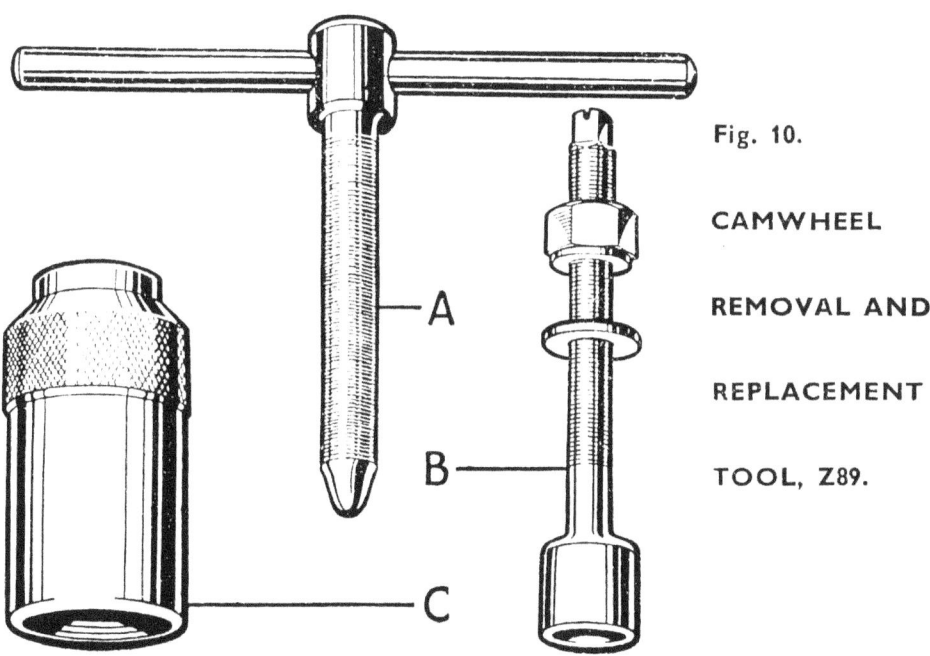

Fig. 10.

CAMWHEEL

REMOVAL AND

REPLACEMENT

TOOL, Z89.

Removing Camwheels

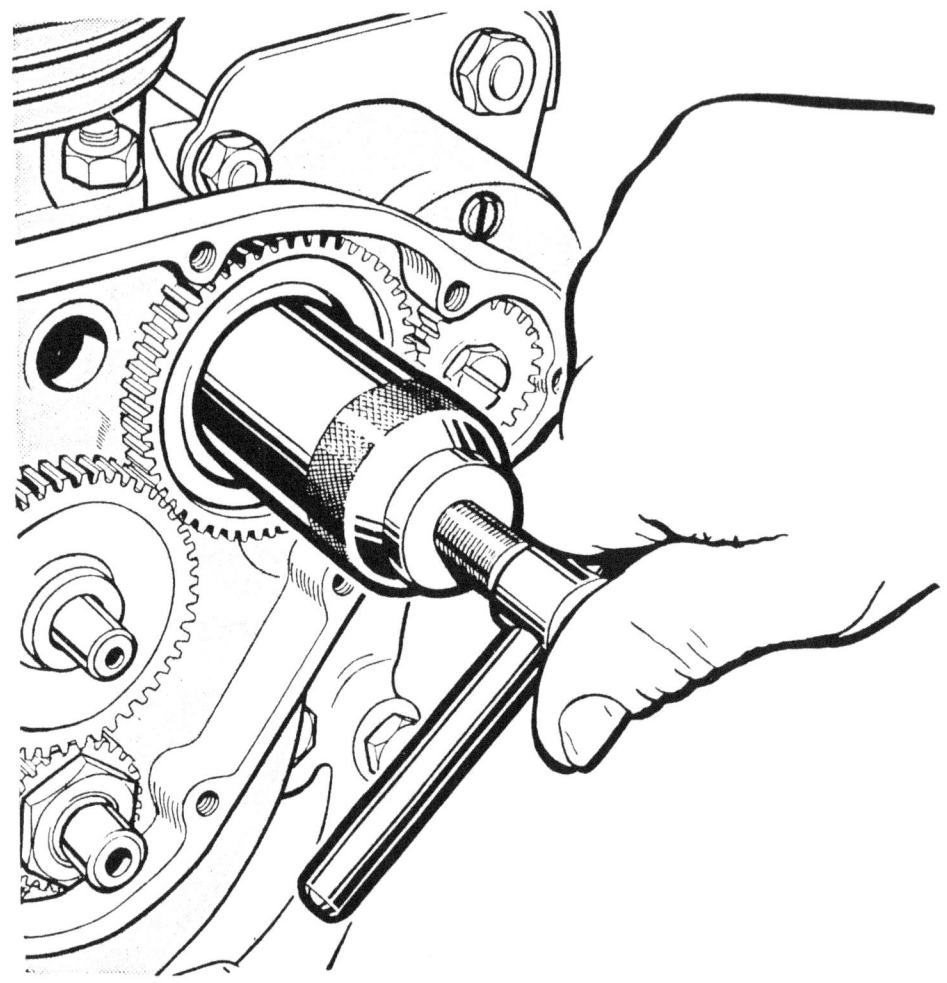

Fig. 11. **REMOVING THE CAMWHEEL**

Crankshaft Pinion. Again a special tool must be employed to withdraw this gear from the crankshaft. Fig. 12 clearly illustrates its application. To assemble to the gear, withdraw the collar "A" from the jaws, fit the plug "C" into the crankshaft end and then fit the jaws "B" over the gear. Close the jaws and re-fit the collar to retain them in position. Now turn the tommy bar clockwise when the gear will be drawn from the shaft. Do not attempt to shock the gear off the shaft by striking the extractor tommy bar with a hammer. This method will only cause damage to the extractor jaws. Remove the key from the shaft.

Cylinder Head and Rocker Boxes. This unit should be removed as an assembly. Unscrew the four rocker oil drain adaptors and the eight cylinder head holding bolts, when the unit can be removed from the cylinder block.

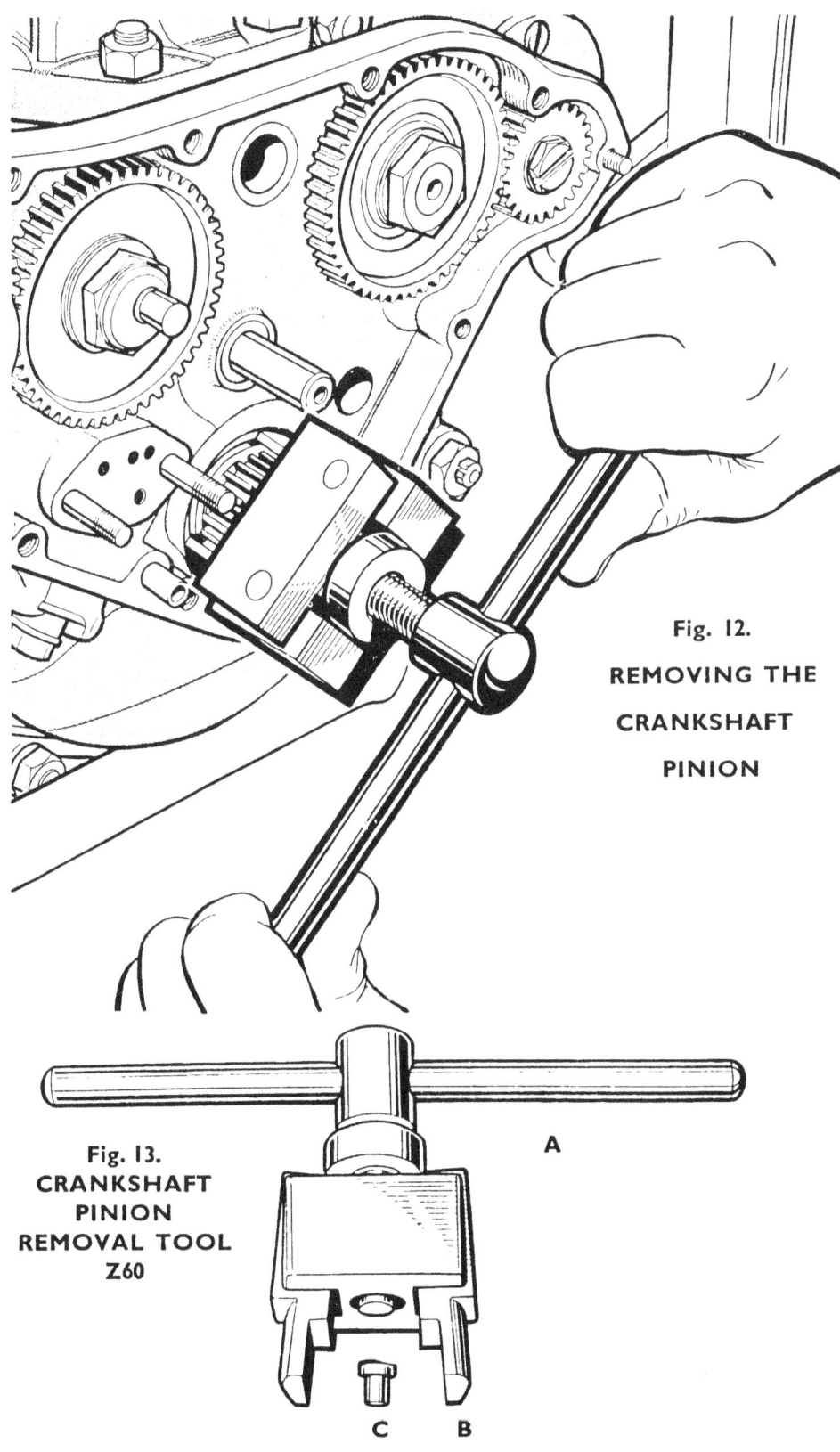

Fig. 12.
REMOVING THE CRANKSHAFT PINION

Fig. 13.
CRANKSHAFT PINION REMOVAL TOOL Z60

Dismantling Cylinder Head

Push Rods and Covers. Remove from the tappet blocks.

Cylinder Block. Unscrew the eight nuts; secure the tappets in the blocks by placing a rubber wedge between them, taking care not to use undue force. Carefully lift the cylinder block off the pistons.

Pistons. Remove a circlip from each piston and then press the gudgeon pins out from the opposite end. The fit of the gudgeon pins in the pistons is fairly tight; if a gudgeon pin extractor is available, it should be employed. The pistons should be suitably marked on the inside to ensure replacement to their original positions.

Magneto or Distributor. Unscrew the securing nuts and remove the unit.

Crankcase Bolts. Remove the remaining bolts and screws. NOTE.—Do not forget to remove the two screws from the internal bosses.

Crankcase Filter. Slacken off the vice jaws and remove the crankcase. Unscrew the four nuts holding the filter base and remove the base and filter gauze.

Crankshaft and Camshafts. To split the crankcase, bump the drive shaft onto a piece of wood when the two halves will readily part. The crankshaft and camshafts can now be removed.

In the drive side crankcase the breather rotary valve and spring is located in the camshaft bush. Care should be taken not to lose these.

DISMANTLING, PREPARATION AND ASSEMBLY OF THE ENGINE UNITS

CYLINDER HEAD

Rocker Boxes. Unscrew the four nuts and then the four screws when the rocker boxes can be removed from the head. Wash the rocker boxes thoroughly and inspect the parts for wear. Check the ball ends, adjuster pins, and rockers on the spindles for wear. Examine the rocker boxes for cracks or pulled studs. Normally, wear on the rocker spindles is negligible as they are fully lubricated. The adjuster pins sometimes show slight wear or indentation which can be removed by lightly stoning the hardened pad. If the markings are too deep, the pins should be replaced. Carefully inspect the ball ends, if the spheres are mis-shapen the ball ends must be changed. This operation will necessitate dismantling the rocker box or boxes. To do this, knock out the rocker spindle from the threaded end using a hide hammer or similar soft tool to prevent damage to the thread. After withdrawing the rocker levers the ball ends can be pressed out of the housings and the new ball-ends fitted. When replacing the spindles, a new rubber seal must be employed; Fig. 6 shows the position of the various washers.

Valves and Springs. Compress the valve springs sufficiently with a compressor tool, when the split cotters can be eased away with a narrow screwdriver or similar tool. Release the tool and withdraw both valve and valve springs. Repeat the operation to the other valves; mark the valves for replacement. Inspect the springs for signs of fatigue (Free length Outer, 2.031" (5.16 cms.); Inner, 1.625" (4.13 cms.)); If in doubt, a new set of springs should be obtained.

Clean the valves and remove any burnt oil from the stems; if the valve faces are pitted they can be re-ground, but excessive grinding by machine is not advisable as the heat transference of the valve will be adversely affected. The stem of the valve should be inspected for wear and scuffing and if either is pronounced, it should be replaced.

Removing Carbon from Cylinder Head. Remove the carbon with a flat round headed scraper from the head spheres and ports. Take particular care when cleaning around the valve seatings to avoid damage to the faces. Inspect the valve seats for pitting or pocketing and the valve guides for ovality. Remember, if the valve guides are changed, the valve seatings must be re-cut. The same applies to a valve replacement or a valve which has had the seating face re-ground.

Replacing the Valve Guides. To remove the old guide place a shoulder drift into the guide from the inside of the combustion chamber and drive out. When fitting the new guide, grease the outer diameter and drive into the cylinder head from the top. Always use a shoulder drift when doing this operation and drive in the guide carefully to avoid damage.

Re-cutting the Valve Seats. A job such as this can normally be undertaken by your dealer at a moderate cost. After the seats have been re-cut, they should be blended to give an even seating of approximately $\frac{3}{32}$" (2.38 mm.)

Grinding-in the Valves. This should be done with a fine carborundum grinding-in paste. First smear a little grease around the valve face and insert the stem into the new valve guide. Attach the valve grinding tool to the stem tip and commence to grind the valve face to the valve seating, using a semi-rotary movement, occasionally lifting the valve and turning through 180°. Continue this process until a uniform seat results. Remove the valve and wash thoroughly in petrol or paraffin and examine the seating. A surer method is to apply a thin even smear of "Engineers marking blue" to the face of the valve. Rotate the valve one complete revolution and then remove it for inspection.

A thin uniform line, free from pit marks or other surface blemishes on valve face and valve seat indicates that the seating is satisfactory. After completion, the part must be thoroughly washed to remove all traces of the grinding-in compound.

Assembling the Cylinder Head. First ensure that all parts are thoroughly clean, then oil the valve stems and guides. Place a valve into its respective guide (Note inlet are marked "IN" and exhaust "EX") and holding the valve head against the seat, turn the head on its side and fit the lower spring cup over the guide and then the inner and outer spring and finally the top collar. Compress the springs with a compressor tool until the split cotters can be fitted into the collar and around the valve stem cut-away. Release the pressure on the compressor tool and remove. Tap the stem head of the valve smartly to ensure correct replacement of the cotters. Repeat the operation to the other valves. The exhaust pipe stubs on the T100, are screwed into the exhaust ports and tightness must be ensured before replacing the cylinder head. Do not replace the rocker boxes at this stage.

Cylinder Block

CYLINDER BLOCK AND PISTONS

Cylinder Block. Remove all traces of carbon from the upper wall of the bores and then wash thoroughly in a cleaning solvent. Check the amount of wear in the upper part of the bore by comparing it with the measurements in the lower. Anything over 0.005" (0.13 mm.) will denote that re-boring is necessary. A rough check can be made by checking the piston ring gap in various sections of the cylinder bores. Normally, the wear at the bottom of the bore is very light.

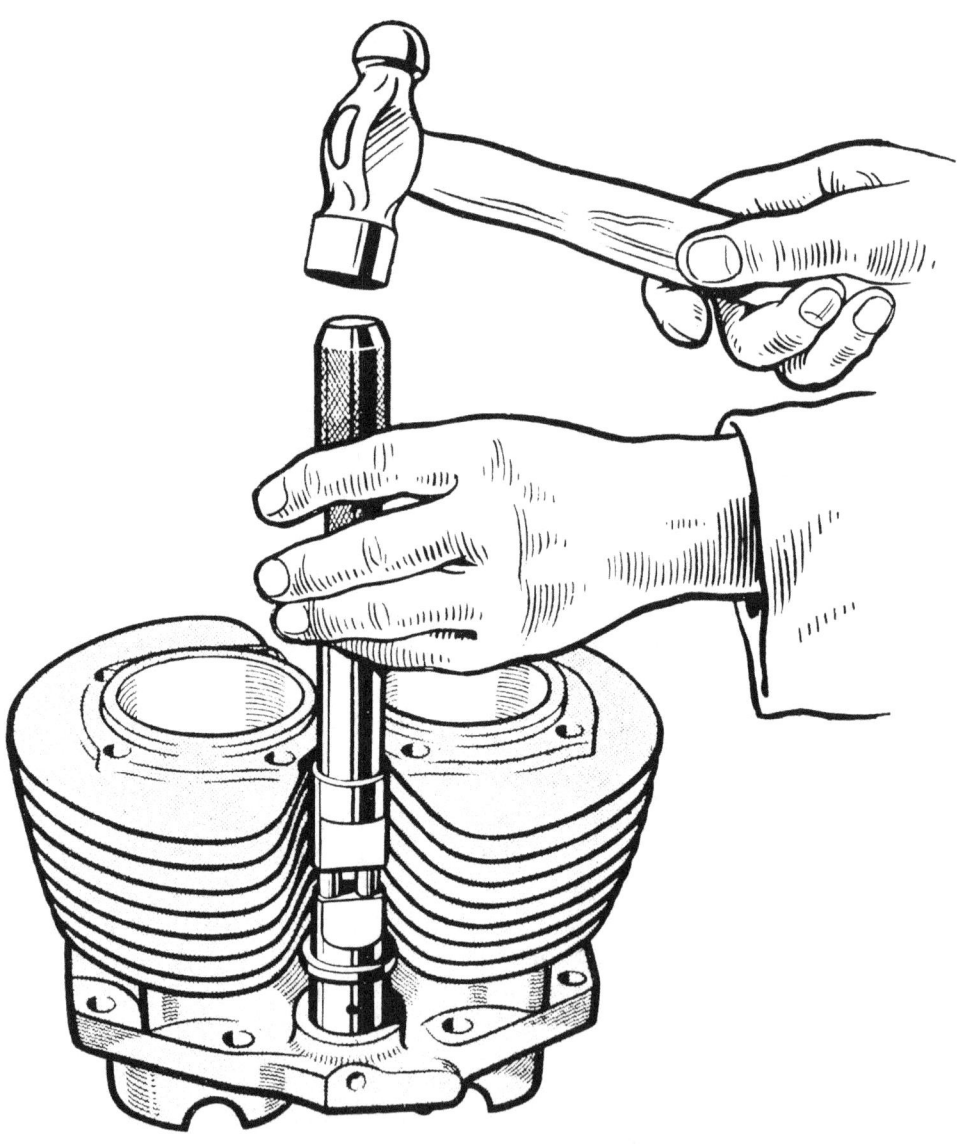

Fig. 14. ASSEMBLING THE TAPPET BLOCK

Inspection of Pistons and Tappets

RECOMMENDED REBORE OVERSIZES ARE AS FOLLOWS:—

Cast Iron Block	+.010"/+.020"/+.040"	500 c.c.
Cast Iron Block	+.010"/+.020"	650 c.c.
Alloy Block	+.010"/+.020"	500 c.c.

It will be noted that the alloy block can only be re-bored to a maximum of + .020" this is due to the fact that cylinder liners are fitted. Further re-boring would thin down the liner beyond safety limits. It is possible to change the liners, but work such as this should only be entrusted to a competent engineering concern, who will have the necessary equipment.

Tappets. The base of the tappets have a "Stellite" tip fitted; this material has great resistance to wear and under general running conditions, the tappets will not require changing until a considerable mileage has been covered. The centre of the tip may show signs of indentation which is caused by the peak of the cam. This does not however indicate wear and the tappet can be re-installed.

Tappet Blocks. It is not necessary to remove the tappet blocks from the cylinder base for inspection; the amount of wear can be estimated by rocking the tappet head. The tappet stem should be a sliding fit in the tappet block bores and the tappet base must fit snugly in the block base. Slackness at these points will cause excessive mechanical clatter. To remove the tappet blocks from the cylinder base flange, place the cylinder block downwards on the bench, remove the locking screw and drift the tappet block out of the cylinder flange. When fitting the new tappet block, grease the outer surface and if possible support the cylinder flange (See Fig. 14). Do not forget to line up the locking screw hole in the tappet block to that in the flange. Replace the locking screw.

Pistons. If the pistons are to be further employed, the rings and gudgeon pins when removed from each piston should be kept separate to ensure correct replacement. Carefully clean away the carbon deposit from the piston crown, taking particular care not to scratch the metal surface. The light deposit of burnt oil in the piston skirt should be removed by rubbing with a rag which has been dipped in petrol. Never in any circumstances use an emery cloth. To clean the ring grooves, it is advantageous to use an old broken ring by inserting the broken end into the groove and working it around the circumference. Clean out the oil drain holes in the scraper ring groove and thoroughly wash the piston. On the inside surface of the piston rings will be found a light deposit of carbon which must be removed if the rings are to be re-fitted.

Now roll each ring around its respective groove to ensure that it does not stand proud of the piston after being fitted correctly and compressed. Before fitting new rings, the gap must be checked in the lowest part of the cylinder bore. The ring must lie square to the bore for checking purposes and to ensure this, place the bottom of the piston skirt onto the ring and ease it about $\frac{1}{2}$" (13 mm.) down the bore. Check the gap by feeler gauge.

	Min.	Max.
Compression Ring Gap	0.010" (0.25 mm.)	0.014" (0.35 mm.)
Scraper Ring Gap (500 c.c.)	0.007" (0.18 mm.)	0.011" (0.28 mm.)
„ „ „ (650 c.c.)	0.010" (0.25 mm.)	0.014" (0.35 mm.)

Piston Rings

When replacing the piston rings on the models 5T and 6T, note that the second compression ring has tapered sides and must be fitted in the middle piston ring groove. The face with (TOP) etched on it must be towards the piston crown. The models T100, T110 and TR5 are fitted with a chrome taper ring in the top piston ring groove. This ring may be identified by its bright chrome appearance and should also be fitted with the etched word (TOP) towards the crown, but in the top ring groove.

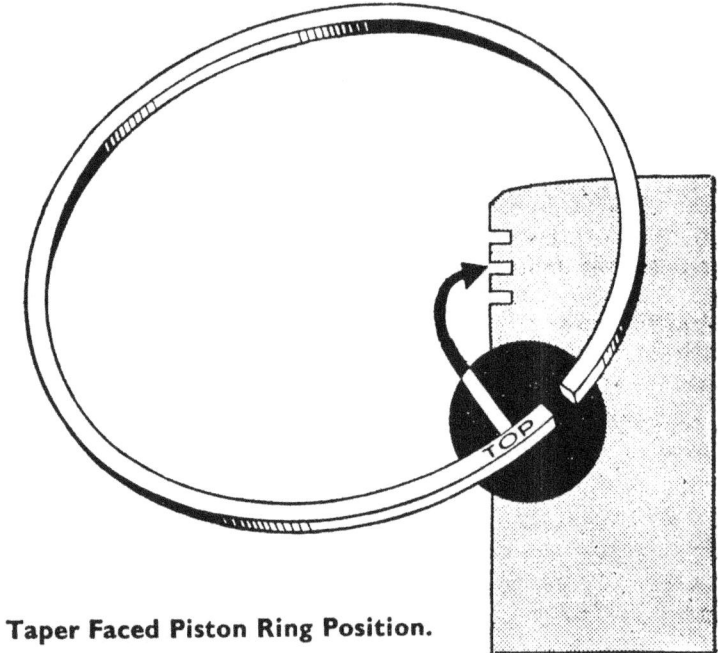

Fig. 15. Taper Faced Piston Ring Position.

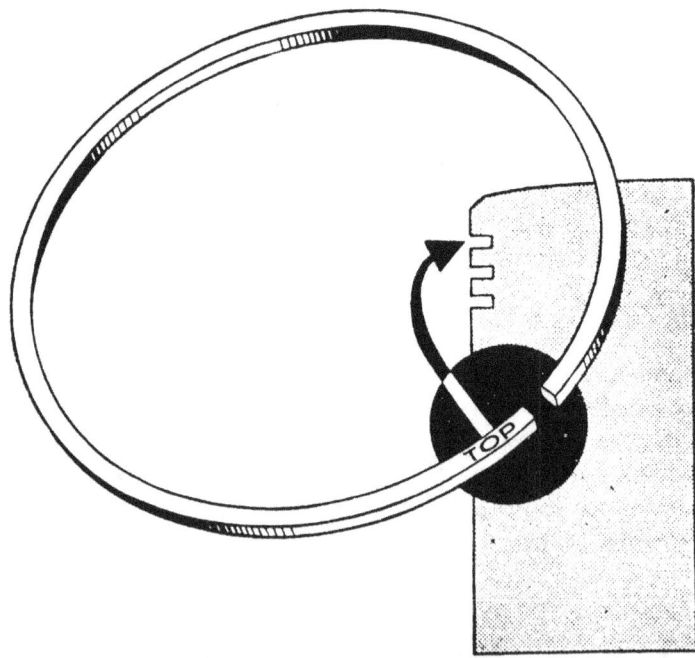

Fig. 16. Chrome Taper Faced Ring Position.

VALVE PUSH RODS AND COVER TUBES

Push Rods. Examine the end cups for chips around the edge, slackness on the tube and general wear inside the cups. For any of these faults, the push rods must be renewed. Bent push rods can cause undue noise and loss of power, so before replacing them to the engine, examine each one for straightness by rolling them on a true surface which could show up any irregularity.

Cover Tubes. If oil leakage is to be avoided after an overhaul, always ensure that the ends are tight on the tubes and in no way damaged.

CRANKCASE UNIT

Main Bearing. Remove the timing side bearing retaining ring (where fitted), and press out the timing and driving side main bearings. This can be more easily accomplished by warming the crankcase. Wash thoroughly and dry out with compressed air if possible as this will tend to remove any small particles of foreign matter. Spin the outer race to test the bearing for roughness and then inspect the balls and track for signs of indentation or pitting. Finally, test the end float which should be negligible in a good bearing. Replace if any fault is shown.

Crankcase. Wash the crankcase halves and inspect all stud fixings for security and the casting for cracks or damage. Remember, if one half of the crankcase is damaged, a complete new crankcase must be purchased as these are machined in pairs. The camshaft bushes normally show very little signs of wear until a considerable mileage has been covered. To make a rough check, fit the camshaft into the bearing and ascertain the up and down movement. If it is desirable that the bushes are changed, proceed as in the following paragraph.

Camshaft Bushes. To remove the bushes in the timing side half, heat (100°C approx.) the crankcase around the bush housing when the bushes can be easily pressed out. While the case is still warm, press in the new bushes, ensuring that the oil hole is lined up with the drillway in the housing. The removal of the drive side bushes is a little more difficult and it is necessary to cut a thread in the bushes with a tap before heating the crankcase. When this is done, re-insert the tap and hold the square end in the vice when the crankcase can be gently tapped away with a hide hammer leaving the bush attached to the tap. Located behind the rear bush is the breather valve porting disc. Before replacing the new bush, ensure that this disc is correctly positioned on the locating peg.

If the temperature of the crankcase half has dropped, re-heat and then press In the new bushes. The phosphor bronze bushes are machined to size before pressing in, and only the smallest amount of metal need be removed when reamering. To ensure accurate alignment, the two halves should be bolted together before reamering.

Scavenge Pipe. Check this pipe for security and ensure that a perfect oil seal is made where it enters the crankcase at the pump position. Failure at this point would reduce oil scavenge to the minimum.

Servicing Crankcase

Refitting the Main Bearings. On all models previous to 1954 and the 1954 model 5T, a bearing chipshield is inserted before the timing side main bearing and a disc and circlip following the bearings. It will be found easier to fit the bearings on all models if the crankcase is heated in the area of the bearing housing before pressing the bearings into position.

Timing Cover. This Cover houses a very important bush which seals the crankshaft oil supply. If this bush is worn, the pressure from the oil pump will be released directly into the timing cover, thus reducing the quantity and pressure of oil to the big ends. The bush should always be changed when overhauling the engine. Press out the old bush and press in the new bush. Reamer in position. (New crankshaft end diameter = 0.622" - 0.623". Bush internal diameter = 0.6235" - 0.624").

Timing Gears. Timing gear wear is negligible; the only part which will require changing after considerable mileage is the intermediate gear bush. To change, push out the old bush and insert the new. It may be necessary to lightly reamer the bush to suit the spindle diameter. If the timing gears are noisy, it is futile to purchase an odd gear to overcome this fault. A far better plan is to consult your Triumph dealer who will be able to remedy this trouble by selective assembly of gears from his stocks.

Oil Pump. As previously stated under "Lubrication Maintenance", Page 25, only the oil pump block will show signs of wear after considerable mileage. When doing an engine overhaul however, completely dismantle the pump by removing the two plungers and the two body plugs when the non-return ball valves and springs will be released. Wash the pump body and examine the ball seatings; if these show signs of heavy indentation, pitting or wear to one side of the seat, they can be re-cut with a 45° cutter or drill suitably sharpened. Inspect the balls and springs and if in doubt about their condition, new ones should be fitted. When replacing the balls, they should be given a sharp tap onto their seatings to ensure a good seat. After assembling the pump, submerge the body in oil and operate the plungers. This will prime the pump and at the same time give some indication of its pumping ability.

Oil Release Valve and Indicator. The illustration, Fig. 5, indicates the construction of the valve and indicator and should be closely followed during the dismantling and assembly procedure. First remove the valve cap and indicator assembly by unscrewing from the main body when the piston valve can be withdrawn. To remove the indicator, grip the shaft nut and unscrew the shaft from it. Withdraw the shaft to release the springs and rubber seal. Carefully clean all parts and ensure that the piston valve works freely in the body. Do not tamper with the springs by stretching to increase the tension as the spring poundage is set to give the correct pressure. When replacing the indicator always fit a new oil seal. Assemble in the following manner: Place indicator shaft into the cap and slide the new oil seal over the shaft followed by the main spring (large) and auxiliary spring (small) and finally screw on the shaft nut. Oil the piston valve and enter into the body, position the joint washer on the body and screw on the cap assembly.

Servicing Crankcase

Crankshaft and Connecting Rod Assembly. The dismantling, overhaul and assembly of this unit is a job that is normally undertaken by the dealer, or at the works. If the owner wishes to carry out this work, he must have a certain amount of mechanical ability and a good workshop.

Dismantling. Grip the bottom end of the flywheel in the vice and carefully mark each rod so that they can be replaced in exactly the same position relative to the cranks and the connecting rod cap to the rod itself. Unscrew the two nuts securing each rod and remove the rods from the cranks. Replace the cap to the rods for the time being. Identify the cranks to the flywheel and then remove the six bolts and nuts when the assembly can be parted.

Inspection and Identification. Wash all parts thoroughly and examine the bearing surfaces.

			New.	
Crank big-end journal size:	Earlier pattern		1.4360"	(3.6484 cms.)
			1.4365"	(3.6497 cms.)
,, ,, ,, ,,	Current models		1.6235"	(4.1237 cms.)
			1.6240"	(4.1250 cms.)
Connecting rod big-end size:	Earlier pattern		1.4370"	(3.6510 cms.)
			1.4375"	(3.6522 cms.)
,, ,, ,, ,,	Current models		1.6250"	(4.1275 cms.)
			1.6255"	(4.1288 cms.)
Connecting rod small end (All)		... ...	0.6885"	(1.7488 cms.)
			0.6890"	(1.7501 cms.)
Gudgeon pin size (All) ...	... ...	...	0.6882"	(1.7480 cms.)
			0.6885"	(1.7488 cms.)
Connecting rod end float (All)		... ...	0.0290"	(0.737 mm.)
			0.0320"	(0.813 mm.)

Light score marks on the crank big-end journals can be carefully eased down with smooth emery but after this operation the parts must be carefully washed again. If the cranks are scored, the connecting rod big-ends will also show similar signs, these should be carefully removed by using a scraper and if necessary a minute amount of metal can be removed from the mating surfaces of the cap and rod to enable the rod to be refitted to its original clearances. If any metal is removed from the mating surfaces, the bearing will have to be re-bedded by removing all high spots (use engineers marking blue on the journal bearing to detect high spots) with a scraper. Remember, the maximum amount of white metal in the connecting rod cap is 0.025" (0.635 mm.). This operation should only be done by a mechanic who is fully conversant with this type of engineering procedure.

If the damage is beyond repair, service re-ground cranks and connecting rods to fit can be obtained from a dealer in the following UNDERSIZES:—

Cranks	... ...	0.010"—0.020"
Connecting rods	... ...	0.010"—0.020"

The small end bush wear can be detected by inserting the gudgeon pin into the bush. If in good condition the pin should be a smooth working fit in the bush, no rock being in evidence. To replace the bush, press out the old one and at the same time

Connecting Rod

insert the new. Ensure that the oilways are aligned. When reamering the bush, care must be taken to ensure that the bore is parallel with the big-end.

The final examination is the fit of the main bearings on the crank timing and driving shafts. The bearings should be a tight push fit; a loose fitting bearing would tend to cause crankcase "rumble".

Assembly. Place the bottom end of the flywheel in the vice and position the timing and driving side cranks to their respective sides. Fit six NEW bolts and nuts (the old parts should never be re-used) and fully tighten. Lock the nuts by centre punching the periphery of the thread. Oil the journal bearings and fit the respective connecting rods. Before doing this, measure the overall length of the connecting rod bolt with a micrometer; during the tightening process the bolt will be stretched. Again the micrometer should be employed and when the bolt has stretched .007" (0.178 mm.)—.008" (0.203 mm.) it is then under correct tension and must not be further tightened. Apply the nozzle of an oil gun to the timing shaft oilway and pump oil through the crankshaft until it passes the connecting rod bearings.

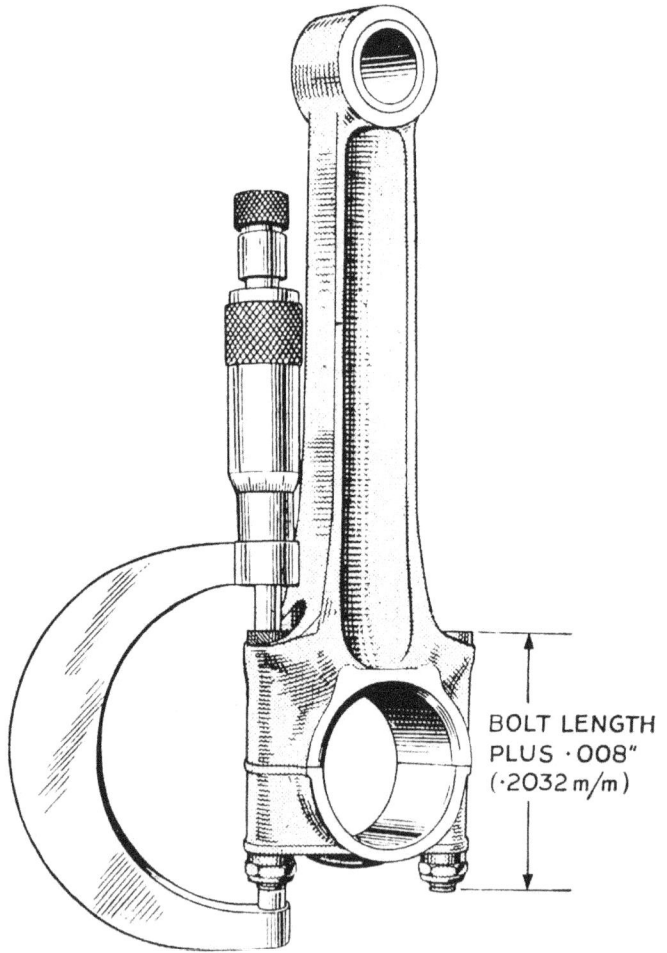

BOLT LENGTH
PLUS ·008"
(·2032 m/m)

Fig. 17.

CHECKING CONNECTING ROD BOLT STRETCH

ASSEMBLING THE ENGINE

Before commencing this operation, clean down the work bench and lay out the engine units and parts in assembly order. Also check the nuts, bolts and washers, etc., and have the gaskets and jointing compound available. When the engine is being erected, each working surface must be liberally oiled. This can be done with the use of a clean paint brush or an oil can. The operator should not rub on the oil with his fingers, otherwise a certain amount of grit etc. may be picked up during the process.

Crankcase, Driving Side. Lubricate the main bearing and the camshaft bushes.

Crankshaft Assembly. Enter the driving side shaft into the ball-race in the drive side crankcase. Ensure that the shaft is fully located. (It is advantageous to allow the shaft to protrude vertically through a convenient hole in the bench and then the outer face of the drive side crankcase will take the weight on the flat surface of the bench).

Camshaft. As both camshafts are identical, the mechanical breather can be fitted into either. First insert the spring and then the breather disc valve engaging the projections into the camshaft slots. Enter this assembly into the inlet (rear of engine) camshaft bush and test the engagement of the disc valve by depressing the camshaft. Insert the other camshaft into the exhaust (front of engine) camshaft bush.

Crankcase Timing Side. Lubricate the main bearing and camshaft bushes. Lightly smear jointing compound on the inner mating face, then thread this half over the crankshafts and camshafts. Bolt the two halves together, ensuring that these meet without undue force being applied. If any difficulty is encountered, suspect the breather disc in the inlet camshaft being out of position. To remedy, rotate the camshaft until the slot is engaged. Two internal screws are located in the crankcase just above the camshaft; be sure to replace these.

Aligning the Crankcase Halves. The top of the crankcase must present a perfectly flat face to the cylinder base. There must be no step between the halves. If a step is evident, a sharp tap on the stud boss nearest to the proud face with a hide hammer, will bring it flush. Do not strike the base face itself. When the two faces are properly mated, the bolts and screws should be fully tightened. Rotate the crankshaft to check for freedom of movement.

Sump Filter. Fit the filter with a new joint washer to the sump and over the scavenge pipe, then the cover with a joint washer. Replace the four washers and nuts but do not over-tighten, otherwise a broken stud may result, a trouble which can be well avoided at this stage.

Crankcase. Place the crankcase in the vice as in the dismantling procedure and pour into it an egg-cupful of engine oil.

Replacing Camwheels

Crankshaft Pinion. Fit the Woodruff key to the engine shaft and assemble the pinion (shoulder side to the engine) to the shaft. When the pinion is correctly positioned to the key it must be fully located by tapping it onto the shaft with a hollow punch. Do not fit the nut at this stage.

Camwheels. To fit these, special tool Z89, Fig. 18 must be employed. First assemble the keys to the camshafts then screw on the centre tool (B). Slide the camwheel over the tool and engage the keyway onto the key. Screw onto the camwheel thread the outer tool (C), and onto (B), the left hand nut. Screw down the nut until it contacts the outer tool, then, to prevent the camshaft turning when the nut is screwed down, hold the end of the rod (B) with a suitable tool. When the camwheel is fully located remove the tool and then fit the opposite camwheel. Do not attempt to punch the camwheels onto the shafts, as the key will be brought into contact with the shaft bushes and may cause considerable damage. If the operator cannot avail himself of the special tool, the camshafts and camwheels can be assembled before the two halves of the crankcase are fitted together. Fit the camshafts to the timing side crankshaft half and then support them, when the camwheels can be aligned to the keys and punched into position.

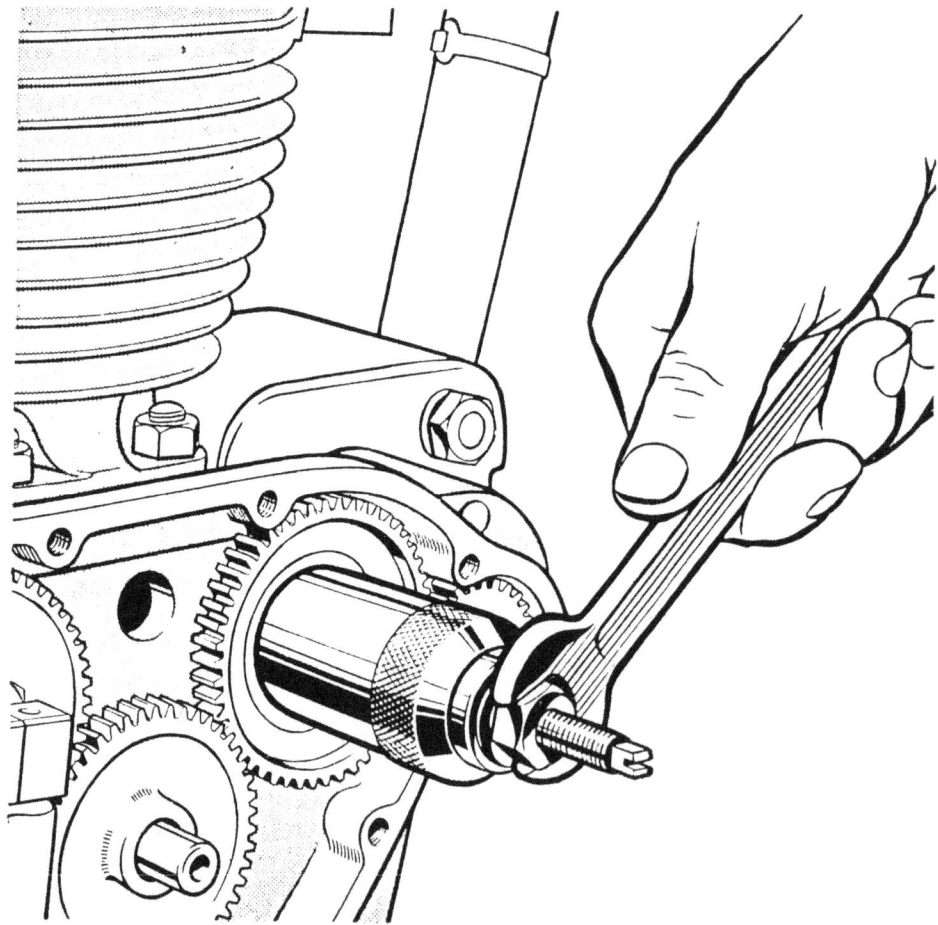

Fig. 18. REPLACING THE CAMWHEEL

Timing Gear Markings

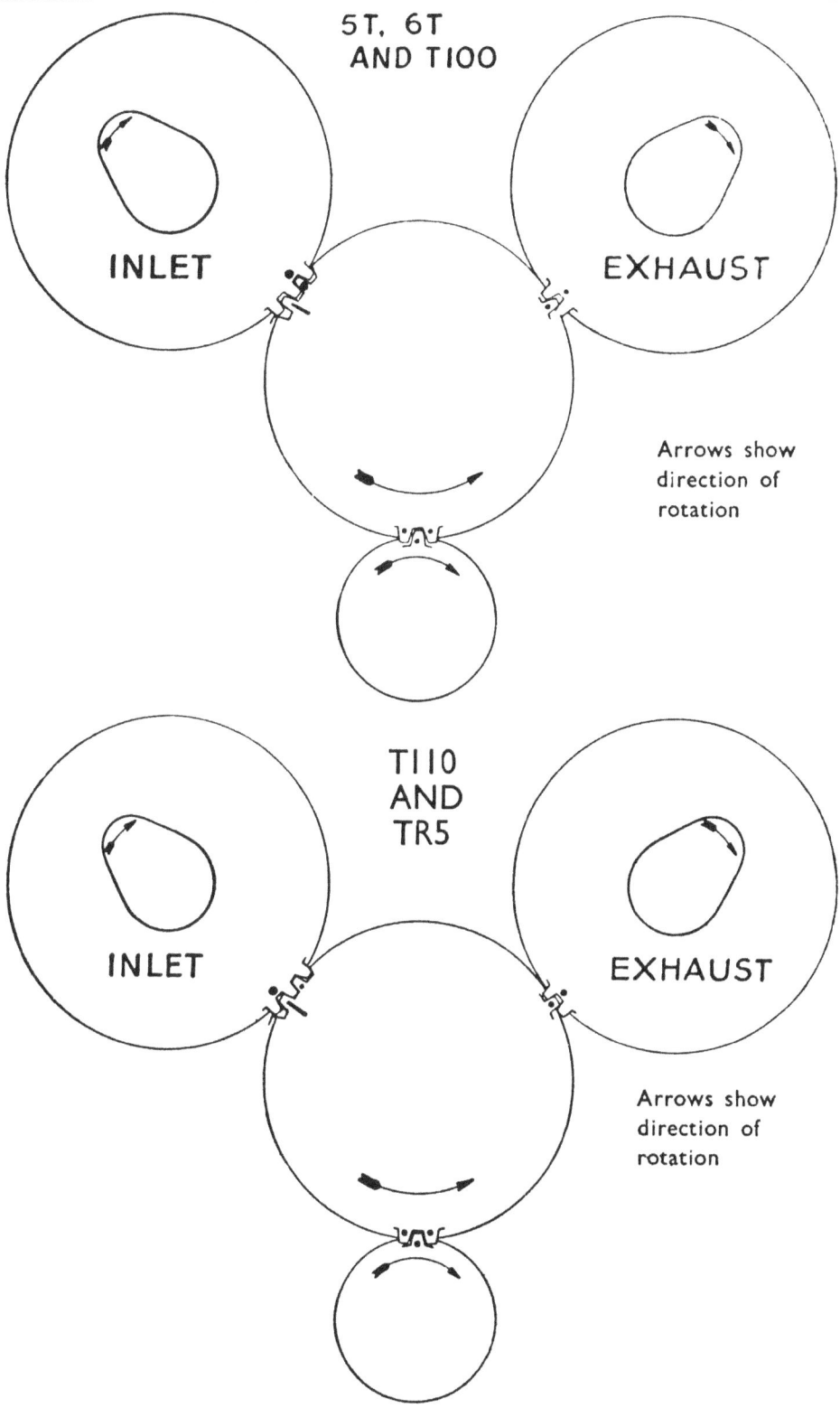

Fig. 19
Position of Timing Pinion in relation to Camwheels and Crankshaft Pinion

Timing Diagrams

Valve Timing. Assemble the intermediate wheel in the same manner shown on page 57, for your particular model.

Pinion and Camshaft Nuts. Replace the pinion nut (R.H.), followed by the exhaust camshaft nut (L.H.), and finally the inlet camshaft nut (L.H.), which has the eccentric drive peg for the oil pump. Ensure that these nuts are well secured.

Oil Pump. Prime the pump with oil and fit to the crankcase with a new joint washer. Ensure that the washer is positioned correctly and not covering any oilways.

Magneto. Assemble the magneto to the crankcase and secure with the three nuts.

Magneto Driving Gear. Fit the gear to the magneto shaft and loosely screw on the nut.

Distributor. See Ignition Timing, page 60.

Pistons. If replacing the old pistons, they must be fitted to their appropriate connecting rods. Lubricate the small end bushes and fit the pistons to the rods. Carefully insert the gudgeon pins until they abut against the circlips already in the piston boss. Now fit the two remaining circlips and ensure that they are in grooves. If in doubt regarding the serviceability of the circlips, always fit new ones, the cost of

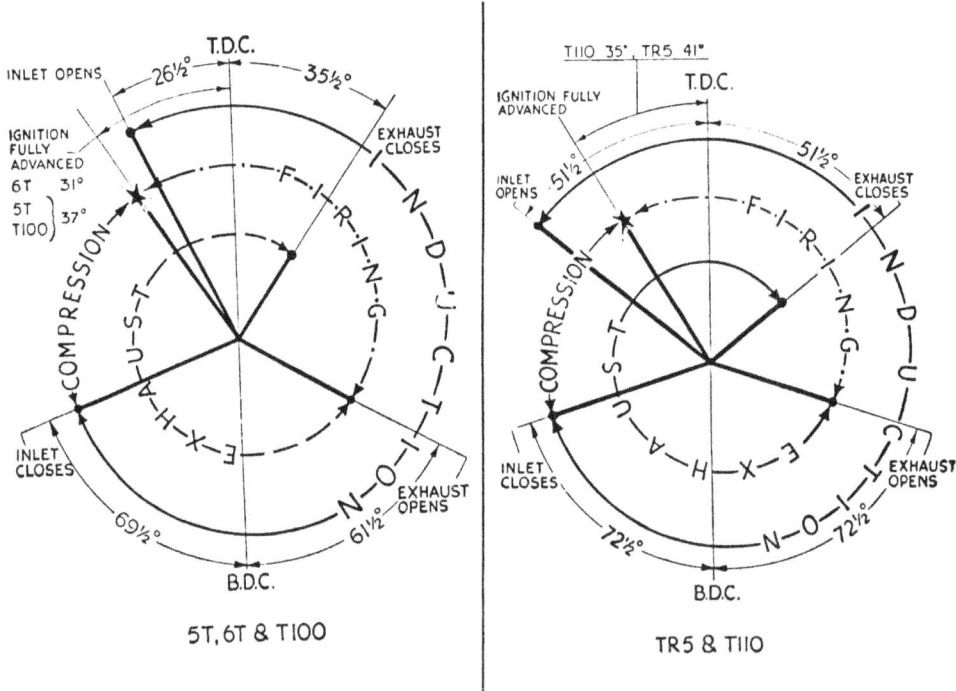

Fig. 20. TIMING DIAGRAMS

See pages 6—18 for checking figures.

Fitting Cylinder Block

which is extremely small when compared with the damage which can result from a badly fitting circlip. Lubricate the piston rings and skirts and turn the rings so that the gaps do not coincide. Place the piston ring clip over the rings and allow the base of the pistons to rest on the forward top face of the crankcase (see Fig. 21).

Cylinder Block. Grease the cylinder block base washer and fit to the block. Lubricate the tappet blocks and assemble the tappets. Place a rubber wedge between the tappet stems to prevent them falling into the crankcase during assembly (see Fig. 21). Liberally oil the cylinder bores and then lower the block over the pistons until the piston rings enter the bores.

Support the block in one hand and turn the crankshaft with the other, forcing the piston up into the bores. As the pistons enter the bores, the piston ring clips will fall clear and can be withdrawn over the connecting rods. Guide the block over the base studs and then remove the wedges from the tappets. Fit the eight holding nuts and securely tighten.

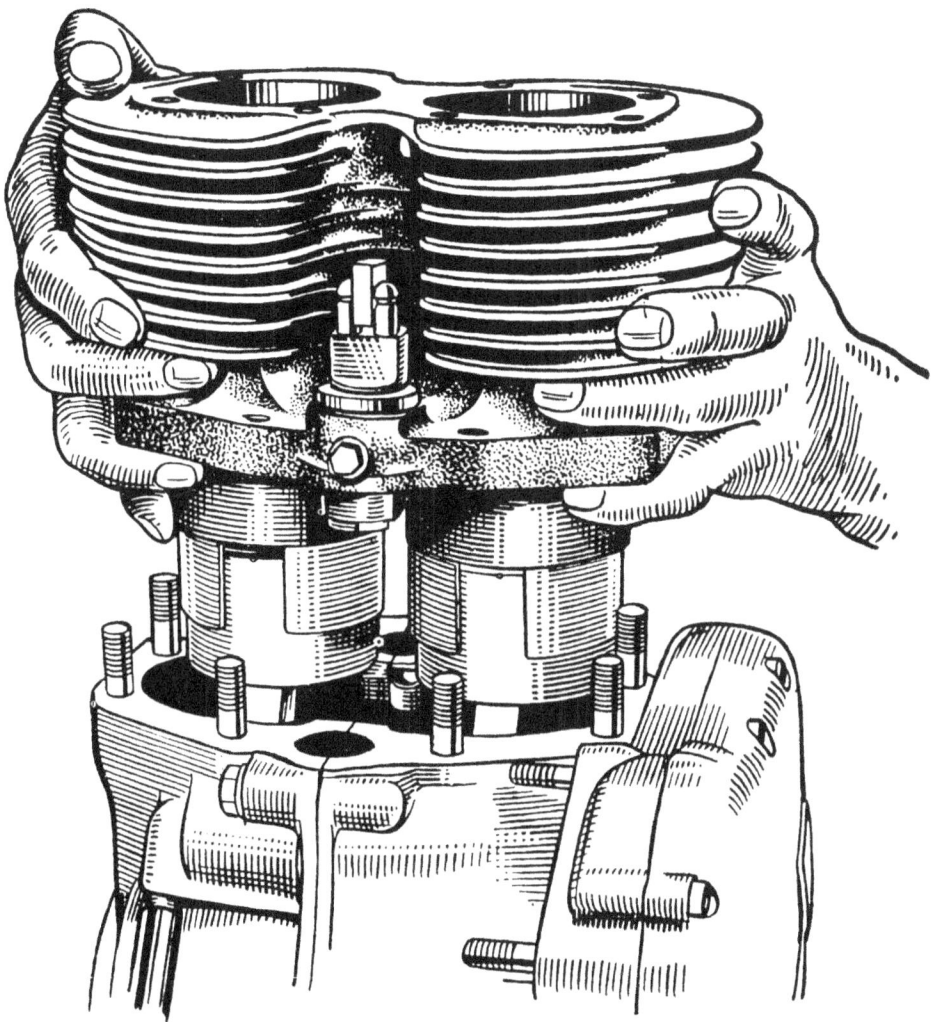

Fig. 21. FITTING THE CYLINDER BARREL
(Note the cork wedge holding the tappets)

Fitting Cylinder Block

Ignition Timing. *The timing of the engine can be carried out at this stage if desired. The information given on page 67 (Magneto) and page 68 (Coil) applies when the cylinder head is fitted. The marked timing stick should be discarded in favour of a depth gauge, by which means an accurate measurement can be made directly on top of the piston.*

Inlet Push Rods and Covers. Fit the rubber oil seal to the tappet block and then assemble to the tappets and block the push rods and cover. The oil drain pipes should be assembled to the cover tube before re-positioning to the engine.

Inlet Manifold. Assemble the inlet manifold to the cylinder head with the new joint washers. In the case of the cast iron cylinder head, we recommend the use of jointing compound with the joint washers. The reason for this is that as the manifold and cylinder head are manufactured from dissimilar metals, a slight amount of "weave" takes place between them which may cause the washer to become dislodged.

Cylinder Head. Grease the head gasket and fit to the cylinder block. Assemble the head to the block and lightly tighten down the four short bolts.

Inlet Rocker Box. Grease the rocker box gaskets and upper push rod cover washer and assemble to the rocker box. Turn the engine over until both inlet push rods are nearly level and then assemble the rocker box to the cylinder head and push rod cover. Check that the gaskets have not been misplaced during assembly and then enter the two short rocker box holding bolts and firmly screw down. Fit and tighten the two rocker boxes to cylinder head nuts.

Exhaust Rocker Box. Fit the push rods and covers (with drain pipes fitted) to the tappet block. The rocker box can then be assembled in exactly the same manner as the inlet rocker box.

Rocker Oil Drain Adaptors. Ensure that the oil drain adaptor bolts are clean and then fit a copper washer between the oil drain banjos. Insert the adaptor and tighten (care should be exercised when tightening into an alloy head, TR5 & T100).

Cylinder Head Holding Bolts. Position the remaining four bolts (the torque stay bolts to the rear) and screw down until a grip is felt. All eight bolts should now be evenly tightened but do not use excessive force on the spanner. The actual force required is 18 foot pounds; if tightened beyond this figure, distortion may take place.

Ignition Timing. If the timing has been left until this stage is reached, reference should be made to page 67 (Magneto) or page 68 (Coil).

Timing Cover. Smear the joint face with jointing compound and assemble the cover to the crankcase. Employ a well fitting screwdriver when tightening the screws.

Oil Release Valve and Indicator. Fit the joint washer and screw the assembly into the timing cover.

Installing the Engine

Tappet Adjustment. Adjust as described on page 36 and replace the four inspection caps.

Carburetter. This unit can be fitted now, or after the engine has been installed in the frame. Do not forget to replace the tufnol block on the TR5 and T100 models.

Sparking Plugs. Replace and connect H.T. leads.

Rear Engine Plate. Loosely assemble the rear engine plates to the crankcase on the rigid frame models.

The engine is now ready for installation into the frame.

INSTALLING THE ENGINE
(RIGID FRAME MODELS)

ENGINE. When the engine is ready for installation, ensure that the rear lower stud is fitted in position with the nuts loosely assembled. Check that the footrest spindle is positioning the distance piece between the rear engine plates. Place a box under the frame and lift the engine into position. Ensure that the rear lower stud engages with the rear engine plates.

Front Engine Plates. Tilt the engine back and swing the plates into position. Re-fit all studs and nuts to both front and rear engine plates and attach the cover plates on the 5T and 6T models.

Dynamo. Replace to the crankcase and secure with the timing cover domed nut and tighten the clip screw.

Torque Stays. Replace to engine bolts and secure with the nuts.

Torque Clip (TR5). Remove the relevant engine bolt and then pass it through the clip back to the engine. Securely tighten.

Oil Pipes. Connect the main oil pipes from oil tank to engine and the rocker feed pipes to rocker spindles.

R.H. Footrest. Re-position the spindle and assemble the short distance piece to the L.H. side, which fits between the engine plate and inner primary case.

Primary Chaincase Inner. Smear jointing compound around the crankcase mating surface and assemble to the crankcase and over the shafts. Replace the primary chaincase to rear chainguard screw.

Installing the Engine

Air Filter, Battery Carrier and Battery. Fit the air cleaner to the frame and re-connect the rubber connector to the carburetter. Fit the battery carrier over the air filter and secure both to the frame at the seat lug. Tighten up the nut. Secure the carrier to the chaincase with the two bolts and tighten down. Place the battery in the carrier and tighten the retaining strap. Re-connect the leads and test the lights. (It is most important that the leads are not crossed. The positive lead must be secured to the earthing point).

Primary Chaincase, Clutch, Alternator and Engine Sprocket. Re-fit as described on page 90.

L.H. Footrest. Assemble to spindle and tighten both L.H. and R.H. spindle nuts.

Footbrake Pedal. Fit to the spindles and replace the securing nut.

Control Cables. Re-connect the respective cables to the handlebar and frame fittings.

Exhaust System. Fit to engine and frame and ensure that all bolts are fully tightened.

Petrol Tank. Replace the tank and secure with the bolts and rubber pads. Connect the petrol pipes. The bolts should be locked by wiring the two rear and the two front together.

Twinseat or Saddle. Fit in position; replace and tighten the front and rear connection bolts.

Oil Tank. REPLENISH.

INSTALLING THE ENGINE
(SWINGING ARM FRAME MODELS)

Engine. When tne engine has been prepared for installation, ensure that the rear lower stud is fitted in position with the nuts loosely assembled. Check that the footrest spindle is positioning the distance piece between the rear engine plate. Now lift the engine into the frame and engage the rear lower stud into the rear engine plates. A box placed under the engine will retain it in this position. When the stud is engaged, fit the remaining two studs and loosely assemble the nuts and washers.

Front Engine Plates. Replace the dynamo clip if not already in position. Re-fit the front engine plates and loosely replace the lower studs and nuts.

Dynamo. Insert the dynamo through the engine plate and secure the stud to the timing cover with the domed nut and tighten the clip screws. Connect up the electrical terminal.

Installing the Engine

Front Engine Plates Cover. Position over the studs and insert the two remaining studs and secure with their respective nuts. At this stage, tighten both rear and front engine plate stud nuts.

Torque Stays. Fit the stays to the engine bolts and tighten the bolt nuts and frame lug bolt.

Oil Pipes. Connect the main oil pipes from oil tank to crankcase and the rocker pipes to the rocker spindles.

R.H. Footrest. Loosely assemble to spindle.

Primary Chaincase, Alternator, Clutch and Engine Sprocket. Fit the short distance piece over the footrest spindle and assemble the primary chaincase inner. Fit the primary chaincase outer, clutch and engine sprocket as described on page 90.

L.H. Footrest. Assemble to spindle and tighten both L.H. and R.H. spindle nuts.

Footbrake Pedal. Fit to the spindle and replace the spring washer, plain washer and finally secure with the nut. Connect the operating rod to pedal and secure with the plain washer and split-pin. Ensure that the split-pin is locked. Engage the stop lamp switch spring to the pedal fixing.

Control Cables. Re-connect the respective cables to handlebar and frame fittings.

Exhaust System. Fit to engine and frame the exhaust pipe and silencer assemblies making sure that the connecting bolts etc., are fully tightened.

Petrol Tank. Replace the tank and secure with the four bolts and eight rubber buffer pads. Connect the petrol pipes. The bolts should be locked by wiring the two rear and the two front together.

Twinseat. Fit in position and replace and tighten the front and rear fixing bolts.

Oil Tank. REPLENISH.

NOTE

When the motorcycle has covered the first 250 miles after its overhaul; it is wise to check all nuts and bolts to ensure that they have not become loose due to the engine "bedding down".

TIMING THE ENGINE

VALVE TIMING

The camwheels, timing pinion and intermediate wheel which mesh together are suitably marked; when these marks coincide with each other, the valve timing is correct. Fig. 19 clearly illustrates the timing for the respective models.

NOTE: When the engine crankshaft has been rotated the marks on the gears will not coincide due to the uneven number of gear teeth until the crankshaft has been turned a considerable number of times. The timing of course, is not affected.

T100 FITTED WITH RACING CAMS E.3134

The marking on the camwheels is not sufficiently accurate for timing the valve operation for racing purposes. It will be noted that the camwheel has three keyways provided to enable the operator to obtain accuracy of approximately plus or minus $2\frac{1}{2}$ degrees.

The following valve timing instructions are given assuming that the engine has been fitted with racing cams and is now installed in the vice (Fig. 9, page 42) with the rocker boxes, timing gears and timing cover still to be fitted.

Exhaust Rocker Box. Assemble the exhaust rocker box and the timing side push rod to the cylinder head. Fit the holding bolts and nuts and tighten down.

Tappet Adjustment. Ensure that the tappet is on the base of the cam and then adjust the rocker pin to give 0.020" (0.50 mm.) clearance between the pin and the valve tip.

At a later stage, to check the opening of the valve a D.T.I. (dial test indicator) should be fixed to the engine. If the operator is not in possession of such an instrument the clearance given above should be increased to 0.025" (0.60 mm.) when checking.

Checking T.D.C. Fit a degree timing disc to the drive side engine mainshaft and fix a pointer in any convenient location. Turn the crankshaft until the pistons are at T.D.C., then set the disc and pointer to read 0 degrees and clamp up firmly. To ensure that the pistons are at true T.D.C., turn the crankshaft backwards until the piston is say $1\frac{1}{2}$" (4 cms.) down the stroke. Note the reading on the disc. Now turn the crankshaft forward until the pistons are again $1\frac{1}{2}$" (4 cms.) down the stroke. The disc reading should be the same. If not correct, re-adjust the disc or pointer. Particular care should be exercised to ensure accurate T.D.C. setting.

EXHAUST CAMSHAFT TIMING

Setting the Crankshaft. Turn the crankshaft forward until the disc reading is 55 degrees before B.D.C.

Setting the Exhaust Camshaft. Rotate the camshaft "CLOCKWISE" until all play between the rocker adjuster pin and valve tip is taken up.

Timing the Engine

Fitting the Camwheel. First fit the intermediate wheel. It is now necessary to fit the camwheel to the shaft without disturbing it or the intermediate wheel. This is made possible by aligning one of the three keyways with the camshaft key and the teeth in line with the teeth on the intermediate wheel. When aligned press on the camwheel (See Fig. 18).

Checking the Valve Closing. Turn the crankshaft backwards until the rocker adjuster clearance is nil which should give the point of closing of the valve as 34 degrees after T.D.C.

The opening and closing of the valve can be more accurately determined by clamping a D.T.I. in a convenient position and allowing the plunger button to rest on the valve collar. Any movement of the valve is then immediately seen on the clock face. Another method is to use a feeler gauge. First re-set the rocker adjuster to give a 0.025" (0.60 mm.) clearance. The "nip" on the valve can now be felt by inserting a 0.005" (0.10 mm.) feeler.

It should be appreciated that due to tolerances in manufacture, wear, etc., it may not be possible to obtain the exact degree figures quoted. Points of opening and closing should be within 3 degrees either way, if the error is more, the camwheel must be extracted and one of the remaining two keyways tried. Do not forget to mark the keyway already tried with an indelible pencil to prevent it being accidentally tried again.

INLET CAMSHAFT TIMING

Repeat the exhaust procedure by fitting the inlet rocker box, timing side push rod and adjusting the clearance between rocker adjuster and valve to give 0.020" (0.50 mm.).

Setting the Crankshaft. Turn the crankshaft backwards until the exhaust valve closes and the disc reading is 55 degrees after B.D.C.

Setting the Inlet Camshaft. Rotate the camshaft "ANTI-CLOCKWISE" after all play between the rocker adjuster pin and valve tip is taken up (valve closing).

Fitting the Camwheel. Assemble in the same manner as in the exhaust camshaft procedure.

Checking Valve Opening. Rotate the engine forward until there is no play between the rocker adjuster and valve tip when the point of opening should be approximately 34 degrees before T.D.C. (The exhaust valve is now open).

As a final check, the drive side cylinder push rods may be fitted and the timing of the drive side cylinder checked. If any discrepancy (up to 4 degrees) is found between the two cylinders, it should be equalised. To do this, it will be necessary to remove the camwheel and re-select another keyway. When the timing has been corrected, insert the new figures in the "Record Table" overleaf thereby obviating this last operation for subsequent assemblies.

Timing the Engine

VALVE TIMING RECORD TABLE

.... INLET VALVE OPENS ... ... B.T.D.C.

.... INLET VALVE CLOSES ... ... A.B.D.C.

.... EXHAUST VALVE OPENS ... ... B.B.D.C.

.... EXHAUST VALVE CLOSES ... ... A.T.D.C.

TAPPETS SET AT 0.020" (0.50 mm.)

Remove the timing disc and pointer. Detach the rocker boxes and push rods for final assembly (See page 55).

TAPPET ADJUSTMENT

When the rocker boxes and push rods are finally assembled, RE-ADJUST THE TAPPET CLEARANCE TO:—

INLET	... ...	0.002" (0.05 mm.)
EXHAUST	... ...	0.004" (0.10 mm.)

IGNITION TIMING (RACING)

In order to ensure accuracy, a degree timing disc should be employed when timing the ignition for racing purposes. Fit the disc to the engine shaft and find the true T.D.C., then clip the pointer to indicate ZERO degrees. Set the magneto with the contact points just breaking and the cam ring in the fully advanced position; turn the crankshaft to give the following readings on the compression stroke:

For Petrol or Petrol-Benzole ... ... 42° before T.D.C.

*For Methanol or other alcohol fuels ... ... 38° before T.D.C.

*If this fuel is used for the T100 the alloy cylinder block MUST be replaced by a cast-iron type.

Accuracy of the ignition timing can be finally checked by running the engine at full throttle and moving the ignition lever slowly from the fully advanced position and noting the increase or decrease in R.P.M.

IGNITION TIMING (MAGNETO)

(Assuming that the magneto is in position and the timing cover is removed).

Magneto Wheel. Unscrew the securing nut and screw into the gear centre the withdrawal tool DA50/1 which is supplied with the toolkit. When the tool is in position, tighten the centre bolt and the gear will be withdrawn from the shaft. Set the contact breaker points to .012 ins. fully open.

Sparking Plugs. Remove both plugs.

Piston Positioning. Unscrew the rocker inspection caps. Engage TOP gear and then rotate the rear wheel in the correct direction for forward travel, watching the valve operation in the L.H. (DRIVE SIDE) cylinder. When the INLET valve closes, continue gently to rotate the rear wheel until the piston reaches the top of the stroke (This is known as "TOP DEAD CENTRE—T.D.C.). The correct piston position can be felt with the timing stick by rocking the rear wheel to and fro. When the T.D.C. has been found, mark the lowest part of the timing stick which is visible at eye level and remove the stick; make a further mark ($\frac{5}{16}$" or $\frac{3}{8}$" (8 mm. or 9.5 mm.) as the case may be) above the first mark. Now re-insert the timing stick into the cylinder and rotate the rear wheel backwards until the piston has fallen about 1" (2.5 cms.), then reverse the rotation and slowly bring the piston up to the desired mark on the timing stick. This procedure eliminates any error due to backlash in the timing gears.

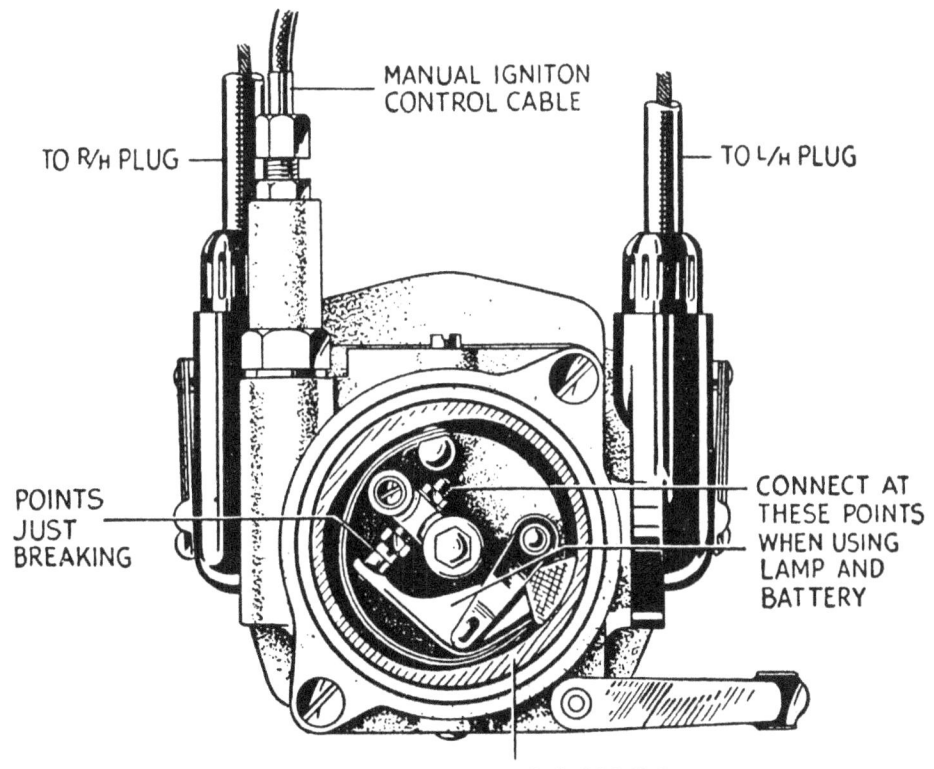

Fig. 22. **MAGNETO IN TIMING POSITION**

Coil Ignition Timing

Positioning the Contact Breaker. Remove the contact breaker cover and advance the manual control lever on the handlebar (Close anti-clockwise to advance). Rotate the contact breaker until the points are in the upper position and just breaking (See Fig. 22). In order to ascertain accurately the exact point of opening, slip a 0.0015" (0.04 mm.) feeler gauge or a piece of tissue paper between the points. Rotate the contact breaker and the gauge will be released immediately the points start to open.

Magneto Gear. Carefully retain the contact breaker in the set position and fit the gear to the magneto shaft (ensure that the shaft and gear bore is free from oil). Tap the gear gently to engage the taper and fit and secure the washer and nut.

Automatic Timing Device (A.T.D.). 5T and 6T machines with magneto ignition are fitted with an automatic timing device. This is removed by unscrewing the central bolt which has a self-extracting action. When replacing the unit hold the central portion and twist the gear against the spring. Use a pencil as a wedge to hold it in this position while fitting the unit to the shaft.

Final Operation. Re-check the timing and if correct, replace the timing cover, contact breaker cover, sparking plugs, H.T. lead (See Fig. 22) and the four rocker inspection caps.

Sparking Plug Leads. If the timing operation has been carried out correctly, join the plug leads as follows:—

    The lead nearest the engine to the R.H. cylinder (Timing side).
    The opposite lead to the L.H. cylinder (Drive side).

IGNITION TIMING (COIL)

REPLACING THE DISTRIBUTOR AND DRIVING PINION

Replacing the Distributor, Adaptor and Coil. Assemble the distributor complete with the clamping lever to the adaptor and tighten the retaining bolt. Fit the adaptor to the crankcase with the clamping nut and bolt towards the crankcase and with the slotted head pointing downwards. Fit the lower retaining nut but do not tighten at this stage.

Clamp the coil onto the bracket and ensure that the two bolts are tight. Assemble the coil and bracket onto the upper two distributor adaptor studs and fit the remaining nuts. Tighten up all three retaining nuts. The distributor clamp nut and bolt should be loose enough to allow the distributor to rotate for final positioning.

Replacing the Distributor Drive. The position of the distributor should be adjusted to give the easiest position for timing the ignition, and subsequent maintenance. Rotate the distributor body until the contact breaker points are approximately at 11 o'clock when looking from the left hand of the machine. Tighten the lever clamping bolt in this position. If a long screwdriver is held against the slotted head of the clamping bolt from the underside of the engine, the nut can be tightened more easily. With R.H. cylinder (Timing Side) at T.D.C. on compression stroke (both valves closed) rotate the rotor arm clockwise until the contact breaker points are just beginning to open, when the rotor arm is pointing to the rear of the machine. Holding the rotor arm in this position, slide the thrust washer, followed by the drive pinion, onto the distributor shaft so that the hole in the pinion boss lines up with the hole in the distributor shaft. Mesh the pinion into the nearest position on the mating pinion and slide the locking pin through the wheel and shaft, retaining it in position by placing the circlip in the groove in the pinion boss. The distributor is now in the best position for final timing and adjustment of the contact breaker points.

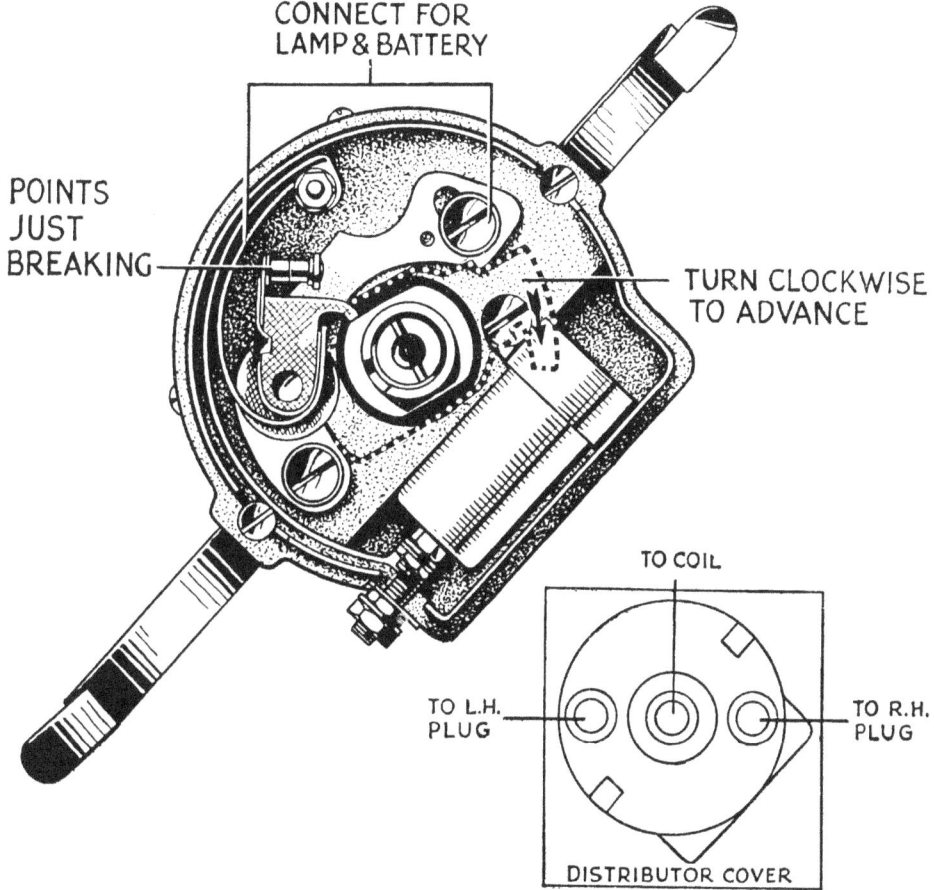

Fig. 23. **DISTRIBUTOR IN TIMING POSITION**

TIMING
Setting the Contact Breaker Points. Slacken the distributor clamp bolt and rotate the distributor slowly until the contact breaker heel is on the peak of the cam lobe, when the point should be separated. To adjust the points, slacken off the two screws securing the fixed contact plate and move the plate to give a 0.014-0.016" (0.36 mm.-0.40 mm.) gap between the contact points. Tighten up the screws and re-check the gap adjustment.

Piston Positioning. Unscrew the rocker inspection caps. Engage TOP gear and then rotate the rear wheel in the correct direction for forward travel, watching the valve operation in the R.H. (Timing Side) cylinder. When the INLET valve closes

Coil Ignition Timing

continue gently to rotate the wheel until the piston reaches the top of the stroke (This is known as "TOP DEAD CENTRE"—T.D.C.). The correct piston position can be felt with the timing stick by rocking the rear wheel to and fro. When the true T.D.C. has been found, the 1954 Model 6T should be timed with the piston in this position, whereas for the Model 5T and 1955 6T, mark the lowest part of the timing stick which is visible at eye level and remove the stick; make a further mark $\frac{1}{32}''$ (0.80 mm.) above the first mark. Now re-insert the timing stick into the cylinder and rotate the rear wheel backwards until the piston has fallen about $\frac{1}{4}''$ (6 mm.) then reverse the rotation and slowly bring the piston up to the desired mark on the timing stick. This procedure eliminates any error due to backlash in the timing gears.

Correct Positioning of the Distributor. Stand over the right hand side of the machine and place the left hand under the distributor, holding it in such a manner that it can be freely turned to the left or right. Now lean across the saddle or twinseat and rotate the distributor housing slightly (contact breaker points nearly vertical) until the points just visibly open. Retaining the distributor in position tighten up the clamp bolt and make a further check.

Check the Timing. Check the setting by placing a 0.0015" (.040 mm.) feeler gauge (or if not available a cigarette paper or tissue paper) between the points. Rotate the rotor arm against the springs on the fully advanced position when the feeler gauge should just be released. Finally check that the lever clamp bolt is fully tightened. A long screwdriver should be held against the slotted head of the clamping bolt from the underside of the engine to prevent it from rotation when the nut is being tightened.

Sparking Plug Leads. If the timing operation has been carried out correctly, join the plug leads as follows:—

The lead nearest to the engine the L.H. cylinder (Drive Side).
The opposite lead to the R.H. cylinder (Timing Side).

Distributor Protective Cover. Fit the P.V.C. sheet over the distributor with cut-away hole on the L.H. (drive side) of the engine. Fit the H.T. leads from the distributor cap into the cut-away.

GEARBOX

The gearbox employed has four speeds and is very robustly constructed. It will require very little attention, and, if its oil change intervals are strictly adhered to and the security of its clamping bolts occasionally checked, the life of the gearbox will be greatly prolonged.

For the rider who wishes to use his machine in one or more of the various competitions or for road racing, a set of gears can be made available to suit the particular conditions. To change from STANDARD to WIDE ratio, four gears are required, namely—mainshaft high, mainshaft second, layshaft high and layshaft second. The speedometer driven gears will also have to be changed to correct the speedometer to gearbox ratio. To fit CLOSE ratio gears a complete set is required and as no provision is made for the speedometer gears, a sealing plug is supplied. A tachometer driven off the exhaust cam gear is employed for the purpose of checking the engine revolutions when close ratio gears are fitted. On page 207 an "Engine Revolution" and "Gear Ratio" chart will be found which will assist the rider in choosing a suitable combination of gears.

Briefly, the gearbox operates in the following manner:

Gear selections are made by depressing or raising the pedal. The pedal is attached to the plunger quadrant which is spring loaded on either side of its axis. After the pedal has been operated, it will automatically return to the central position for the next selection. When the pedal is depressed the upper quadrant plunger moves under the guide plate, whereas the lower one, being released, connects with the gear operating quadrant which is geared to the camplate.

The camplate is rotated by the gear quadrant, the movement being arrested by a spring loaded plunger which is sprung into a notch in the camplate periphery. As the camplate rotates, the gear selector forks which are connected, move along their spindle and in turn shift the gears. Fig. 24 shows clearly all the working parts and before attempting to dismantle the gearbox, the illustration should be carefully studied.

FAULTY GEAR SELECTION

A badly adjusted clutch is one of the chief causes of faulty gear selection. Always ensure that the clutch plates spin true and that the correct grade of oil is employed (See page 200 for further information).

Gearchange pedal springs may be fatigued or broken, thus preventing the pedal from centralising itself. Remedy—change both springs.

Quadrant Plunger Sticking. To remedy, remove the plunger and polish the bearing surface with smooth emery until the plunger will move freely in its housing. It is a good plan to renew the plunger springs if this fault occurs.

Camplate Plunger Sticking. To remedy, remove the domed nut from the bottom of the gearbox casing and apply the same remedy as for Quadrant Plungers. Slackness of the nuts securing the kickstarter assembly or clutch centre.

As both these parts are attached to the gearbox mainshaft, either becoming loose would allow the mainshaft to float and cause a faulty selection. Remedy—obvious.

Gearbox

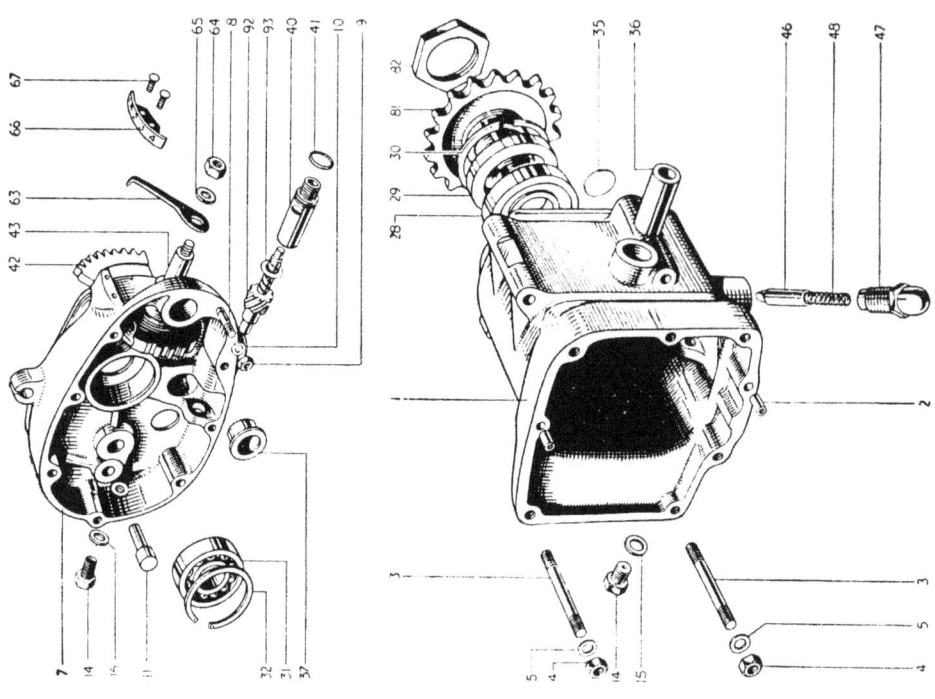

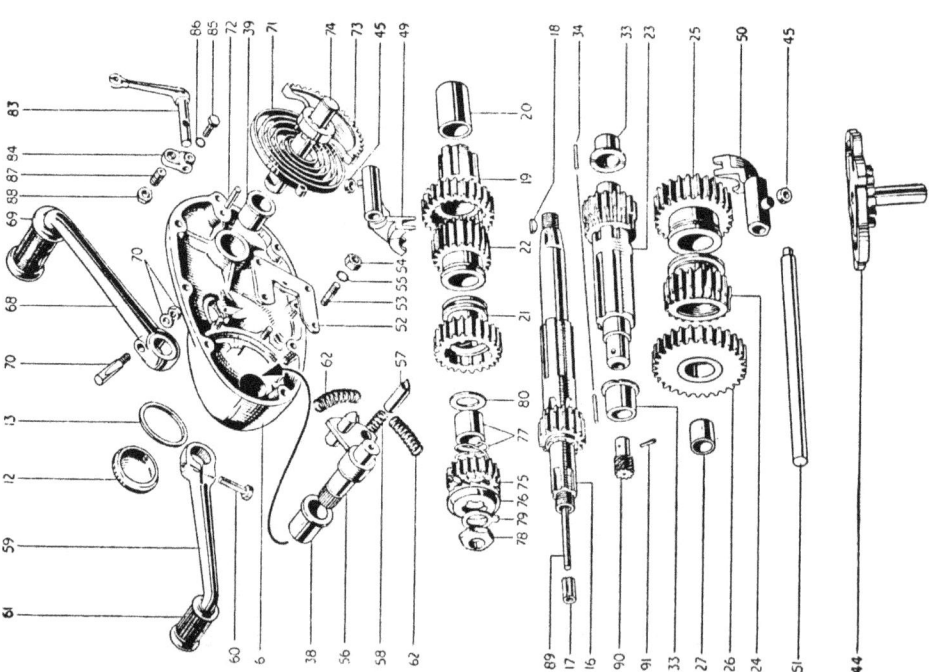

Fig. 24. GEARBOX (COMPONENT PARTS)

INDEX TO FIG. 24. GEARBOX (COMPONENT PARTS)

Index No.	Description.	Index No.	Description.
1	Casing.	47	Bush, plunger.
2	Dowel, inner cover.	48	Spring, plunger.
3	Stud.	49	Fork, gear selector mainshaft.
4	Nut.		
5	Washer.	50	Fork, gear selector layshaft.
6	Cover, gearbox outer.	51	Rod, gear selector fork.
7	Cover, gearbox inner.	52	Plate, gearchange guide.
8	Stud.	53	Stud.
9	Nut.	54	Nut.
10	Washer.	55	Washer.
11	Stop, kickstarter quadrant.	56	Plunger assy. gear quadrant.
12	Cap, oil filler.	57	Plunger, gear quadrant.
13	Washer.	58	Spring, plunger.
14	Plug, oil level and drain.	59	Pedal, gearchange.
15	Washer.	60	Set screw.
16	Mainshaft and low gear.	61	Rubber.
17	Bush.	62	Spring, pedal return.
18	Key.	63	Finger, gear indicator.
19	Gear, mainshaft high.	64	Nut.
20	Bush, mainshaft high gear.	65	Washer.
21	Gear, mainshaft third.	66	Quadrant, gear indicator.
22	Gear, mainshaft second.	67	Pin, quadrant fixing.
23	Layshaft with high gear.	68	Crank, kickstarter.
24	Gear, layshaft third.	69	Rubber, kickstarter crank.
25	Gear, layshaft second.	70	Cotter pin, with nut and washer.
26	Gear, layshaft low.		
27	Bush, layshaft low gear.	71	Spring, crank return.
28	Bearing, high gear.	72	Peg, spring anchor.
29	Oil seal.	73	Quadrant, kickstarter.
30	Circlip.	74	Shaft, kickstarter axle.
31	Bearing, mainshaft.	75	Pinion, kickstarter.
32	Circlip.	76	Ratchet, kickstarter.
33	Bush, layout.	77	Sleeve and spring, pinion.
34	Peg, layshaft bush.	78	Nut, kickstarter ratchet.
35	Disc, layshaft bush.	79	Lockwasher.
36	Bush, gear selector camplate.	80	Washer, plain.
37	Bush, gearchange spindle inner.	81	Sprocket, gearbox.
		82	Nut, sprocket locking.
38	Bush, gearchange spindle outer.	83	Lever, clutch operating.
		84	Arm, clutch operating.
39	Bush, kickstart outer.	85	Peg, clutch operating lever.
40	Bush, speedo drive.	86	Washer.
41	Washer.	87	Pin, clutch lever adjusting.
42	Quadrant, gear operating.	88	Locknut.
43	Spindle, gear operating quadrant.	89	Rod, clutch operating.
		90	Pinion, speedo drive.
44	Camplate, gear control.	91	Peg, pinion to layshaft.
45	Roller, gear control camplate.	92	Gear, speedo drive.
		93	Washer, gear thrust.
46	Plunger, gear control camplate.		

REMOVING THE GEARBOX FROM THE FRAME
(RIGID FRAME MODELS)

Battery Carrier and Air Cleaner Assembly. Disconnect the cable and remove the battery. Remove the two base screws and strap nut and remove the battery carrier, together with the air cleaner.

Exhaust System. Unscrew the front connections and silencer hanger bolts and remove the two exhaust pipes and silencers complete.

Footbrake Pedal. Unscrew the spindle nut and slide the pedal off the spindle.

Footrests. Remove the left hand footrest securing nut and remove the left hand footrest. Withdraw the other footrest complete with rod. Do not lose the distance piece between the chaincase and the engine plate.

Primary Chaincase Outer Cover. Disconnect the three leads from the stator, underneath the saddle. Remove the screws connecting the outer cover to the inner. Place a tray under the chaincase to catch the oil and remove the outer cover, pulling the stator lead through the inner cover.

Engine Sprocket and Rotor. Bend back the locking tab on the rotor retaining washer and loosen the retaining nut.

Clutch. Remove as indicated on Page 83 when the clutch housing is free on the shaft. Unscrew the nut on the engine shaft and remove the clutch, engine sprocket, rotor and primary chain together. Remove the Woodruff key from the gearbox mainshaft.

Primary Chaincase Inner Cover. Unscrew the nut and bolt connecting the rear chain guard to the inner cover. Unscrew the three screws connecting the inner cover to the crankcase and remove the inner cover.

Rear Chain. Take out the spring link and remove the rear chain from the gearbox sprocket.

Clutch Cable. Disconnect the cable nipple from the gearbox clutch lever and completely unscrew the adjuster from the inner cover, to release the cable.

Speedometer Cable. Unscrew the cable nut at the gearbox end and withdraw the cable.

Primary Chain Adjuster. Unscrew the nut which secures the adjuster to the frame.

Gearbox Clamp Bolt. Remove the clamp bolt nut and tap the bolt through the frame lug.

Gearbox Pivot Bolt. Unscrew the bolt from the frame. Remove the gearbox from the right hand side of the frame complete with the two clamp plates which should be removed afterwards.

REMOVING THE GEARBOX FROM THE FRAME
(TR5)

The removal procedure for the TR5 model is exactly the same as for the 5T and 6T with the following exceptions:—

Exhaust Systems. Slacken off the branch pipe clip. Unscrew the front connection and silencer hanger bolt and remove the exhaust system complete.

Alternator Assembly. This assembly is not fitted to the TR5 Model, and all reference to electrical equipment can be disregarded when dealing with the gearbox on this model.

REMOVING THE GEARBOX FROM THE FRAME
(SWINGING ARM FRAME MODELS)

Exhaust System. Remove both exhaust pipe and silencer assemblies by slackening the finned clip bolts, the bracket to frame bolts and the silencer bolts when the assembly can be eased off the exhaust stubs.

Footrests. Remove the left hand footrest; withdraw the right hand footrest and spindle as an assembly. Take care not to lose the distance piece between the primary chaincase and the left hand rear engine plate, and the distance piece between the engine plates.

Footbrake Pedal. Take out the split pin securing the operating rod to pedal, unscrew the pedal spindle nut when the pedal can be withdrawn.

Primary Chaincase—Clutch and Engine Sprocket. Remove these parts as described on Page 83.

Clutch Cable. Disconnect the cable nipple at the gearbox end, unscrew the cable adjuster and detach the cable from the gearbox inner cover lug.

Speedometer Cable. Unscrew the attachment nut at the gearbox when the cable can be withdrawn.

Oil Tank Air Cleaner Unit. Disconnect the oil pipe block at the engine and plug the feed hole in the block to prevent loss of oil. Remove the oil tank's three fixings and withdraw oil tank and air cleaner from the frame.

Battery Carrier to Engine Plate Bolt. Remove.

Dismantling Gearbox

Rear Engine Plate Studs. Slacken the nuts on the front lower studs and remove all other nuts from the right hand engine plate. (The gearbox adjuster can be left in position). Remove the studs by drifting with an aluminium rod. Remove the cover plate, slacken the pivot bolt and ease the gearbox back, when both plates can be removed.

Pivot Bolt. Remove the nut and withdraw the pivot bolt. The gearbox can now be taken out of the frame.

DISMANTLING THE GEARBOX

Before attempting to dismantle the gearbox, wash it thoroughly to remove dirt, oil and grease, etc. Drain the oil by removing the plug in the rear of the casing. (Note— on the Models equipped with the swinging arm rear suspension, the drain plug is placed at the bottom front of the casing). Place the gearbox in the vice, with the pivot lug gripped between the jaws.

Gearbox Outer Cover. Unscrew the five screws and three nuts holding the outer cover to the inner cover and tap the joint gently, with a hide hammer, to break the jointing compound seal. Grip the gearchange lever and kickstarter crank and withdraw the cover from the gearbox.

Gearbox Inner Cover. Bend back the tab on the kickstarter ratchet and pinion lockwasher and, placing a block between the gearbox sprocket and the vice to prevent the sprocket revolving, undo the securing nut. Withdraw the ratchet and pinion assembly complete. Remove the four screws securing the inner cover to the shell. Tap to break the joint seal and remove the cover. Care should be taken to prevent the contents of the gearbox from coming away with the inner cover.

Gear Cluster. Remove the gear selector fork rod. Slide the mainshaft from the case until the clutch end comes free from the high gear. Taking care not to lose the rollers from the selector forks, remove the gear clusters from the gearbox in one assembly. The only gear remaining is the high gear which is held in position by the sprocket nut (See Page 78).

The gearbox is now completely broken down into units and it is proposed to deal with these units separately in such a way that the fitter can dismantle, overhaul and re-assemble the major unit assemblies.

By doing the work in this manner the assembly of the gearbox is simplified in that there is no sub-assembly to bother about while concentrating on the correct assembly of the complete unit.

DISMANTLING, PREPARATION AND ASSEMBLY OF UNITS

GEARBOX OUTER COVER

Kickstart Assembly. Remove the kickstarter crank cotter pin and slide the pedal off the shaft. Withdraw the quadrant and spring assembly from the bush. Check the quadrant for chipped teeth and spindle wear, and the spring for fatigue cracks especially at the centre. Change if necessary. Replace the assembly in exactly the opposite way, making sure that the centre of the spring re-engages with the same spline on the quadrant spindle shaft (See Fig. 25).

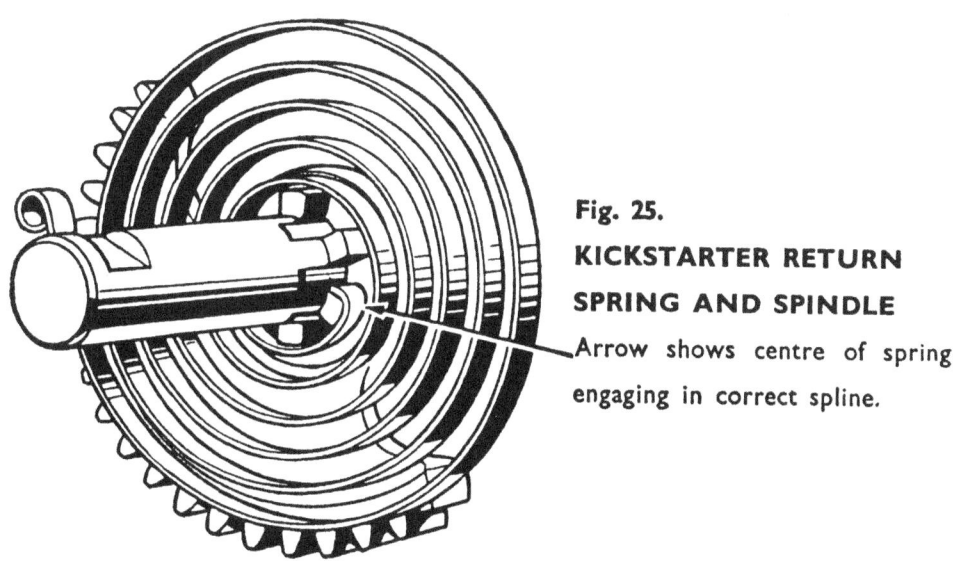

Fig. 25.

KICKSTARTER RETURN SPRING AND SPINDLE

Arrow shows centre of spring engaging in correct spline.

Clutch Operating Lever. If it is necessary to remove this lever the kickstarter assembly must be removed (see paragraph above) and the kickstarter bush pressed in sufficiently to allow the lever to be withdrawn past it after removal of the lever arm peg screw. The peg screw should be changed if the peg shows any signs of wear. Re-assemble in the reverse way.

Gearchange Mechanism. Provided that this mechanism has been working satisfactorily, there is no need to disturb it. If, however, it should become necessary, release the quadrant plungers and springs by raising and depressing the gearchange pedal. Remove the four nuts on the guide plate and slide the plate off the studs. Slacken the gearchange pedal set screw and slide the pedal off the splined shaft. Withdraw the plunger quadrant from its bush. Replace the springs if they have become rusty due to condensation, examine the guide plate for wear and relieve any high spots with fine emery cloth.

Replace the guide plate if the knife edges are worn. If it is necessary to remove any of the bushes, the casing should be heated before they are pressed out. Re-assemble the mechanism in the opposite way to dismantling.

GEARBOX INNER COVER

Gear Operating Quadrant. This quadrant can be inspected for wear on the teeth while still in position. The freedom of the spindle can also be checked. It is, therefore, unnecessary to remove the quadrant unless it requires changing. To do this, remove the split-pin and withdraw the spindle. Replace in the opposite way, using a new split pin.

Bearing. Remove the retaining circlip and press the bearing out; thoroughly degrease it and dry with compressed air if possible. Check for roughness, pitting, indentation and end float; make sure that the inner race is a tight push fit on the mainshaft. When replacing, heat the casing and then press the bearing into position. Re-fit the circlip, ensuring correct engagement in the groove. Liberally oil the bearing.

Speedometer Drive. Using a soft metal drift against the spindle gear, gently tap the drive gear and bush out of its housing. Examine the gear for worn teeth and check the fit in the bush. To replace, fit the thrust washer over the gear spindle and thread the spindle into the bush. Fit the assembly into the cover, gear first. Fit the oil seal into the annular groove in the bush and press the bush into position until the keyway in the bush lines up with the screw hole.

Kickstarter Ratchet and Pinion. This assembly has already been removed to take off the inner cover. The pinion and ratchet should be checked for chipped or broken teeth and the spring for fatigue. Replace after the inner cover is back in place.

GEAR CLUSTER

Gears. Examine all the gears thoroughly for chipped, fractured or worn teeth. Check the internal splines and bushes, making sure that the splines are free on their respective shafts, with no tendency to bind, and the bush in the layshaft low gear is not worn.

GEARBOX CASING

Camplate and Plunger Assembly. Unscrew the acorn nut at the base of the main casing and withdraw the camplate plunger and spring. Remove the camplate from the bush. Make sure that the plunger works freely in its housing. Check the spring for fatigue. Examine the camplate carefully for signs of wear in the roller tracks as such wear will make gear selection difficult and damage to the gears may result. Change the camplate if a worn track is evident. To replace, fit the camplate spindle into the bush and screw the plunger assembly (pointed end engaging the cam) into the plunger housing. Secure the camplate in the TOP (4th) gear positions (See Fig. 26).

Chain Sprocket. Place a small aluminium block between a sprocket tooth and the vice, to stop the sprocket rotating, and unscrew the sprocket nut. It may be necessary to tap the end of the spanner with a hammer to free the nut. Ease away the sprocket.

Dismantling Gearbox

High Gear, Oil Seal and Mainshaft Bearing. Remove the two long casing to outer cover studs and the two dowels, casing to inner cover and press the high gear out and into the casing. Ease the oil seal from the housing and discard.

Remove the bearing retaining circlip and press the bearing out of the housing. Check the gear for chipped or worn teeth and the shaft bearing for wear. Thoroughly clean and degrease the journal bearing and dry with pressure air. Check for roughness, pitting, indentation and float; make sure that the mainshaft high gear is a good fit in the inner race. When replacing, first warm the casing and then press the bearing into the housing, securing it with a circlip. Lubricate with oil when in position. Press a new oil seal into the ball race housing with the part number on the outside and the leather "rolling" towards the inside of the case. Insert the high gear from inside the housing, through the bearing and press it fully home.

Replacing the Chain Sprocket and Nut. Support the high gear from inside the casing and press the sprocket onto the high gear splines. Secure the casing in the vice and with a block between the sprocket teeth and the vice, tighten the locknut to the sprocket.

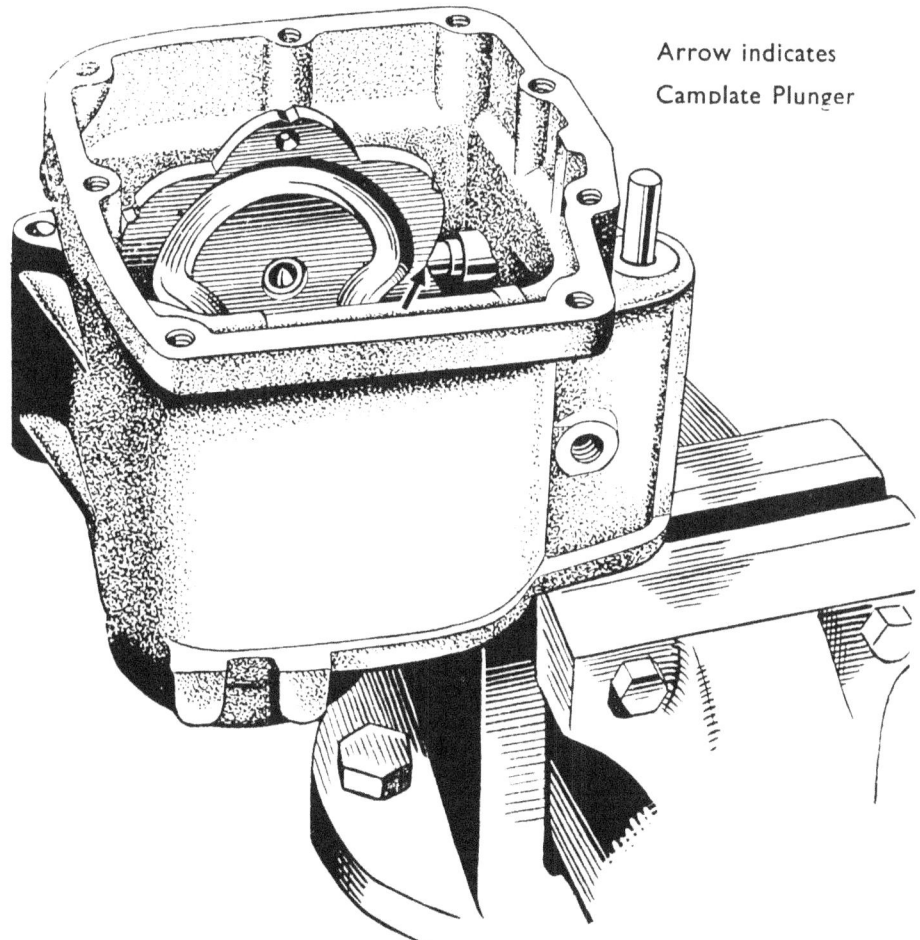

Arrow indicates Camplate Plunger

Fig. 26. GEARBOX CASING IN VICE
Showing the Camplate in the top (4th) gear positions.

ASSEMBLING THE GEARBOX

Mainshaft Gears. Secure the gearbox casing in a vertical position with the open end facing upwards (See Fig. 26). Slide the mainshaft third gear over the mainshaft followed by the mainshaft second gear, with their selector grooves towards the centre. Grease the camplate roller and fit it onto the smaller selector fork peg. Position the smaller selector fork in the second and third gear grooves with the shaft of the selector fork below the mainshaft and the roller towards the clutch end of the casing. Lower the assembly into the case. When the gear cluster is correctly located, turn the selector fork until the camplate roller rests in the selector camplate track. Withdraw the mainshaft slowly, leaving the second and third gears and selector fork in position to assist assembly of the layshaft gears.

Layshaft Gears. Assemble the third and second gear with the selector fork grooves facing inwards to the layshaft and high gear. Appiy grease to the roller and fit to the larger selector fork peg. Fit the larger selector fork into the grooves, with the shaft of the selector above the layshaft and the camplate roller towards the open end of the gearbox. Lubricate the layshaft bush and lightly smear the shaft with oil. Lower the layshaft assembly into the gearbox, small gear first until the camplate roller can be engaged on the camplate track. Oil the selector rod and thread it very carefully through the selector forks, shoulder end first, and engage it in the locating hole in the clutch end of the casing. Oil the mainshaft and thread it through the mainshaft gears. Place the layshaft low gear over the layshaft end with the internal teeth facing inwards. Place a straight edge over the gearbox end and test the clearance between the running face of the layshaft low gear and the outer face of the inner casing. Minimum allowable clearance is 0.005" (0.13 mm.) If the clearance is less than specified, the layshaft bush cannot have been fully located, or, if it has, the face of the bush must be cleaned up. Remember that a layshaft seizure means a locked rear wheel.

Gearbox Inner Cover. Fit the hollow dowels and long casing studs to the casing and lightly smear jointing compound onto the cover inner face. With the selector quadrant held in the high (4th) gear position, assemble the inner cover to the casing. Tighten the casing screws; do not omit the screw adjacent to the selector quadrant inside the cover. The action of the selector assembly can be checked if the quadrant is operated by a screwdriver and the high gear and mainshaft are rotated at the same time. Gear selection should be correct if these instructions have been carried out correctly.

With the selector in high gear, fit the kickstarter ratchet and pinion assembly onto the mainshaft in the following order: plain washer, sleeve, spring, pinion with ratchet face facing outwards, ratchet, lockwasher and nut. Lock the gears by placing a block between the chain sprocket and the vice and tighten up the ratchet nut. Bend the locking washer tab over when the nut is tight.

Gearbox Outer Cover. Smear jointing compound onto the face of the inner cover. Grasp the gearchange pedal in one hand and the kickstart lever in the other. Wind the kickstart pedal anti-clockwise to prevent the quadrant fouling the stop on the inner cover, when the outer cover is slid into position. Fit and tighten up the nuts and screws. Test the action of the kickstarter pedal, making sure that there is sufficient tension in the spring to return the pedal smartly and that it is not becoming "coil bound" when the pedal is depressed fully. Check that the gear selection is correct. Re-fill with oil until it begins to overflow from the level plug hole. Screw the level plug into the hole and replace the filler cap.

INSTALLING THE GEARBOX

(RIGID FRAME MODELS)

Positioning the Gearbox in the Frame. Re-fit the clamp plates and chain adjuster to the gearbox with the chamfered nut on the right hand end of the upper stud. Tighten up fully. Fit the gearbox into the frame and slide the pivot bolt and clamp bolt into position. Fit the clamp bolt nut and tighten both bolts slightly. Screw the frame adjuster bolt end nut into the frame and tighten.

Rear Chain. Replace the chain over the drive sprocket and fit the spring link.

Cables. Fit the speedometer cable to the drive and tighten up the securing nut. Screw the clutch cable adjuster into the lug on the inner cover and fit the cable nipple into the clutch lever.

Footrest Rod. If the removal process was carried out as described, the rod and right hand footrest and footrest nut should have remained as one assembly. Enter the free end into the engine plates from the right hand side making sure that the rod passes through the distance tube between the rear engine plates.

Primary Chaincase Inner Cover. Fit the oil retaining plate under the spring plates. Place the engine plate to chaincase distance piece in position on the footrest rod and fit the chaincase to crankcase and over the gearbox mainshaft. Make sure that the footrest rod projects into the chaincase. Secure the front end with the three screws (not fitted to TR5). Position the rear chainguard to the chaincase and secure with the set screw.

Battery Carrier and Air Cleaner. Replace the air cleaner and battery carrier and secure to frame and chaincase. Fit the battery and connect the leads.
For assembly of the Clutch and Engine Sprocket, etc., see page 90.

L.H. Footrest. Fit to spindle and securely tighten the nut.

Footrest Pedal. Grease the pedal spindle and fit the pedal. Replace the spring washer, plain washer and secure with the nut.

Exhaust System. Re-fit the exhaust pipe and silencer assemblies.

Installing Gearbox

INSTALLING THE GEARBOX (SWINGING ARM FRAME MODELS)

Frame. Ensure that the link securing the centre stand spring is correctly positioned in the frame lug.

Pivot Bolt. Fit the gearbox into the frame and insert the pivot bolt. Replace the bolt nut, finger tight.

Rear Engine Plates. Re-position to engine and frame (plate with adjuster fitted on the R.H.). Fit the plate cover and then enter the studs (nut fitted at one end) from the L.H. side. Do not omit the footrest spindle and lower rear stud and distance pieces. Fit the R.H. stud nuts and securely tighten all except the adjuster securing nut which should be only finger tight at this stage.

Battery Carrier to Engine Plate Bolt. Re-fit.

Oil Tank and Air Cleaner Unit. Fit the air cleaner to the oil tank and shroud and replace the assembly to the frame fitting the three securing nuts and bolts. Re-connect the air cleaner to the carburetter. Remove the plug from the oil block and re-fit the block to crankcase using a new joint washer.

Speedometer Cable. Insert the cable end into the gearbox ensuring that it mates with the driving spindle and then tighten up the attachment nut.

Clutch Cable. Connect cable nipple to clutch operating arm and screw the cable adjuster into the inner cover lug.

R.H. Footrest and Spindle. Insert the spindle through the engine plates from the R.H. side ensuring that the distance piece is correctly located. Fit the short distance piece between the primary inner cover and engine plate over the footrest spindle.

Primary Chaincase, Clutch and Engine Sprocket. Replace as described on page 90, but before replacing the chaincase outer cover, check the primary chain adjustment. If out of adjustment, correct as described on page 94 and then tighten the adjuster stud and the pivot bolt nut.

L.H. Footrest. Fit to spindle and securely tighten the nut.

Footbrake Pedal. Grease the pedal spindle and fit the pedal. Replace the spring washer and secure with the nut. Connect operating rod to pedal, placing the plain washer over the rod end, and secure with a split pin.

Exhaust System. Re-fit the exhaust pipe and silencer assemblies.

CLUTCH AND SHOCK ABSORBER UNIT

The clutch is the multi-plate cork type incorporating a transmission shock absorber. The pressure on the plates is made by four equally disposed springs which can be varied by screwing in or out the four slotted nuts which secure them. The clutch is designed to operate in oil and it is therefore essential that the oil level in the chaincase is maintained otherwise the cork inserts may burn and disintegrate under heavy loading. Always use the recommended grade of oil (SAE 20 see lubricant chart, page 200). If a heavier grade of oil is used, the clutch plates will not readily separate when disengaged which will cause difficult and noisy gear selection when the gearchange pedal is operated. Even with the thinner grades of oil, the kick-starter should always be operated a few times with the clutch extracted before attempting to start the engine. This procedure ensures that the plates separate freely when a gear selection is made.

The shock absorber unit which is incorporated in the clutch is robustly constructed and is designed to give many thousands of miles of trouble free service. Briefly, it operates in the following manner: the drive is transmitted through the clutch plates in the normal manner, then through the drive rubbers to the four armed spider which is keyed to the clutch shaft; this also being keyed to the gearbox mainshaft. The spider is free to oscillate inside the clutch centre but is restrained by eight rubber pads, two on either side of each arm. The larger of these pads is the drive rubber, the smaller the rebound. The drive and rebound rubber effectively level out all the engine speed variations at low speeds, providing an extremely smooth and pleasant torque, which reduces transmission wear due to the absence of "snatch".

REPLACEMENT OF THE CORK INSERTS

It is not recommended that replacement of the cork inserts in the clutch plates is made by the owner. This operation calls for precision and special equipment to reduce the new inserts to the correct thickness at each side of the plate and to ensure an even overall surface. The better method is to exchange the old plates for service replacement plates at the nearest Triumph Dealer.

OVERHAULING THE CLUTCH
DISMANTLING

Exhaust Pipe and Silencer L.H. Remove.

Footrest. Remove the left footrest.

Footbrake Pedal. Remove the unit from the pedal spindle.

Primary Chaincase. On the Rigid Frame 5T and 6T A.C. equipped models the stator leads must first be released from under the saddle mounting and then freed from the frame. Place an oil drip tray under the chaincase and proceed to remove the securing screws (all models). Ease the outer casing away and where an alternator is fitted take care to avoid damaging the stator windings.

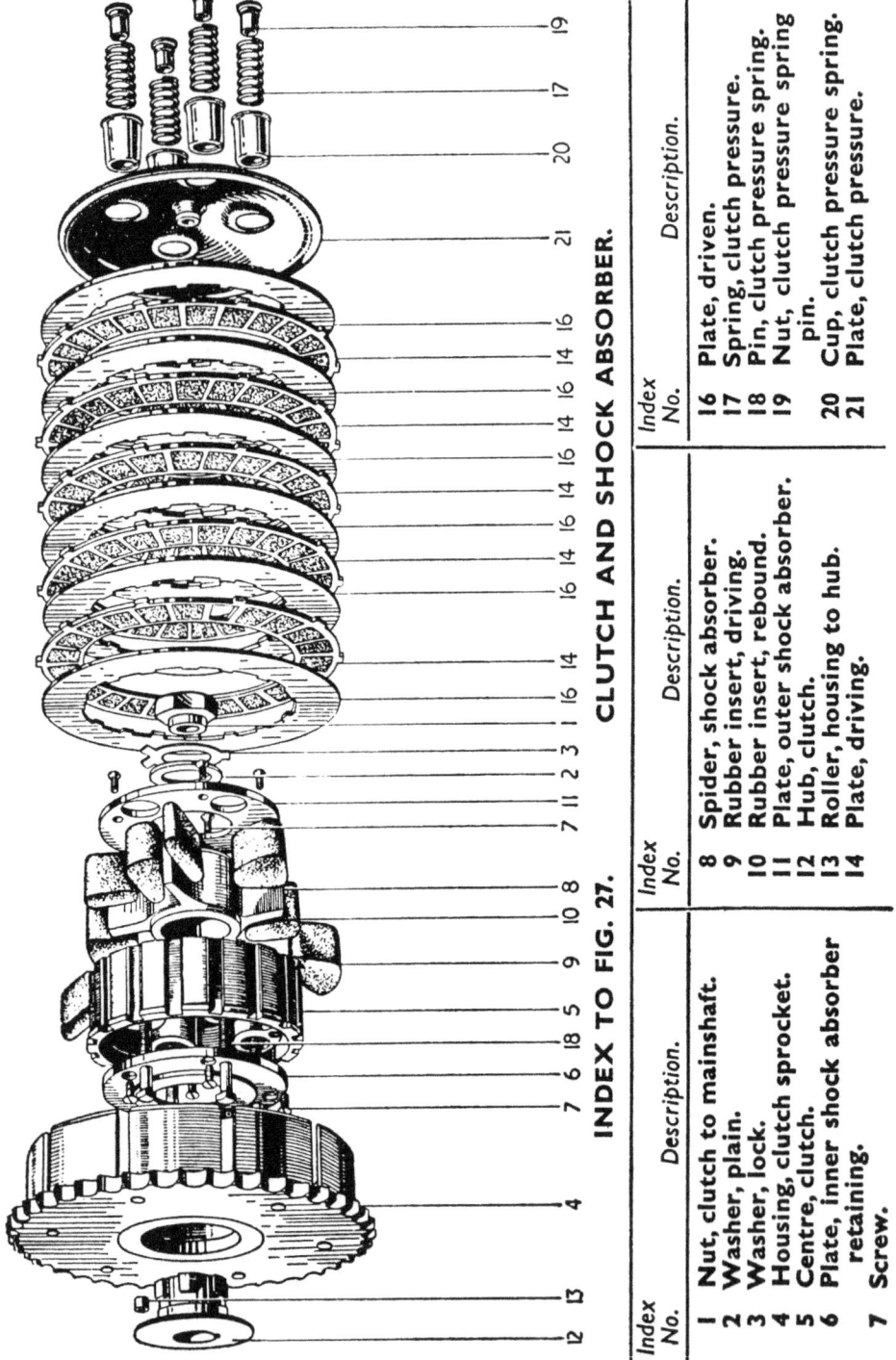

INDEX TO FIG. 27. CLUTCH AND SHOCK ABSORBER.

Index No.	Description.	Index No.	Description.	Index No.	Description.
1	Nut, clutch to mainshaft.	8	Spider, shock absorber.	16	Plate, driven.
2	Washer, plain.	9	Rubber insert, driving.	17	Spring, clutch pressure.
3	Washer, lock.	10	Rubber insert, rebound.	18	Pin, clutch pressure spring.
4	Housing, clutch sprocket.	11	Plate, outer shock absorber.	19	Nut, clutch pressure spring pin.
5	Centre, clutch.	12	Hub, clutch.	20	Cup, clutch pressure spring.
6	Plate, inner shock absorber retaining.	13	Roller, housing to hub.	21	Plate, clutch pressure.
7	Screw.	14	Plate, driving.		

Dismantling Clutch

Clutch Slotted Nuts (See Fig. 28). Unscrew these by using the special key "B" provided in the toolkit. On the underside of the nut head is a small "pip" which contacts the ends of the spring coil, thus making an effective locking device which prevents the nut unscrewing when in service. To facilitate removal, insert a knife blade "A", under the head of the nut in order to hold the spring away from the "pip" while the nut is being unscrewed.

Pressure Springs. Withdraw from the cups.

Pressure Plate. Remove complete with cups.

Fig. 28. REMOVAL OF CLUTCH NUTS
Using special screwdriver and knife blade.

Dismantling Clutch

Clutch Plates. Withdraw the bonded and plain plates from the housing.

When this stage is reached, no further dismantling is necessary if only service relined plates are to be fitted. On the other hand, if it is desirable to overhaul the shock absorber unit, proceed as below. For the average owner the changing of the shock absorber rubbers can be more easily effected with the clutch in situ.

If the shock absorber shows no sign of wear, the unit should not be disturbed, the operator proceeding with dismantling from (Clutch Push Rod, page 87).

Shock Absorber Outer Retaining Plate. Unscrew the four 2 B.A. countersunk screws and remove the plate.

Engine Mainshaft Nut. Remove the mainshaft nut and withdraw the rotor or sleeve as the case may be.

Brake Pedal. First engage TOP gear and then replace the pedal on its spindle; connecting up the operating rod. Depress the pedal to its fullest extent and wedge by inserting a suitable tool between the arm and the stop.

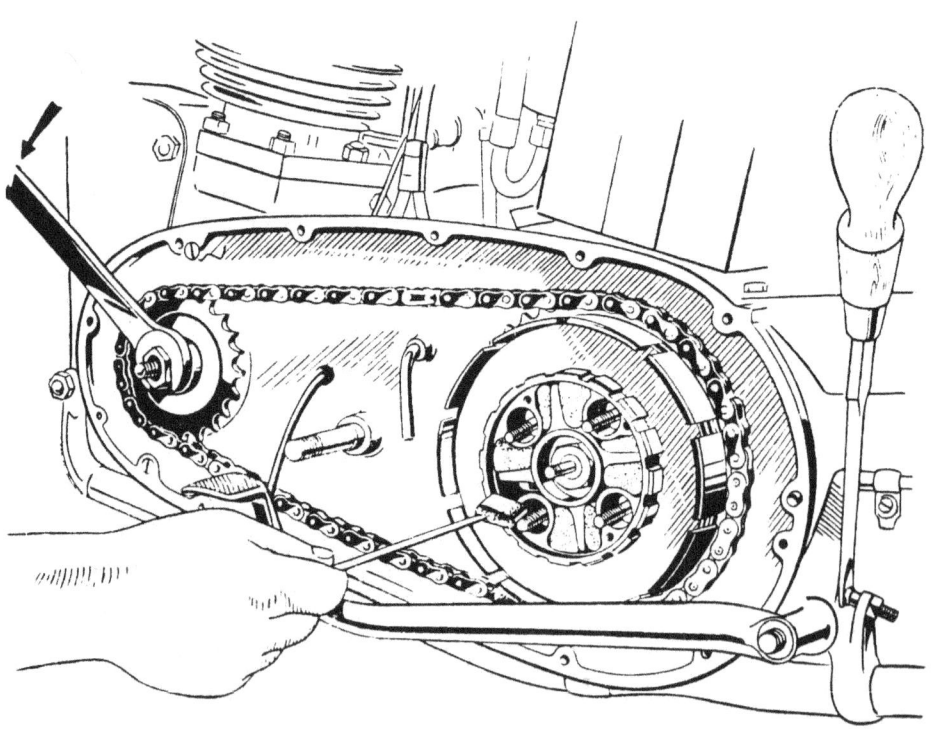

Fig. 29. METHOD OF REMOVING SHOCK ABSORBER RUBBERS

Servicing Shock Absorber

Removing the Shock Absorber Rubbers. Engage the clutch locking tool (See Fig. 33) in the clutch housing and clutch centre. Slide the driveshaft adaptor, Part No. Z90 (Fig. 32), onto the engine mainshaft, engaging the "dogged" end into the exposed sprocket splines. On the 6T model the mainshaft nut must be replaced to keep the adaptor in position for the next operation. Place a suitable spanner onto the adaptor hexagon so that the mainshaft can be rotated anti-clockwise to compress the other rubbers. Ease the rebound rubbers out and then release the pressure on the spanner when the drive rubbers can be removed.

Although this chapter deals with the dismantling of the clutch and shock absorber, it is desirable at this point to explain the assembly of the shock absorber unit.

Replacing New Shock Absorber Rubbers. Position the four drive rubbers (See Fig. 29) and exert pressure on the spanner to replace the rebound rubbers.

Outer Retaining Plate. Ensure that the rubbers are correctly positioned and fully in their housing and then replace the plate, securing with the four 2 B.A. countersunk screws.

To dismantle the remainder of the clutch proceed as follows:—

Clutch Push Rod. Remove from mainshaft.

Fig. 30.
VIEW OF CLUTCH SHOWING RUBBER INSERTS IN POSITION.

Removing Clutch

Clutch to Mainshaft Nut. First lock the clutch housing to the clutch centre by inserting the tool illustrated in Fig. 33. Bend back the locking washer tab and then place a good box spanner on the nut and shock it loose by striking the spanner tommy bar a few sharp blows with a hammer. Unscrew the nut and remove the plain and lock washers.

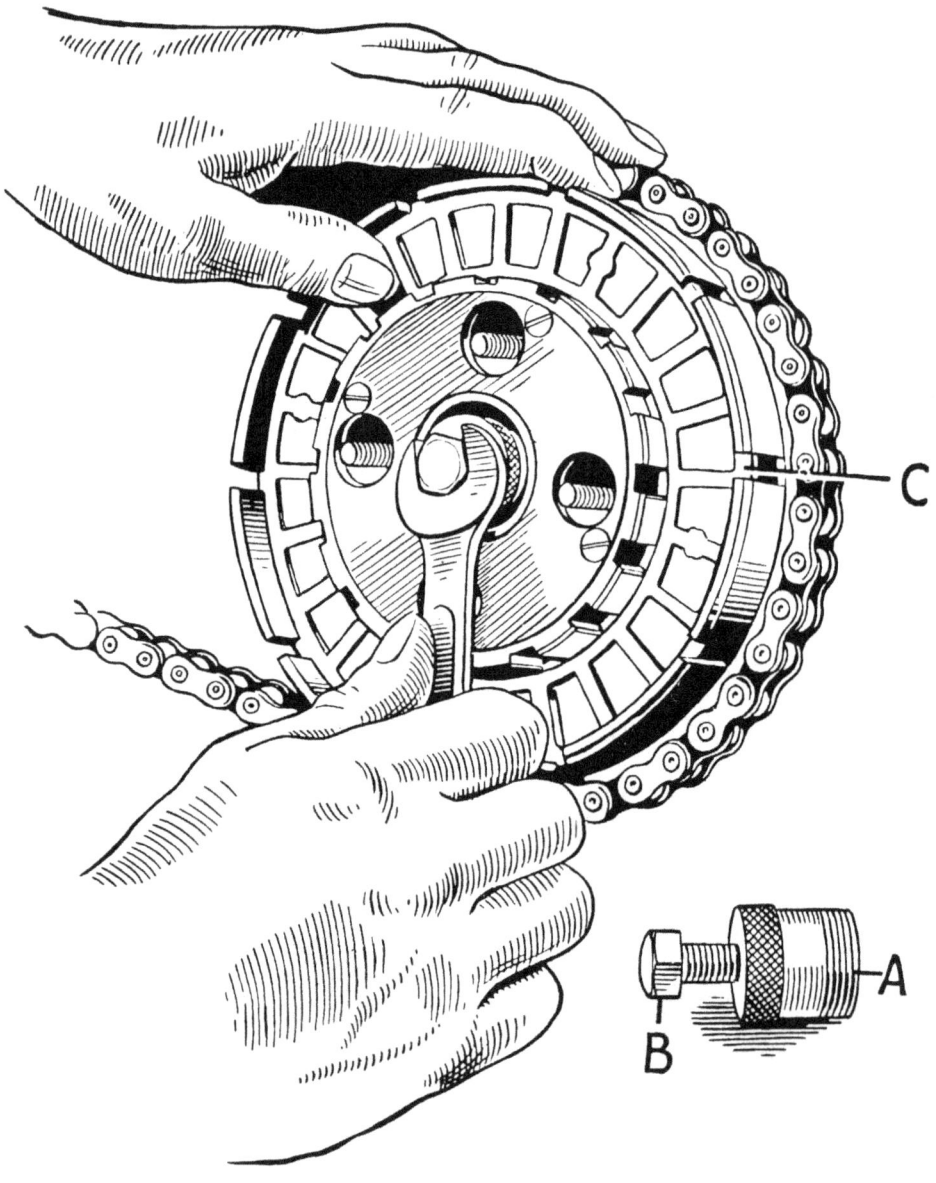

Fig. 31.
USE OF CLUTCH EXTRACTOR "AB" AND LOCKING TOOL "C"

Removing Clutch

Clutch Housing. To remove this unit, screw the tool Part No. DA50/1 seen in Fig. 31 into the clutch centre and by turning the centre bolt the clutch housing assembly will be extracted from the shaft. Holding the extractor tool in the right hand and gripping the engine sprocket in the left; remove both sprockets and chain as an assembly.

Clutch Hub. If the sprocket play on the hub is excessive, split the assembly by simply pressing out the hub from the clutch centre when the sprocket, hub and rollers can be examined (see page 90).

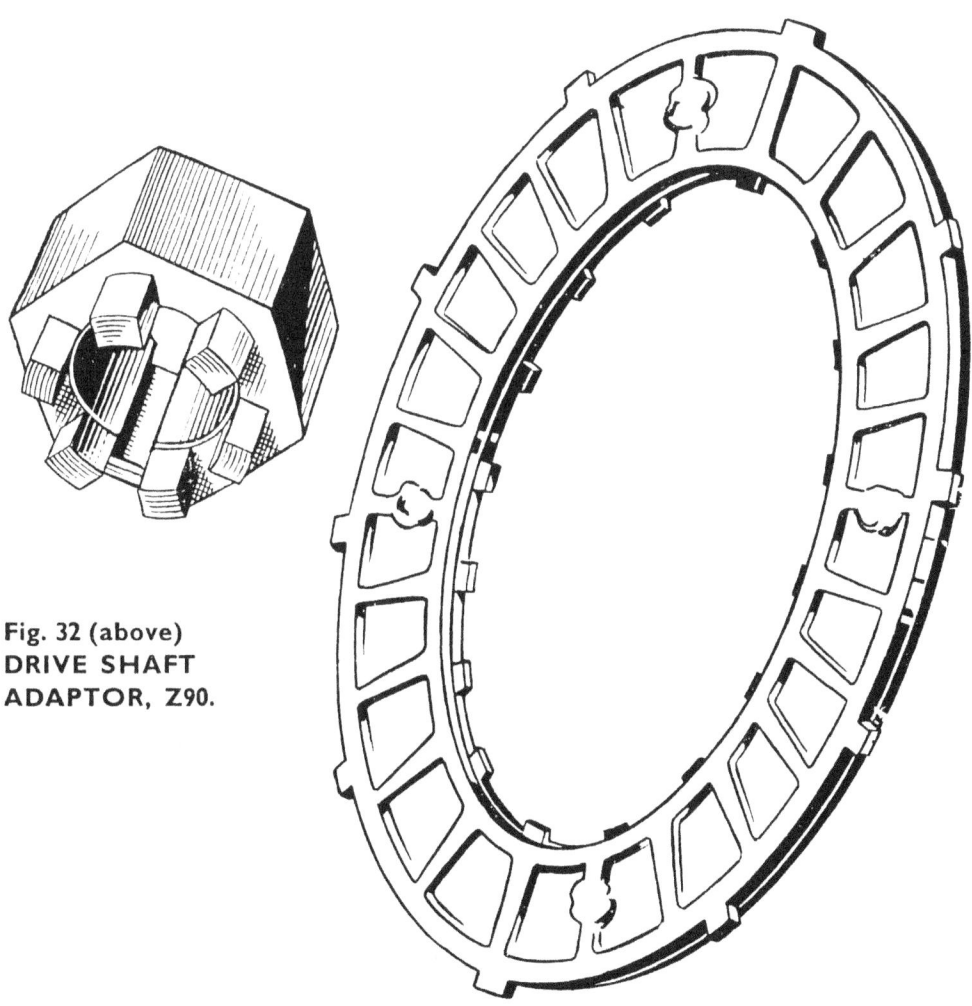

Fig. 32 (above)
DRIVE SHAFT ADAPTOR, Z90.

Fig. 33. **CLUTCH LOCKING TOOL**

PREPARATION AND INSPECTION

Clutch Springs. Check carefully for distortion. The free length of the spring is: 4 plate clutch, 1.5" (3.81 cms.); 5 plate clutch, 1.969" (5.0 cms.). If a spring measures less than 1.4" and 1.869" (3.56 and 4.75 cms.) respectively, a new one should be employed, or better still a complete set.

Cork Plates. Wash in paraffin and examine the cork inserts for wear and general condition. The corks should protrude $\frac{1}{32}$" (0.8 mm.) on each side of the plate and show no signs of burning. The engagement projections on the plate should be unworn and a good fit in the clutch housing.

Steel Plates. These must be perfectly flat and neither surface scored.

Clutch Hub. Inspect the bearing surface for pitting and indentation and replace if either fault is evident.

Clutch Roller. Check diameter with a micrometer 0.2495" (6.337 mm.), 0.25" (6.350 mm.), and if below the former, fit a new set. Also carefully inspect for signs of rust.

Clutch Sprocket. First inspect the condition of the sprocket teeth. If these are "hooked" or "chipped" a new sprocket must be fitted to avoid excessive chain wear, or, in extreme cases, chain failure. If the teeth are in good condition, inspect the bearing spool for pitting or indentation. Failure at this point can be rectified by pressing out the old spool and replacing it with a new one which must be ground after fitting. Lastly, check the housing slots in which the clutch plates operate. If worn the clutch will be noisy in operation and in extreme cases the plates may not free properly when the clutch is disengaged.

ASSEMBLING THE CLUTCH

It is assumed that the primary chaincase has been fitted and the clutch housing assembly has been dismantled, but the shock absorber unit has been dealt with as on page 87.

Clutch Housing and Hub. Apply grease to the centre hub bearing track and assemble the twenty rollers to the hub. Fit the hub into the clutch sprocket. Place the assembly on the bench with the open end of the housing facing upwards.

Shock Absorber Assembly. Position the four clutch pins into the shock absorber unit and press the latter onto the hub splines. Before finally pressing into position, ensure that the heads of the pins are correctly located against the flange on the shock absorber inner plate.

Primary Chain. Place the engine sprocket and clutch sprocket on the bench in their relative positions and assemble the chain to them with the spring link fastener facing upwards and its security checked. Fit the key to the gearbox mainshaft and assemble the engine and clutch sprocket as one unit to their respective shafts.

Assembling Clutch

Clutch. Fit the clutch locking plate into the housing and to the clutch centre, then assemble the plain washer, locking washer and nut to the gearbox mainshaft. Well tighten the nut and lock by bending down the locking washer tabs. Remove the locking plate.

Engine Sprocket. To this part on the models 5T and 6T, first fit the key to the shaft and then the plain washer, rotor, locking washer and finally the securing nut. TR5, T100 & T110—Fit the key, distance piece, locking washer and securing nut.

Clutch Plates. If new corked plates are to be fitted, first soak them in oil (SAE 20). First assemble a steel plate to the housing and then a corked plate and so on until all the plates are in position.

Clutch Push Rod. Fit into the gearbox mainshaft.

Outer Pressure Plate. Assemble this complete with cups to the clutch. Hold in position and enter the four springs and then secure with the four slotted nuts. Each nut should be just started on the pin thread to aid assembly. When all the nuts are in position, screw them down until the thread of the pin is level with the outer face of the nut.

Clutch Cable Adjustment. Screw in the adjuster inside the gearbox filler cap until the lever leans out about 15°. Now adjust the cable at the lug on top of the gearbox to give $\frac{1}{8}$ in. free movement in the cable.

Trueing the Clutch. The clutch outer pressure plate must spin true, otherwise the plates will not separate when the clutch is disengaged, thus causing faulty gear changing and the engine to stall in traffic due to "creep". To check, disengage the clutch by operating the handlebar clutch lever and depressing the kickstarter when the pressure plate can be observed rotating. If the pressure plate "wobbles" mark the place which projects the furthest and screw in, half a turn, the nearest slotted nut. Repeat the test. It must be emphasized that extra care taken with this operation will make for a smooth and effective clutch engagement.

Primary Chain Adjustment. Check, and if necessary carry out the adjustment as described on page 92.

Chaincase Outer Cover. Grease the paper gasket and fit to the outer cover. Position the outer cover to the inner cover but on the models 5T & 6T thread the alternator cables through the hole in the inner cover and then secure the cover with the fixing screws. Pull the alternator leads through the inner chaincase to prevent them fouling the primary chain. Connect the alternator leads and slide the grommet down the cable and press the boss on the outside of the inner cover.

Footrest and Brake Pedal. Replace the left hand footrest and tighten the nuts on both sides of the footrest rod. Fit the brake pedal and secure.

Exhaust Pipe and Silencer. Replace.

Oil. Remove the chaincase filler cap and pour $\frac{1}{3}$ pint of oil (SAE 20) into the casing Replace the filler cap.

Chains

SPEEDOMETER DRIVE

The drive on all models is taken from the gearbox layshaft and is situated in the gearbox inner cover. To disconnect the drive it is only necessary to unscrew the cable nut at the gearbox end and withdraw the cable.

If an oil leak occurs at the drive bush in the outer cover, this indicates that the bush oil seal has broken down. To remedy this fault, remove the outer cover (See page 77) when the bush can be removed to enable the fitting of a new oil seal (See page 78). For owners who wish to convert the gearbox to close ratio, no speedometer drive is available as it is usual to incorporate a R.P.M. indicator which is driven off the exhaust camshaft wheel in lieu of the dynamo drive. For this condition, a special plug and washer can be supplied to replace the original drive.

TACHOMETER DRIVE

A tachometer and drive can be installed on the T100 and T110 to indicate the engine R.P.M. The tachometer head replaces the speedometer head in the nacelle and the tachometer gearbox replaces the dynamo. The drive between the two units is by cable. When close ratio gears are employed a plug is supplied to blank off the speedometer drive in the gearbox inner cover.

CHAINS

Slack or badly adjusted chains are a prolific cause of harsh running and excessive wear. It is therefore of the greatest importance that the adjustments are made correctly, both front and rear chains are adequately lubricated and all clamping nuts are securely tightened.

Tension. Primary chain $\frac{1}{2}''$. Rear chain $\frac{3}{4}''$.

PRIMARY CHAIN ADJUSTMENT (RIGID FRAME MODELS)

Gearbox Pivot Bolt. This bolt locates the gearbox to the lower frame and it must be slackened off before making an adjustment.

Gearbox Clamp Bolt. To gain access to the clamp bolt nut, remove the R.H. footrest and push the spindle out of the way. It is then possible to apply a spanner to the clamp nut.

Adjuster. This is located above the gearbox and to SLACKEN the chain, turn the adjuster ANTI-CLOCKWISE and to tighten turn CLOCKWISE. When tightening the chain always pull the gearbox back after adjusting, then test the chain tension. The reason for this is that the loading on the rear chain pulls the gearbox towards the rear, thus altering the chain tension.

Securing Gearbox. Re-tighten the clamping nut and pivot bolt and ensure absolute security.

Chains

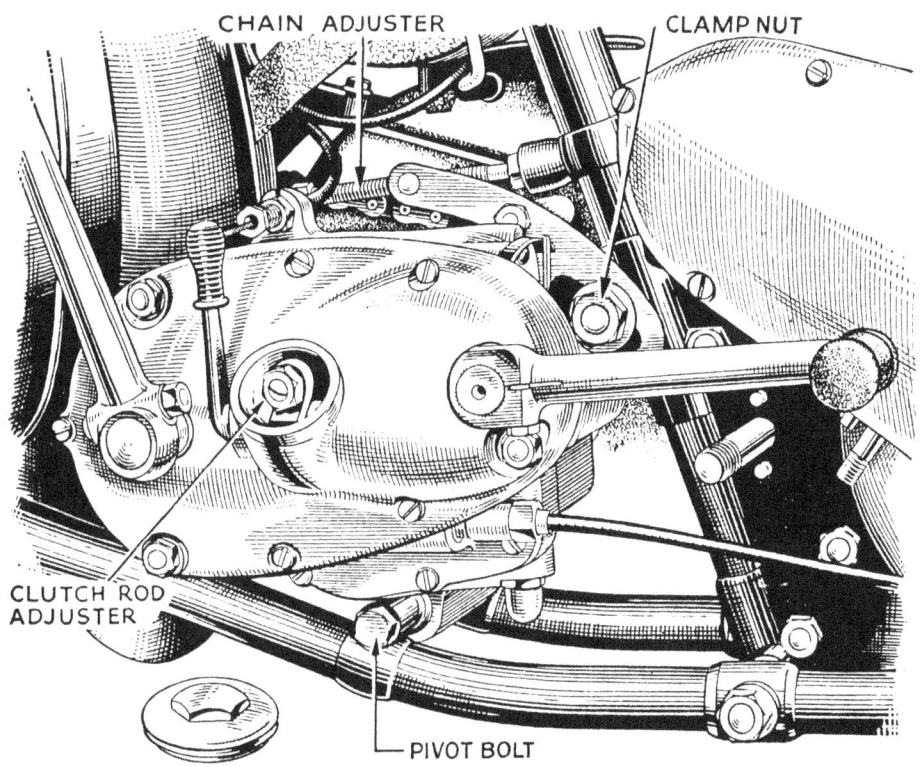

Fig. 34. GEARBOX IN POSITION (RIGID FRAME MODELS)

Showing adjustment points.

REAR CHAIN ADJUSTMENT (RIGID FRAME MODELS)

Wheel Nuts. Slacken off both nuts.

Adjusters. These are located in the rear frame fork ends. To TIGHTEN the chain slacken off the adjuster locknuts and tighten (clockwise) the adjusters. Particular care must be taken not to disturb the alignment of the rear wheel, therefore the adjusters must be turned an equal number of turns. To SLACKEN the chain reverse the procedure.

Securing Wheel. Tighten adjuster locknuts and spindle nuts.

Brake. Check adjustment.

Chains

PRIMARY CHAIN ADJUSTMENT (SWINGING ARM FRAME MODELS)

Gearbox Pivot Bolt. This bolt locates the gearbox to the lower frame and must be slackened off before making an adjustment.

Gearbox Clamping Bolt. Slacken the securing nut which also positions the adjuster.

Adjuster. If the primary chain is to be TIGHTENED, slacken off the front locknut a few turns and then tighten up the REAR LOCKNUT until the chain tension is correct. To SLACKEN the chain, reverse the locknut procedure.

Securing Gearbox. Re-tighten the clamp nut, locknuts and pivot bolt and ensure absolute security.

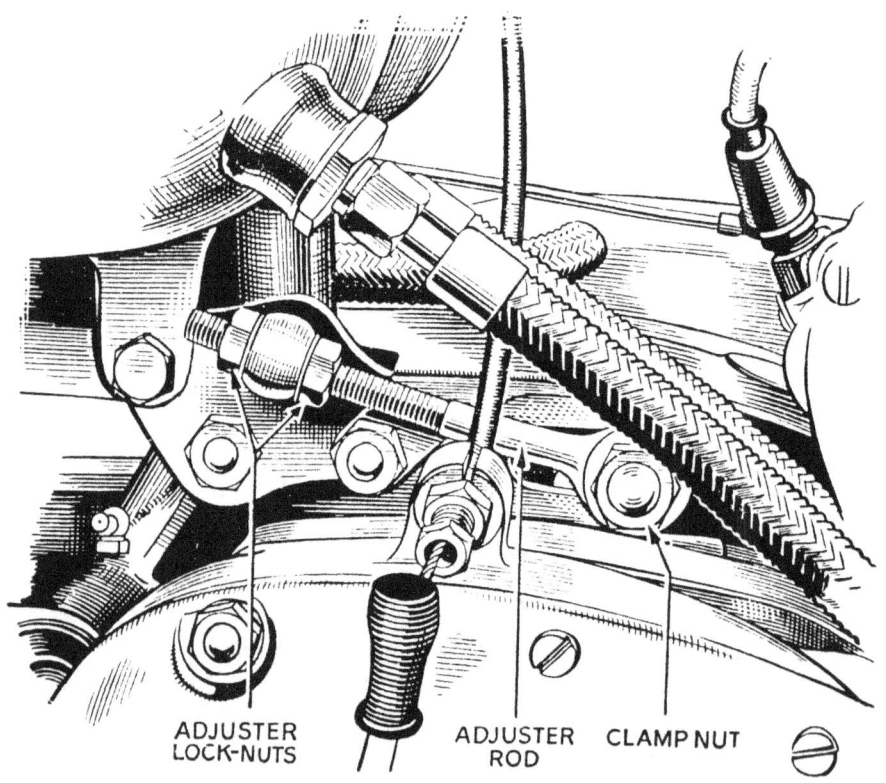

Fig. 35. GEARBOX IN POSITION (T100 & T110)

Showing adjustment points.

REAR CHAIN ADJUSTMENT (SWINGING ARM FRAME MODELS)

This adjustment may be made with the machine off the stand, $\frac{3}{4}''$ vertical play or on the stand, $1\frac{1}{4}''$ vertical play.

Wheel Nut. Slacken off both nuts.

Adjusters. These are located on the wheel spindle and swinging fork end lugs. To TIGHTEN the chain, turn the adjuster nuts clockwise an equal number of turns until the chain tension is correct. To SLACKEN the chain tension, reverse the procedure and push the wheel forward against the adjuster end plates.

Wheel Securing. Tighten adjuster locknuts and wheel spindle nuts.

Brake. Check adjustment.

CHAIN MAINTENANCE

Although both chains are lubricated, it is advisable to remove the rear chain at intervals and thoroughly clean and re-grease (See below).

Cleaning and Greasing the Rear Chain. Remove all external dirt by brushing vigorously with a wire brush. Soak the chain in a paraffin bath, moving it about until the joints are washed clean. Finally rinse in clean paraffin and leave to drain and dry. The chain after drying will then be ready for lubricating. Immerse the chain in a bath of grease which has been melted over a pan of boiling water. The chain should remain in the bath for five to ten minutes, being moved about freely to ensure penetration of the grease into the chain bearings. Allow the grease to cool to its normal state, then take the chain out of the bath, wipe off the surplus grease and replace the chain on the machine. When fitting the spring clip fastener on the connecting link, care must be taken to ensure correct fitting. The fastener is roughly the shape of a fish, and, if it is remembered that a fish swims nose first and the fastener is fitted so that the nose (closed end) is always proceeding in the forward direction when the machine is running, the fitter will have an easy aid to memory. It is a good plan to carry out this cleaning and greasing service at the beginning of the winter, half-way through the winter and at the commencement of the summer.

Chain Maintenance

ALTERATIONS AND REPAIRS

If the chains have been correctly serviced, very few repairs will be necessary. Should the occasion arise to repair, lengthen or shorten a chain, a rivet extractor and a few spare parts will cover all requirements.

To SHORTEN a chain containing an EVEN NUMBER OF PITCHES remove the dark parts shown in No. 1 and replace by cranked double link and single cranked link, No. 2.

To SHORTEN a chain containing an ODD NUMBER OF PITCHES remove the dark parts shown in No. 3 and replace by a single connecting link and inner link as No. 4.

To REPAIR a chain with a broken roller or inside link, remove the dark parts in No. 5 and replace by two single connecting links and one inner link as No. 6.

Fig. 36. **CHAINS**

RIVET EXTRACTOR

The rivet extractor can be used on all motorcycle chains up to $\frac{3}{4}''$ pitch, whether the chains are on or off the wheels.

When using the extractor:—

1. Turn screw anti-clockwise to permit the punch end to clear the chain rivet.

2. Open the jaws by pressing down the lever (See Fig. 37).

3. Pass jaws over chain and release the lever. Jaws should rest on a chain roller free of chain link plates (See Fig. 38).

4. Turn screw clockwise until punch contacts and pushes out rivet and through chain outer link plate. Unscrew punch, withdraw extractor and repeat complete operation on the adjacent rivet in the same chain outer link plate.

    The outer plate is then free and the two rivets can be withdrawn from opposite sides with the opposite plate in position. Do not use the removed part again.

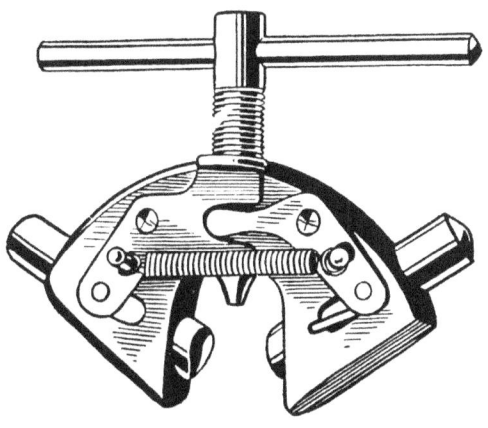

Fig. 37.

RIVET EXTRACTOR WITH JAWS OPEN

Fig. 38.

RIVET EXTRACTOR IN POSITION

TRIUMPH TELESCOPIC FORK

MAINTENANCE

The Triumph telescopic hydraulically controlled fork will require little attention other than an occasional check of the external nuts, screws and washers. At no time during normal service will the forks need topping up with oil; slight leakage that may have taken place will not affect the fork action.
Periodic draining and re-filling every 5,000 miles (8,000 kms.) should be carried out and if the leakage has become excessive, it will be necessary to drain and re-fill the forks before this distance.

Draining. To drain the oil from the fork, remove the two drain plugs at the base of the bottom cover tubes and compress the forks two or three times. This causes the oil to be expelled at a greater rate.

Re-filling. Replace the drain plugs. Remove the headlamp rim assembly from the nacelle, exposing the upper part of the stanchions. Unscrew the two screwed oil plugs in the stanchion and pump 1/6 Pint (100 c.c.) oil (See Lubrication Chart, page 200) into each fork leg by means of a pressure can or gun.

Re-filling the TR5 Forks. To re-fill the forks on the TR5, unscrew the two large cap nuts, securing the stanchions to the fork head lug and pour in the oil past the springs.

It is estimated that, under normal conditions, the time between fork overhauls should be about 20,000 miles (30,000 kms.). This work should be carried out by a dealer or by the Triumph Service Department.

ADJUSTING THE STEERING HEAD RACES

Lower the rear or central stand as the case may be and raise the front wheel clear of the ground by placing a box of suitable height under the crankcase. To test the play in the steering head, slacken off the damper and grip the fork lower tubes; rock the fork in a fore and aft direction. Care must be taken however, to observe that the play felt is in the steering head and not in the fork bushes. By watching the lower portion of the fork crown, any movement in the races will be easily seen. If play is detected, adjust the races in the following manner.

Top Lug Clip Bolt. Slacken off the nut.

Crown and Stem Nut. By swinging the fork to the left or right a spanner can be placed on the nut hexagon. The spanner should be turned clockwise to eliminate play, but only two finger pressure should be applied. Now ease the pressure off by lightly turning the spanner in the opposite direction and then test.

Testing. The fork should move to the full lock position in both directions under its own weight. If the movement is sluggish slacken off the adjuster nut slightly more and test again. Finally, check the steering when riding the machine on the road.

Telescopic Fork

Fig. 39.

TESTING THE ADJUSTMENT OF THE STEERING HEAD RACES

REMOVING THE FORK FROM THE FRAME

The following refers to all models with the exception of the TR5. For this model the operator should disconnect the lighting plug at the headlamp, remove the headlamp, handlebars and steering damper knob and proceed from "Stanchion Cap Nuts". First remove the front wheel, mudguard, headlamp assembly and nacelle top unit as described on pages 109, 174 and 177 and proceed as follows.

Handlebar. Detach control levers and loosen the twistgrip retaining screw. Unscrew four nuts from the handlebar retaining "U" bolts. Slide the handlebar out of the twistgrip sleeve and through the rubber grommets.

Stanchion Cap Nuts. Using a ring spanner to avoid damage to the nut heads, unscrew the two large stanchion cap nuts.

Telescopic Fork

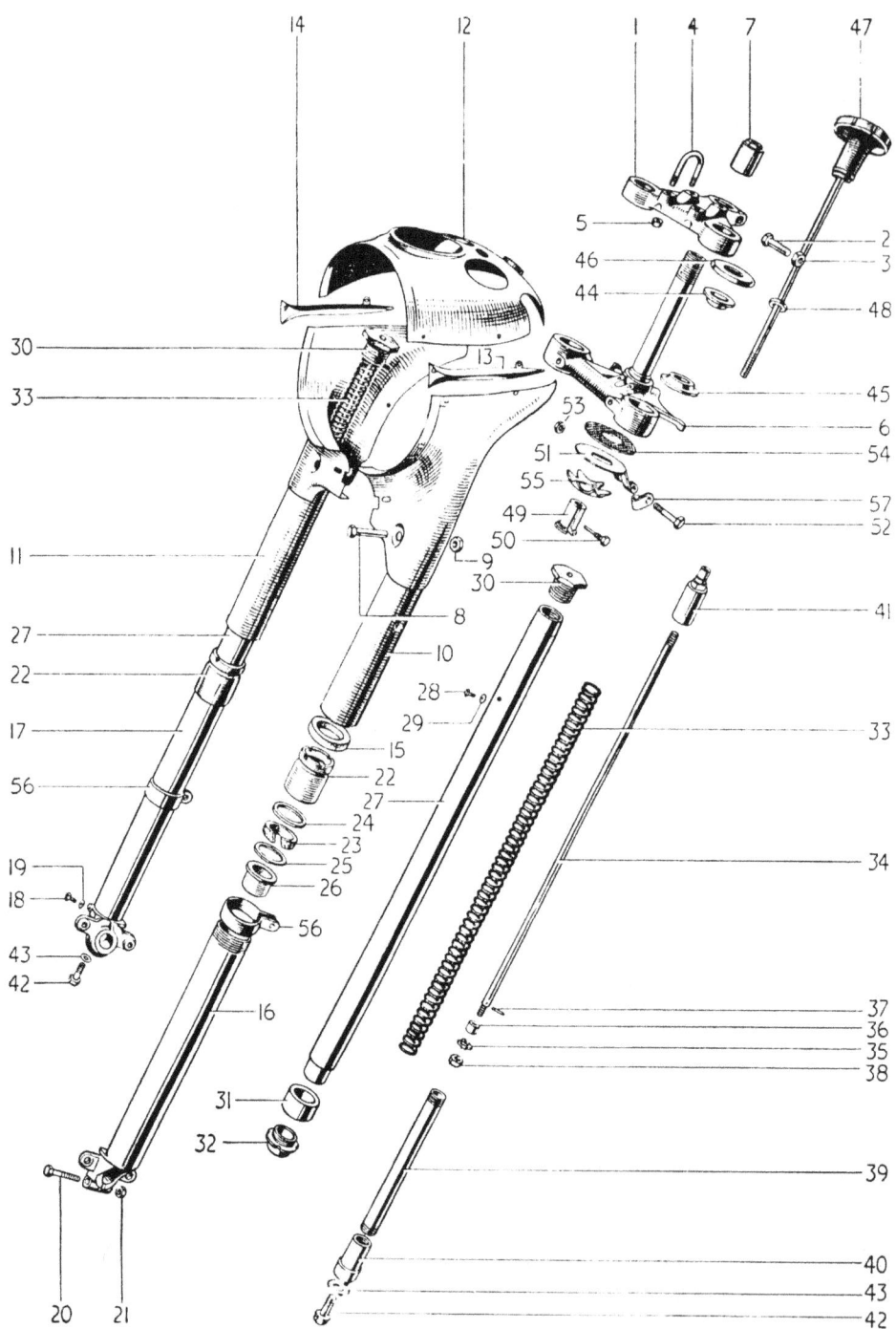

Fig. 40. TELESCOPIC FORK

INDEX TO FIG. 40.   TELESCOPIC FORK

Index No.	Description.	Index No.	Description.
1	Lug, fork head.	29	Washer.
2	Bolt, pinch.	30	Nut, cap.
3	Nut.	31	Bearing, stanchion, lower.
4	"U" bolt.	32	Nut, hydraulic stop.
5	Nut.	33	Spring, fork.
6	Crown and stem.	34	Rod, oil restrictor.
7	Nut, sleeve.	35	Restrictor, oil.
8	Bolt, pinch.	36	Cup.
9	Nut, stop.	37	Pin, cup.
10	Cover, nacelle, N.S.	38	Nut.
11	Cover, nacelle, O.S.	39	Tube, pressure.
12	Nacelle, top.	40	Body, pressure tube.
13	Motif, N.S.	41	Sleeve, pressure tube.
14	Motif, O.S.	42	Bolt.
15	Washer, felt.	43	Washer, aluminium.
16	Cover, bottom tube, N.S.	44	Cone.
17	Cover, bottom tube, O.S.	45	Cone.
18	Plug, drain.	46	Cover, dust.
19	Washer.	47	Knob, damper assy.
20	Bolt, wheel lug pinch.	48	Washer, damper.
21	Nut.	49	Sleeve.
22	Sleeve, dust excluder.	50	Pin, securing.
23	Washer, felt.	51	Plate, damper anchor.
24	Washer.	52	Bolt, anchor plate.
25	Washer.	53	Nut.
26	Bearing, upper.	54	Disc, friction.
27	Stanchion.	55	Plate, friction.
28	Plug, oil filler.	56	Clip, mudguard.
		57	Clip, speedometer cable.

Dismantling Telescopic Fork

Top Lug. Remove the crown and stem sleeve nut, undo the top lug pinch bolt, and, using a soft metal drift, give the top lug a sharp blow from underneath to loosen it from the taper of the stanchions. Remove the damper anchor plate bolt and raise the top lug lifting with it the two stanchion nuts which in turn carry the pressure tube and spring assembly, and the lower fork crown is eased downwards from the frame. The complete fork assembly can be withdrawn from the frame as there is sufficient clearance between the top of the fork crown stem and the underside of the top lug. If care is taken, the top ball race can be left undisturbed and the balls collected from the lower race as the clearance becomes sufficient.

If the mechanic does not wish to disturb the steering column, carry out the first two operations and proceed as follows:—

Middle Lug Pinch Bolts. Remove both bolts.

Top Lug. Undo the top lug pinch bolt and loosen the top lug with a sharp blow as described.

Oil. Remove the drain plugs at the bottom tube covers and let the oil drain out.

Pressure Tube Body Bolt. Remove these bolts from the base of the bottom cover tube.

Pressure Tube Assembly and Spring. Withdraw from the forks by lifting the stanchion cap nuts.

Fork Legs. Remove from the middle lug by pulling downwards.

DISMANTLING THE FORK

Pressure Tube Assembly. Unscrew the two pressure tube securing bolts and withdraw the pressure tube assemblies and top lug.

Lower Nacelle Covers. Remove the two middle lug pinch bolts and take off the lower nacelle covers.

Bottom Cover Tubes. Unscrew the dust excluder sleeves from the bottom cover tubes and pull the cover tubes downwards sharply, this will remove the bushes at the same time.

Dust Excluder Sleeves. Remove the two steel rings and the felt strip.

Stanchion Lower Bearing. Grip the stanchion above the bearing surface and remove the hydraulic stop nut and the stanchion lower bearing.

DISMANTLING THE PRESSURE TUBE ASSEMBLY

Main Spring. Compress the main spring and grip the oil restrictor rod in a pair of pliers. Remove the large cap nut and release the spring.

Pressure Tube Sleeve. Grip the pressure tube and unscrew the pressure tube sleeves.

Restrictor Rod Assembly. Remove the restrictor rod from the pressure tube, unscrew the oil restrictor nut and remove the restrictor, restrictor cup and pin.

DISMANTLING, PREPARATION AND ASSEMBLY OF UNITS

First thoroughly degrease all parts and lay out for inspection. If the mileage covered is more than 20,000 (30,000 kms.) it is recommended that all bushes and seals are changed.

Stanchions. Check that the stanchion is true by laying a straight edge along it to find out if there is any distortion. If the stanchion is to be used again after straightening, the bow should not exceed $\frac{3}{16}"$ (4.8 mm.). The owner is not advised to undertake the servicing of a fork in this condition, it should be returned to a Triumph Dealer for an exchange service replacement.

Head Lugs and Middle Lug. If the motorcycle has been involved in an accident the lug will require expert attention. No attempt should be made to carry out this work without jigs.

Bottom Cover Tubes. Examine for indentation and scrap if defective.

Springs. If the coils are not unduly compressed, the springs are fit for further service. The free length of the spring should be within $\frac{1}{2}"$ (12.7 mm.) of the original length which is $19\frac{1}{4}"$ (49 cms.) solo and 20" (51 cms.) s/c.

Ball Races. Cups, cones and balls should be examined for indentation and pitting and changed if necessary.

Top Race	22	$\frac{3}{16}"$ (4.76 mm.) diam. Balls
Bottom Race	20	$\frac{1}{4}"$ (6.35 mm.) diam. Balls
3T only	22	$\frac{3}{16}"$ (4.76 mm.) diam. Balls Top & Bottom

Friction Damper. Examine the friction damper assembly for traces of oil, grease, rust, etc. Renew the friction disc if at all worn and the spring plate if weak or broken.

PRESSURE TUBE ASSEMBLY

Restrictor Rod. Fit the pin to the restrictor rod, then the cup, restrictor, and finally the locking nut.

Pressure Tube. Screw the lower valve body to the pressure tube and insert the restrictor rod assembly. Slide the top support sleeve over the restrictor rod and screw onto the pressure tube.

Checking. To ensure correct operation of the valve, place the assembly in a tin of oil and pump the rod up and down. When the pressure tube is filled, the upward movement of the rod should be restricted and the downward movement unrestricted.

Spring and Cap Nut. Fit the spring over the restrictor rod and compress until the rod can be gripped with a pair of pliers. Screw the cap nut into position and release the spring.

Aligning Telescopic Fork

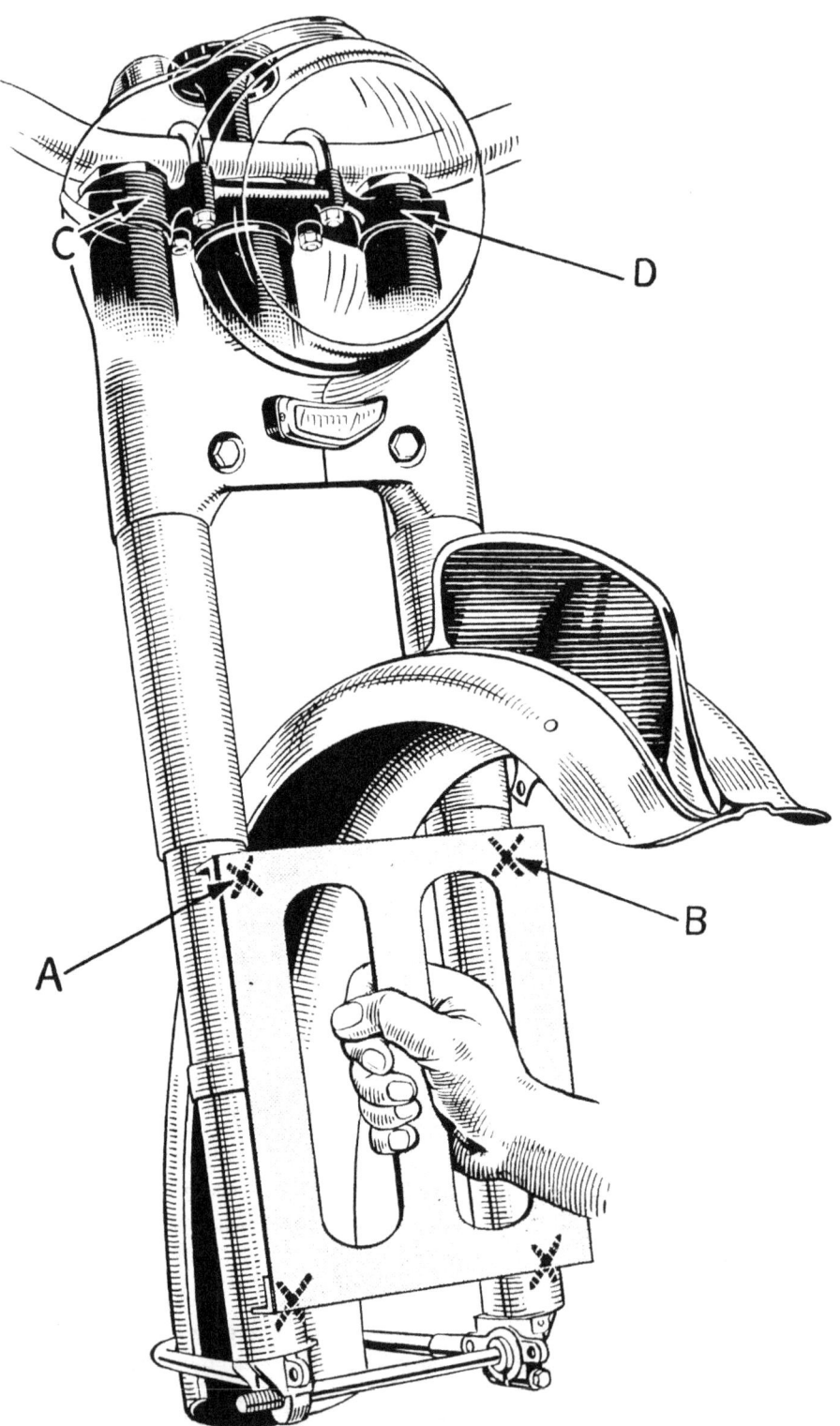

Fig. 41. ALIGNING THE FRONT FORK

Assembling Telescopic Fork

ALIGNMENT INSTRUCTIONS, Fig. 41.

This jig is of simplified form and can easily be made by the distributor, dealer or the private owner. It has the advantage that after the front wheel has been removed, both nacelle and non-nacelle type forks can be checked.

Fit the wheel spindle or a straight $\frac{11}{16}''$ diameter rod in position and place the jig on the lower fork members as indicated in the illustration opposite. To avoid scratching the enamel finish on the fork members, apply a smear of grease at the four points.

Hold it firmly and if the alignment is correct, contact will be made at all four points marked "X". If the jig does not make contact at "A" or "B", it will be necessary with the nacelle type fork to remove the headlamp assembly and instrument top unit to make an adjustment. Slacken off the top lug and middle pinch bolts. If the jig can be rocked at "A" this indicates that "D" is too far forward. To remedy, strike the top lug at point "D" a sharp blow with a hide hammer and then make a further check with the jig. If the error is at "B" the application is the same, only at point "C". When the adjustment is satisfactory tighten the pinch bolts and make another check.

ASSEMBLING AND INSTALLING THE FORK (NACELLE TYPE)

Before commencing to assemble the fork, lubricate all parts.

Stanchion Bearing. Fit the bearing to the stanchions and lock with the hydraulic stop nut. Check the bearings for freedom of movement.

Drain Plugs. Screw the drain plugs into the bottom cover tube, ensuring tightness.

Dust Excluder. Fit a new felt washer to each dust excluder cap making sure that the two thin metal washers are on either side of the felt.

Bottom Cover Tube Assembly. Assemble the stanchion to the bottom cover tube and fit the top bearing. Screw on the dust excluder and check the movement of the stanchions which should be free and smooth.

Steering Races. If the steering column assembly has been dismantled, grease the cups in the frame and press the balls onto them.

Fork and Crown Stem and Top Lug. Assemble the fork crown stem and top lug to the steering column and tighten down the sleeve nut until the steering moves freely from side to side with no up and down movement. Fit and tighten the pinch bolts and lower damper parts.

Horn. Fit the horn to the fork crown and stem (not TR5).

Lower Nacelle Covers. Assemble the lower nacelle covers and position the pinch bolts and nuts, but do not tighten.

Assembling Telescopic Fork

Stanchion and Bottom Cover Tube Assembly. Fit the felt washers into the nacelle covers and slide the stanchions through the fork crown lug into the tapers of the top lug. Lightly tighten the fork crown pinch bolts.

Pressure Tube Assembly. Insert the assembly into the stanchion. In the pressure tube body a dowel is fitted, which must locate in the dowel hole in the bottom cover tube. When it is located, fit the locking bolt with copper washer, through the hole in the bottom cover tube into the pressure tube assembly and lock tight.

Lubrication. Push the bottom cover tube into the upper cover and pour 100 c.c. (1/6 pint) oil past the springs and into the top of each stanchion

Cap Nut. Force the bottom cover tubes down and screw the cap nut into the stanchion, ensuring that it is well tightened. If this precaution is not taken, the stanchion will not be drawn into the top lug and excessive strain will be put on the crown and stem.

Fork Crown Pinch Bolts. Tighten up the pinch bolts. (See Fig. 41 and text describing fork alignment).

Handlebars. Fit the handlebars to the top lug and connect the horn together with all controls and cables.

Nacelle Top Unit. Replace the top unit and connect all wires, speedometer cables, etc., as described on page 177.

Steering Damper Knob. Replace the damper knob, making sure that the steel thrust washer is in position.

Headlamp Assembly. Replace as described on page 177.

Mudguard. Replace to the fork and secure all fastenings.

Front Wheel. Replace the front wheel (see page 114).

ASSEMBLING THE FORK (TR5)

When fitting the TR5 forks, the operator should complete the first six operations listed in the previous paragraph and proceed as follows:—

Fork Top Covers. Fit in the same way as the lower nacelle covers.

Stanchion and Bottom Cover Tube Assembly. Proceed as described.

Pressure Tube Assembly. Assemble as described.

Lubrication. Fill the forks as described.

Cap Nut. Tighten the cap nuts as described.

Fork Crown Pinch Bolt. Tighten the bolts.

Handlebars. Fit the handlebars to the top lug and connect all levers and cables.

Headlamp. Fit the headlamp to the forks and connect the lighting plug.

Speedometer. Re-fit speedometer and cable.

Steering Damper. Re-fit the steering damper knob making sure that the steel thrust washer is in position.

Mudguard. Replace to the fork and secure all fastenings.

Wheel. Replace as described.

CHANGING THE MAIN SPRINGS

In order to change the main springs, or to fit stronger ones for sidecar purposes, the operator should remove the headlamp and nacelle top cover as described on page 177 and the handlebars as described on page 99 and proceed as follows:—

Cap Nuts. Unscrew the two cap nuts in the top lug.

Spring. Grip the spring which should now be showing, and force it down until the restrictor rod can be gripped with a pair of pliers.

Restrictor Rod. Unscrew the cap nuts from the restrictor rod and secure a piece of soft wire to the rod before releasing the spring. This enables the operator to retain control of the restrictor rod during removal and replacement of the spring. Repeat the operation on the other fork leg and re-assemble the forks in exactly the reverse procedure. The fork springs have a colour identification as follows:—

Solo	Red
Sidecar	Blue
Extra-Heavy Sidecar	Purple

WHEELS

ADJUSTING THE BRAKES

Before attempting to make an adjustment, the wheels must be raised clear of the ground by placing the machine on its stand or stands as the case may be.

Front Brake. To adjust the brake shoes closer to the brake drum, turn the knurled thumb nut (See Fig. 42) in a clockwise direction. The brake should be set so that when it is fully applied the lever is just clear of the handlebar. By this adjustment, the rider will be able to exert the maximum amount of grip on the lever. After making an adjustment, spin the wheel to ensure that the brake shoes are not binding on the brake drum.

Rear Brake. The adjustment is made by turning the knurled thumb nut (See Fig. 42) at the rear end of the brake operating rod in a clockwise direction. After adjusting spin the wheel to ensure that the brake is not binding. On the Rigid Frame Models an adjustment can be made to the brake pedal position, but after making an alteration, the brake must be re-adjusted.

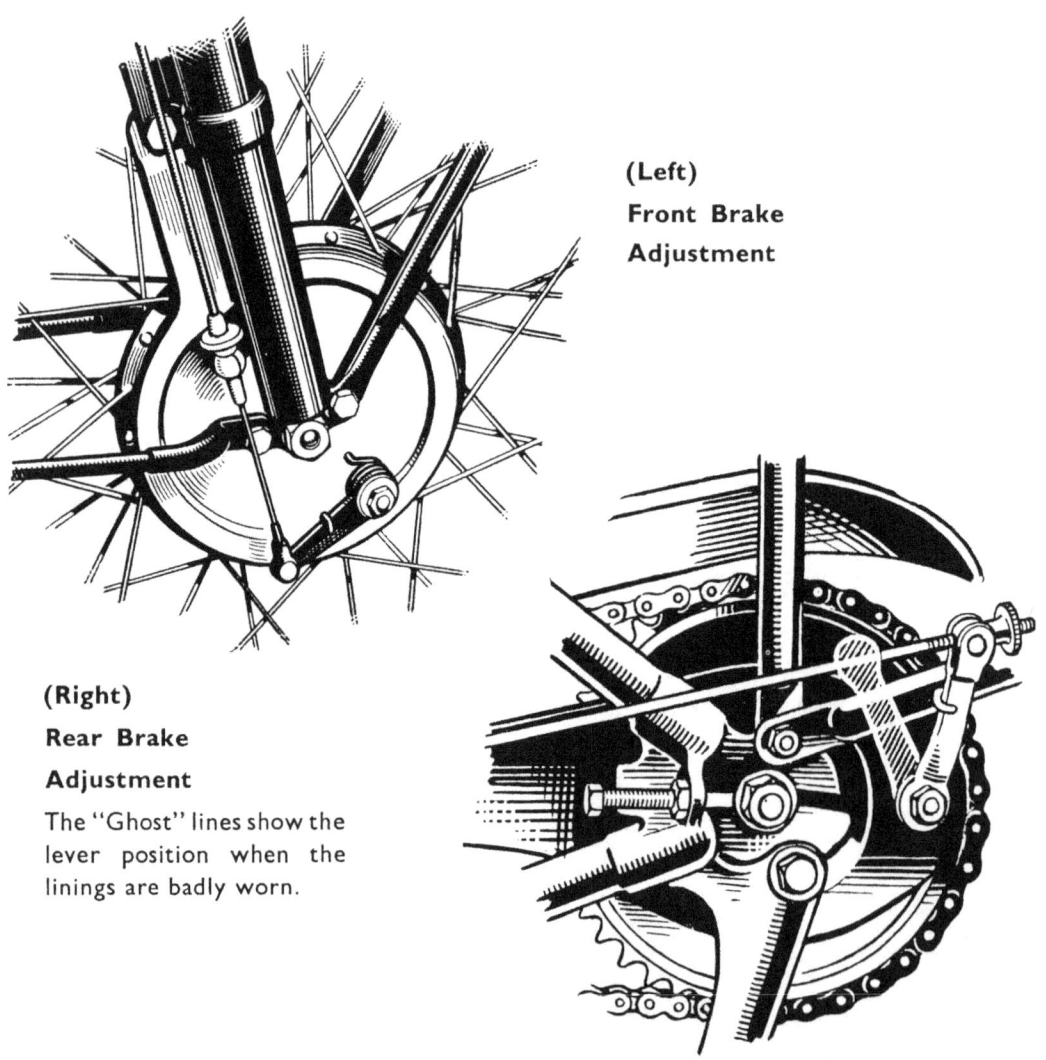

(Left)
Front Brake
Adjustment

(Right)
Rear Brake
Adjustment

The "Ghost" lines show the lever position when the linings are badly worn.

Fig. 42. ADJUSTING THE BRAKES

FRONT WHEEL

The front wheel as fitted to all models requires very little maintenance beyond re-packing the hub with grease every 10,000 miles (15,000 kms.). The wheel bearings are of the ball bearing type and therefore require no adjustment. The rim is 19" in diameter (WM2-19) fitted with 3.25 × 19" tyre, and the hub consists of two parts, the hub itself and the brake drum. It should be noted that the spokes have specially angled heads, ensuring sturdy wheel construction. Four separate head shapes are used and replacements should be the same as the originals. The brakes are internally expanding to a 7" (17.78 cms.) brake drum (Model 5T, 6T & TR5) and an 8" (20.32 cms.) brake drum (T100 and T110) and are mounted on an aluminium alloy (DTD.424) anchor plate as a complete unit.

REMOVING THE FRONT WHEEL FROM THE FORKS

Brake Cable. Remove the split pin from the pivot pin connecting the brake operating lever and the cable. Withdraw the pivot pin.

Anchor Plate Bolt. Unscrew the nut and remove the bolt connecting the anchor plate to the fork leg.

Spindle Nut. Remove from the spindle.

Front Stand. Lower the front stand by loosening the retaining nut at the rear of the mudguard and pivot the stand downwards.

Spindle. Slacken the spindle pinch bolt on the left hand fork and drive the spindle out, when the wheel can be withdrawn from the forks. Do not damage the spindle threads.

DISMANTLING THE FRONT WHEEL

Brake Anchor Plate. Hold the operating lever towards the "ON" position so that the brake shoes do not bind on the drum and lift the anchor plate from the brake drum.

Bearing Retaining Ring Nut. The ring nut has a left hand thread. Remove by turning in a clockwise direction.

Spindle Sleeve and Collar. Drive the sleeve and collar out from the brake drum side.

Wheel Bearing L.H. Drive the bearing out complete with dust cover, using a ⅜" (9.5 mm.) diameter bar inserted through the brake drum side bearing. Remove the bearing distance piece.

Wheel Bearing R.H. Drive this bearing out into the brake drum.

Front Wheel

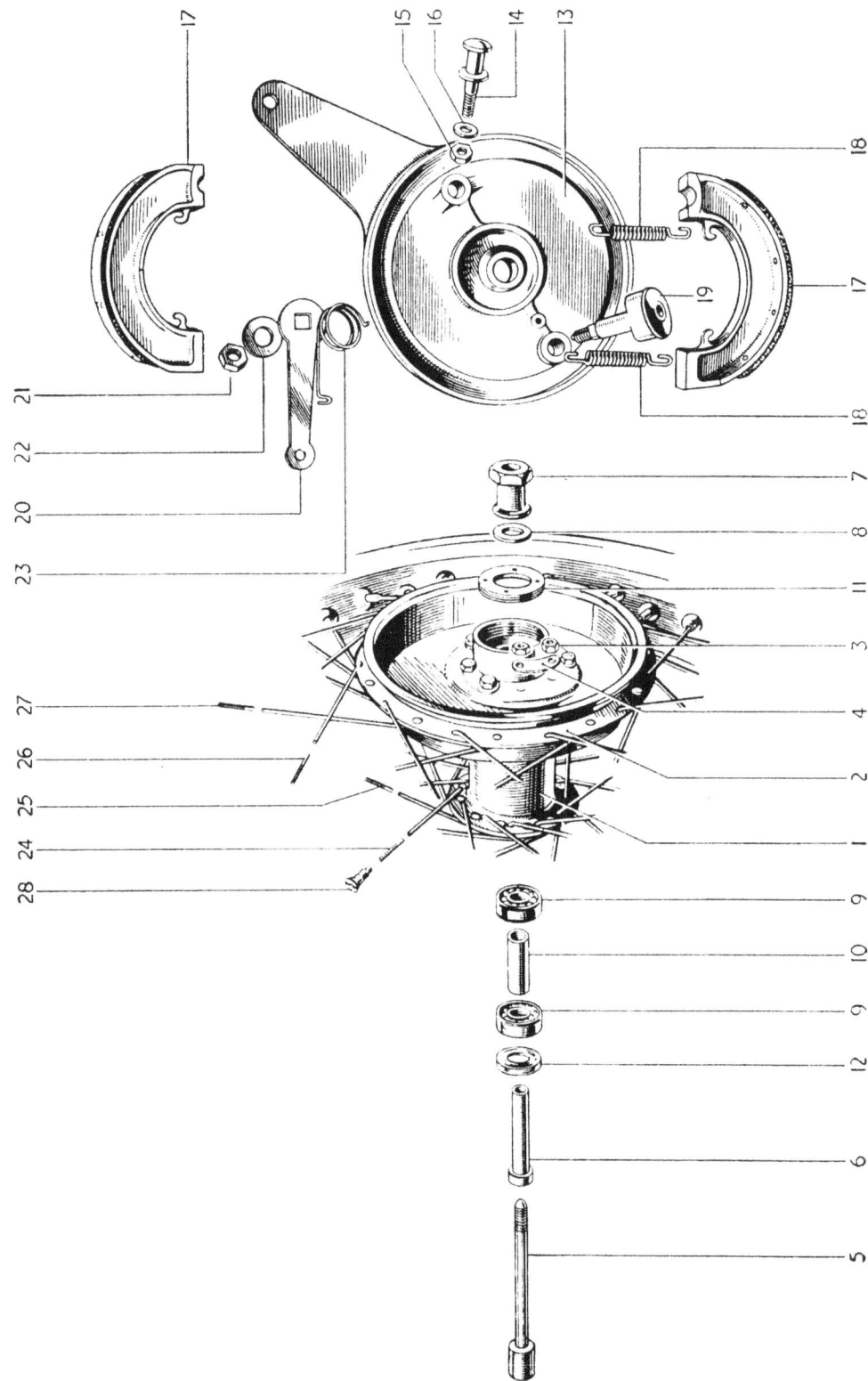

Fig. 43. FRONT WHEEL (5T, 6T & TR5)

INDEX TO FIG. 43. FRONT WHEEL (5T, 6T & TR5)

Index No.	Description.	Index No.	Description.
1	Hub.	15	Nut.
2	Drum, brake.	16	Washer.
3	Nut, drum to hub.	17	Shoe with lining.
4	Lockplate, nut.	18	Cam, brake operating.
5	Spindle.	20	Lever, brake cam.
6	Sleeve and collar.	21	Nut.
7	Nut, spindle.	22	Washer.
8	Washer.	23	Spring, cam lever return.
9	Bearing.	24	Spoke, long, 90° head.
10	Distance piece.	25	Spoke, long, 88° head.
11	Ring nut, bearing retaining.	26	Spoke, short, 83° head.
12	Cap, dust.	27	Spoke, short, 94° head.
13	Plate, brake anchor.	28	Nipple, spoke.
14	Pin, shoe fulcrum.		

TO DISMANTLE THE FRONT BRAKE ANCHOR PLATE

Brake Shoes. Remove the return springs and the brake shoes will be released from the anchor plate.

Brake Operating Lever and Cam Spindle. Unscrew the retaining nut and take off the brake operating lever. Withdraw the cam spindle from the anchor plate. It is unnecessary to remove the brake shoe fulcrum pin.

INSPECTION AND REPLACEMENT OF WORN PARTS

Washing. All parts with the exception of the brake shoes, should be thoroughly washed with petrol or paraffin.

Anchor Plate. This should be examined for cracks and distortion and excessive wear in the brake cam housing.

Brake Cam. Clean out the greaseways and remove any rust. Re-fill the greaseways with clean grease.

Ball Bearings. Clean and dry the bearings thoroughly. Compressed air should be used for drying out if possible. Test the end float and inspect the balls for any signs of indentation or pitting. Change the bearings if they are not up to the required standard. Pack the bearings with grease before replacing in the hub.

Return Springs. Inspect for signs of fatigue and renew if necessary.

Brake Drum. Inspect the brake drum for wear, ovality or scoring. If there is ovality or score marks, the drum will have to be detached from the wheel and skimmed. If it is necessary to skim more than .010" (0.254 mm.) from the drum, it should be scrapped. After skimming the brake drum, the wheel will have to be re-built and trued up.

Front Wheel

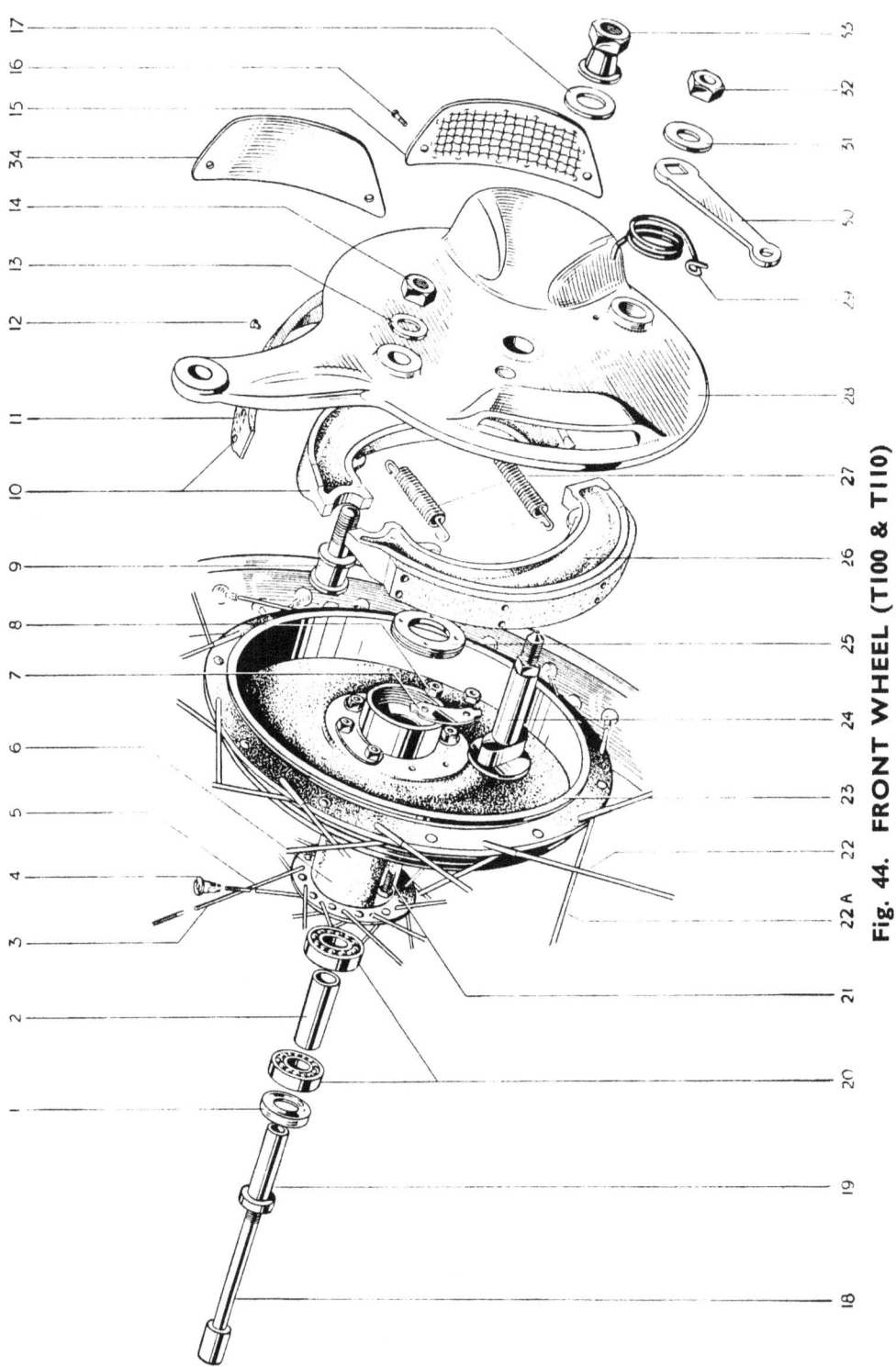

Fig. 44. FRONT WHEEL (T100 & T110)

INDEX TO FIG. 44.   FRONT WHEEL (T100 & T110)

Index No.	Description.	Index No.	Description.
1	Cap, dust.	18	Spindle.
2	Distance piece.	19	Sleeve and collar.
3	Spoke, 90° head.	20	Bearing.
4	Nipple, spoke.	21	Bolt, drum to head.
5	Spoke, 88° head.	22	Spoke, short 80° head.
6	Hub.	23	Drum, brake.
7	Lockplate.	24	Cam, brake operating.
8	Nut.	25	Ring nut, bearing retaining.
9	Pin, shoe fulcrum.	26	Shoe, brake trailing.
10	Shoe, brake leading.	27	Spring, shoe return.
11	Lining, brake shoe.	28	Plate, brake anchor.
12	Rivet, lining to shoe.	29	Spring, cam lever return.
13	Washer.	30	Lever, brake cam.
14	Nut.	31	Washer.
15	Gauze, anchor plate.	32	Nut.
16	Peg, gauze securing.	33	Nut, wheel spindle.
17	Washer.	34	Blanking plate.

Brake Shoes. If the brake adjuster has been fully taken up, the brake shoe linings must be changed. Do not pack the heel of the shoe in an endeavour to make an adjustment. New linings and rivets can be purchased from a Triumph Dealer, but if the owner wishes, he can exchange the brake shoes for a re-conditioned set at very little extra cost. If the old brake shoes are to be used for further service, inspect the rivet heads as these must be below the surface of the lining. Rivets which show signs of contact with the brake drum can be lowered by using a suitable round punch. Support the shoe at the point where the rivet is to be knocked down.

TO ASSEMBLE THE FRONT BRAKE ANCHOR PLATE

Brake Cam. Grease the spindle of the brake cam and insert it into the housing on the brake anchor plate. Fit the return spring over the spindle (long end away from the anchor plate) and tap the lever arm on to the square shoulder with the lever arm in the same line as the cam. Fit the washer and nut and tighten.

Brake Shoes. Place the two shoes on the bench in their relative positions. Fit the return springs to the retaining hooks, then, taking a shoe in each hand and at the same time holding the springs in tension, position the shoes to the anchor plate. By turning the top of the shoes inwards the assembly can be placed over the cam and fulcrum pin and snapped down into position by pressing on the outsides of the shoes.

Wind the brake lever arm anti-clockwise to engage the return spring.

Replacing Front Wheel

ASSEMBLING THE FRONT WHEEL

Preparation. Thoroughly clean the inside of the hub and brake drum. Pack the ball races with grease.

Bearing (Brake Drum Side). Press the bearing into the hub from the brake drum side until it engages on the shoulder in the hub.

Bearing Retaining Ring Nut. Screw up and tighten the bearing retaining ring nut (L.H. thread) using a peg spanner.

Grease. Pack about one egg-cupful of grease into the hub.

Bearing (Opposite Side Brake Drum). Place the wheel with the brake drum, downwards on the bench. Enter the bearing distance piece into the hub and press in the bearings until the distance piece is held firmly between both bearings.

Spindle Sleeve. Slide the spindle sleeve into the bearing, up to the collar.

Bearing Dust Cap. Press the dust cap into the hub end as far as possible.

Anchor Plate. Re-position to brake drum.

FITTING THE FRONT WHEEL TO THE FRONT FORK

The front wheel must be fitted carefully, otherwise the efficient working of the front fork will be impaired. The split left hand cover tube lug which houses the pinch bolt, will align itself correctly on the spindle if the instructions are adhered to.

Spindle. Check that the spindle is a good push fit in the split left hand cover tube lug. If the spindle is too tight, clean out the lug and remove any burrs or enamel. If this is not effective, open up the split lug gap. This procedure must be carried out to ensure that the left hand fork leg aligns itself on the spindle sleeve.

Wheel. Position the wheel between the fork legs and secure in position by passing the spindle through the split lug into the wheel and through the other lug. Do not use force, or both the spindle and the lugs will be damaged.

Anchor Plate. Position the anchor plate and secure the mudguard bridge support clip with the anchor bolt.

Spindle Nut. Fit the spindle nut and plain washer and tighten up. Do not tighten the pinch bolt on the opposite fork leg yet.

Front Brake Lever and Cable. Re-fit the brake cable adjuster to the abutment on the anchor plate and assemble the pivot bolt to the cable fork and brake lever arm. Push a split pin through the pivot bolt and retain it by bending the ends over.

Front Stand. Swing the stand back into position and tighten the securing nut.

Spindle Pinch Bolt. Check that this bolt is loose and that the left hand fork leg can slide on the spindle sleeve. Sit astride the machine, and, applying the front brake, work the fork up and down five or six times. This positions the fork leg on the spindle, and prevents any binding between the stanchions and the cover tubes. Tighten up the spindle pinch bolt.

If this procedure is not adopted, the fork action will be stiff and members distorted. (See Fig. 45).

Aligning Front Wheel

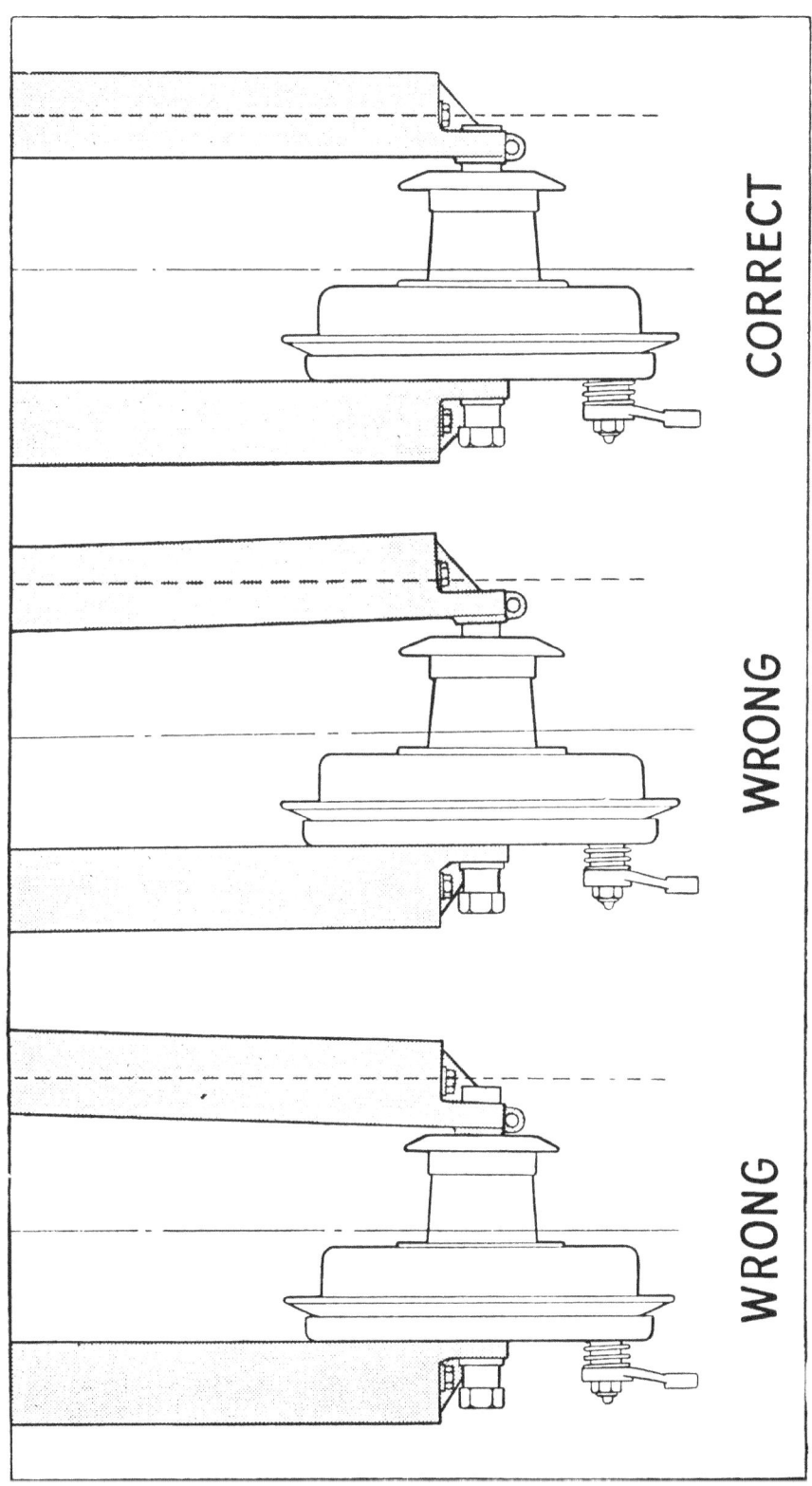

Fig. 45. CORRECT ALIGNMENT OF FRONT WHEEL IN FORKS

Rigid Rear Wheel

REAR WHEEL (RIGID FRAME)

The rear wheel has taper roller bearings and may occasionally require adjustment. If the machine is placed on the rear stand, any slackness in the bearings can be immediately felt. The lateral movement should be "hardly perceptible". The bearings are held in adjustment by locknuts and the lateral movement should always be checked after the locknuts have been tightened. The hubs are packed with grease and only require re-packing every 10,000 miles (15,000 kms.). The rim is 19" in diameter (WM2-19) and has a 3.50 × 19" tyre fitted. The spokes are of four different head shapes as in the front wheel and this should be noted when making replacements. The brakes are 7" (17.78 cms.) internally expanding and are located on a mild steel anchor plate, having a strong external peg which locates in a channel in the frame to withstand the braking torque.

REMOVING THE REAR WHEEL FROM THE FRAME

Mudguard. Disconnect the rear light leads underneath the saddle, unscrew the nuts connecting the mudguard to the frame and take off the mudguard.

TR5. The mudguard of the TR5 is designed to allow removal of the rear wheel and it is therefore unnecessary to remove it.

Rear Chain. Depress the gear lever to make sure that the gearbox is not in neutral. This prevents the chain rotating on the gearbox sprocket and falling off when the spring link is removed. Remove the spring link and clear the chain from the rear sprocket.

Brake Adjusting Nut. Unscrew this nut and remove the brake rod from the lever arm.

Spindle Nuts. Slacken the two rear spindle nuts and withdraw the wheel from the frame.

INDEX TO FIG. 46.   REAR WHEEL

Index No.	Description.	Index No.	Description.
1	Nut, spindle.	13	Nut, bearing adjusting.
2	Nut, brake plate locking	14	Collar, chain adjuster thrust.
3	Anchor plate.	15	Nut.
4	Shoe c/w lining.	16	Lever, brake cam.
5	Lining, brake shoe.	17	Spring, cam lever return.
6	Rivet, lining.	18	Spring, shoe return.
7	Brake drum and sprocket.	19	Cam, brake operating.
8	Lockplate.	20	Cap, dust.
9	Bolt, drum to hub.	21	Ring, bearing backing.
10	Bearing.	22	Hub.
11	Spoke, 76° head.	23	Nipple, spoke.
12	Spoke, 100° head.	24	Spindle, wheel.

Rigid Rear Wheel

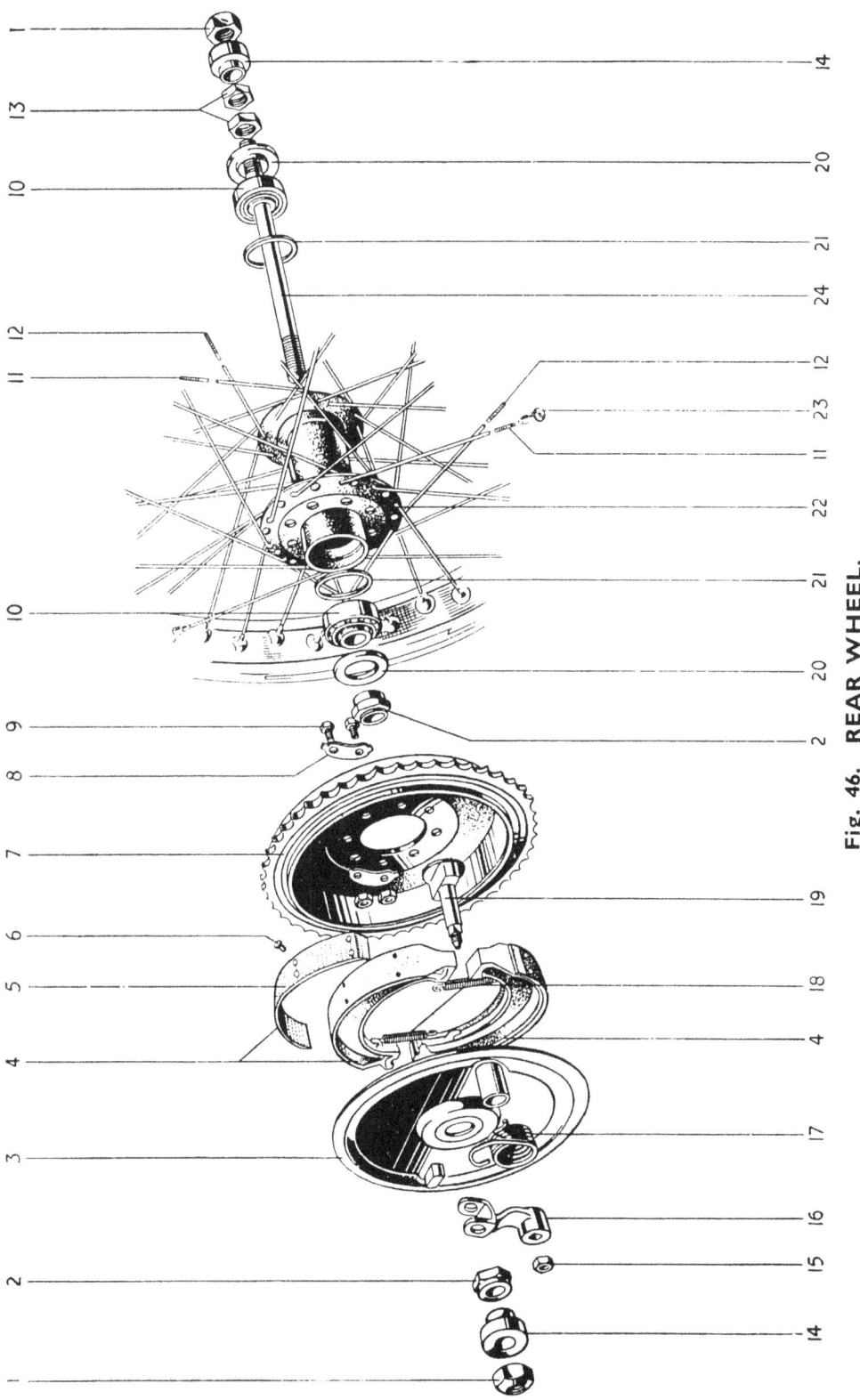

Fig. 46. REAR WHEEL.

DISMANTLING THE REAR WHEEL

Spindle Nuts. Remove both spindle nuts and chain adjuster thrust collars.

Brake Anchor Plate. Unscrew the anchor plate nut and remove the brake anchor plate.

Wheel Spindle. Turn the wheel over and remove the bearing adjusting locknuts and withdraw the rear wheel spindle.

Bearing Inner Races. Remove both bearing inner races. The cages will be retained by the dust caps. The outer races are a press fit and can be removed by tapping out from the opposite side with a drift.

DISMANTLING THE REAR BRAKE ANCHOR PLATE

Brake Shoes. Take off both brake shoe return springs and remove the brake shoes.

Brake Shoe Cam. Remove the nut and washer securing the lever arm to the cam spindle and take off the lever arm. Withdraw the cam from the plate.

INSPECTION AND REPLACEMENT OF WORN PARTS

Cleaning. All parts with the exception of the brake shoes, should be thoroughly washed in petrol or paraffin.

Anchor Plate. Examine the anchor plate for distortion and wear, particularly in the brake cam housing. Check that the locating stud is secure.

Brake Cam. Clean out the greaseways and remove any rust with a fine emery cloth. Re-fill the greaseways with clean grease.

Roller Races. Thoroughly clean and dry the roller races and cages. Inspect the rollers and tracks for pitting and scoring. Change the bearings if they are not up to standard. Pack the races with grease before replacing to the hub.

Bearing Backing Rings. These rings should be examined carefully as they are very liable to damage when the bearings are withdrawn from the hub and will probably require replacing.

Anchor Plate and Bearing Locking Nuts. Examine these nuts for damage to the threads and hexagons.

Spindle. The rear wheel spindle should be checked for bends and signs of the wheel nuts having been overtightened. Do not replace a wheel spindle which shows any sign of damage or distortion.

Return Springs. Inspect for signs of fatigue and renew if necessary.

Brake Drum and Sprocket. Examine the brake drum for scoring or ovality. If the drum needs skimming, it can be removed from the wheel by bending back the tabs on the brake drum lock plates and removing the brake drum bolts. Replacement is the reverse procedure. If it should be necessary to skim more than .010" (0.254 mm.) from the drum, it should be replaced by a new drum. Examine the sprocket teeth for wear. The top of the tooth should be flat and approximately $\frac{1}{8}$" (3.2 mm.) across. When the teeth become worn, the profile becomes pointed and sharp. This condition is dangerous and damage to the chain is likely to follow.

Brake Shoes. See page 113.

ASSEMBLING THE REAR BRAKE ANCHOR PLATE

Brake Operating Spindle and Cam. Grease the spindle of the brake operating cam and insert it into the housing from the inside of the brake anchor plate. Place on the return spring (long end away from the anchor plate) and tap the lever arm onto the square shoulder at right angles to the flat side of the cam. Place on the lever nut and tighten up.

Brake Shoes. Place the two shoes on the bench in their relative positions. Fit the return springs to the retaining hooks, then, taking a shoe in each hand and at the same time holding the springs in tension, position the shoes to the anchor plate. By turning the top of the shoes inwards, the assembly can be placed over the cam and fulcrum pin and snapped down into position by pressing on the outsides of the shoes. Wind the brake lever arm anti-clockwise to engage the return spring.

ASSEMBLING THE REAR WHEEL

Hub. Assemble the brake drum to the hub. Enter the fixing bolts from the hub side and position the locking washers inside the brake drum. Fit the outer lockwasher and the fixing bolt nuts; when fully tightened, lock them by bending up the locking washer tabs.

Bearing Backing Ring. Place the backing ring in the brake drum side of the hub and then insert the bearing outer race. The race should be pressed into the hub. Repeat operation to the opposite side.

Inner Roller Race. Pack the race with grease and enter the brake drum side outer race. Place the dust cover over the bearing and press into position. Turn the wheel over and pack into the hub, a small quantity of grease (egg-cupful). Fit the remaining race and dust cover.

Spindle. If the shoulder nut has been removed from the spindle, it should now be replaced and screwed down to the end of the spindle thread (the smaller shoulder of the nut must be in the outer position). Enter the spindle into the hub from the brake side.

Fitting Rigid Rear Wheel

Bearing Adjusting Locknut. Turn the wheel over and place the spindle between the jaws of the vice (brake drum downwards) taking care to protect the thread with lead vice clamps. Screw both bearing adjusting locknuts onto the spindle and tighten the lower until it contacts the bearing but leaves the wheel free to rotate. Lock the upper nut to the lower, then remove the wheel from the vice. Check that the spindle will rotate freely by hand. Replace the wheel into the vice for the next operation (brake drum uppermost).

Anchor Plate Assembly. Turn the brake lever towards the "ON" position; by doing this the backward pressure on the brake cam is released. The brake shoes are now in the "OFF" position and the anchor plate can be placed into the brake drum. Screw the remaining shouldered locknut (small shoulder towards the brake drum) onto the spindle and tighten fully to that already in position. Ease the brake lever towards the "ON" position and spin the wheel to check for binding of the brake shoes onto the brake drum.

Chain Adjuster Thrust Collar and Spindle Nut. Place the thrust collar onto the spindle with the shoulder inwards and screw the spindle nut on loosely. Repeat for the opposite side.

FITTING THE REAR WHEEL TO THE FRAME
Positioning the Wheel. Lift the rear wheel into the frame with the brake drum to the left hand side. Engage the anchor plate lug "A", into the locating channel "B", on the inside of the left hand fork lug (See Fig. 47). Push the wheel up to the chain adjuster screws and tighten up the spindle nuts.

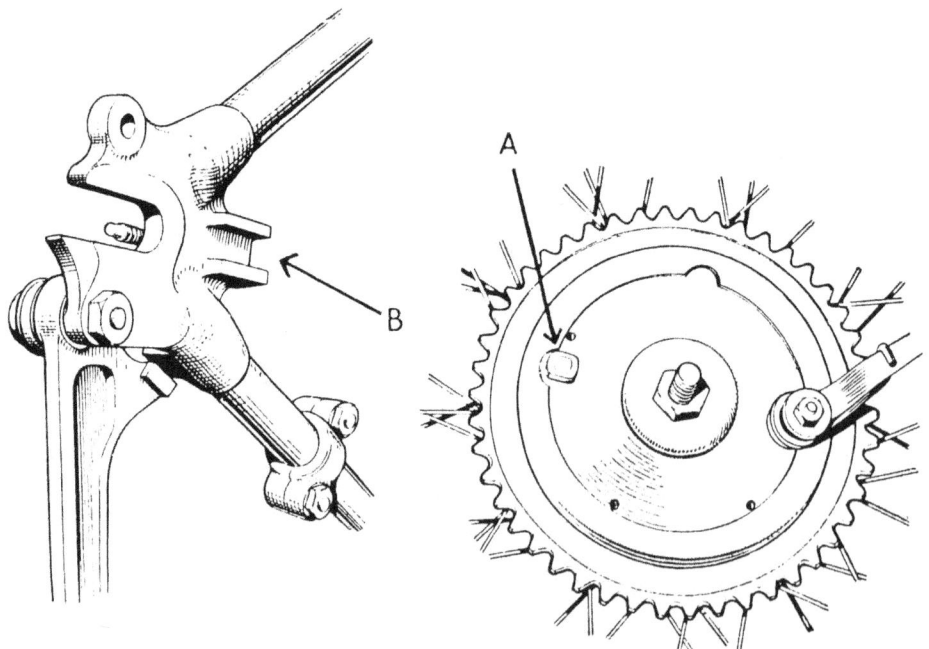

Fig. 47. Stud "A" on Rear Brake Anchor Plate which must be located in Rear Fork Channel "B".

Final Bearing Adjustment. Test the wheel bearings for adjustment now that the wheel is in the frame. Any further adjustment should be made before final assembly. The right hand spindle nut should be undone before any adjustment is made.

Brake. Pull the brake lever arm back, thread the brake rod through the pivot roller in the lever arm and screw on the brake adjusting thumb nut until the wheel can just turn freely without the brakes binding. If new linings have been fitted, it may be necessary to bed the brakes in before adjustment can be made, allowing the wheel to run freely.

Rear Chain. Fit the chain round the sprocket and replace the spring link so that the closed end is facing the direction of chain travel.

Mudguard. Re-assemble the mudguard to the frame and reconnect the tail lamp leads under the saddle.

Road Test. Check the working of the stop light and after road testing, make the final adjustments to the brake.

REAR WHEEL (SWINGING FORK FRAME)

This wheel is mounted on journal ball bearings and therefore requires no adjustment. Slackness in the bearings can be checked by first placing the machine on the central stand and then testing the lateral movement which should be hardly perceptible if the bearings are in good condition. Other details are as the rear wheel fitted in the rigid frame.

REMOVING THE REAR WHEEL FROM THE FRAME

Rear Chain. Depress the gear lever to make sure that the gearbox is not in neutral. This prevents the chain rotating on the gearbox sprocket and falling off when the spring link is removed. Remove the spring link and clear the chain from the sprocket.

Brake Torque Stay. Remove the rear nut and loosen the front nut and bolt.

Brake Adjusting Nut. Unscrew this nut and remove the brake rod from the lever arm.

Spindle Nuts. Unscrew the two spindle nuts and remove from the spindle.

Chain Adjuster Assembly. Pull the wheel back in the frame a short distance and disconnect the adjuster assembly from the spindle.

Wheel. Fig. 49 clearly indicates the method of withdrawing the wheel from the frame. If a prop stand is fitted, it is advantageous to lower it in order to steady the machine during this operation. When the machine is at the right angle, the wheel can be easily removed.

Rear Wheel

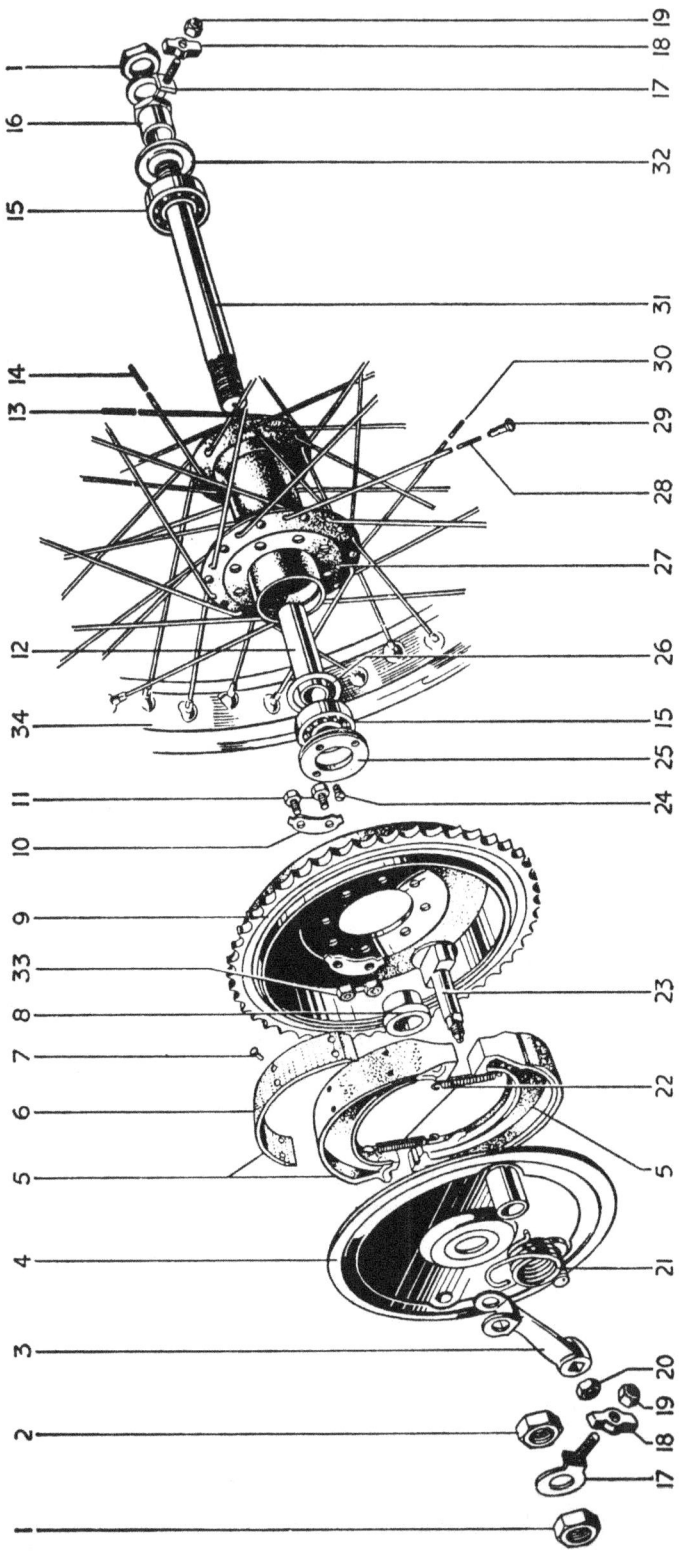

Fig. 48. REAR WHEEL (SWINGING ARM FRAME)

DISMANTLING THE REAR WHEEL

Brake Anchor Plate. Unscrew the anchor plate nut and hold the brake lever against the spring tension just sufficiently to permit the removal of the anchor plate.

Spindle. Remove the anchor plate distance piece and knock out the spindles, taking care not to damage the thread.

Bearing Retaining Ring Nut. Slacken off the ring nut grub screw and unscrew the ring nut. If a suitable peg spanner is not available, the nut can be tapped round with a pin punch.

Bearing and Backing Rings. Remove both bearings by knocking out of the hub from opposite sides with a suitable metal drift. The bearing distance tube and backing rings will now be released.

Brake Drum and Sprocket. This part need not be detached from the hub if the drum does not require attention and the sprocket teeth are not hooked or worn. If removal is necessary, bend back the locking tabs and remove the eight bolts and nuts when the drum can be released.

DISMANTLING THE REAR BRAKE ANCHOR PLATE

Brake Shoes. Take off both brake shoe return springs and remove the brake shoes.

Brake Shoe Cam. Remove the nut and washer securing the lever arm to the cam spindle and take off the lever arm. Withdraw the cam from the plate.

INDEX TO FIG. 48.   REAR WHEEL

Index No.	Description.	Index No.	Description.
1	Nut, spindle.	18	End plate, adjuster.
2	Locknut, anchor plate.	19	Nut.
3	Lever, cam operating.	20	Nut, cam lever.
4	Plate, anchor.	21	Spring, cam lever return.
5	Shoe c/w lining.	22	Spring, shoe return.
6	Lining, shoe.	23	Cam, operating.
7	Rivet, lining.	24	Locking screw, bearing retaining ring.
8	Distance piece, L.H. bearing.	25	Ring, bearing retaining.
9	Brake drum and sprocket.	26	Ring, L.H. bearing backing.
10	Lockplate.	27	Hub.
11	Bolt, drum to hub.	28	Spoke, 76° head.
12	Distance piece.	29	Nipple, spoke.
13	Spoke, 80° head.	30	Spoke, 100° head.
14	Spoke, 97° head.	31	Spindle.
15	Bearing.	32	Cap, dust.
16	Nut, R.H. bearing retaining.	33	Nut.
17	Adjuster, chain.	34	Rim, wheel.

Rear Wheel

Fig. 49. REMOVING WHEEL FROM S/A FRAME

INSPECTION AND REPLACEMENT OF WORN PARTS

With the exception of the bearings, the procedure is the same as that listed for the rigid frame rear wheel on page 118.

Bearings. Clean and dry the bearings thoroughly. Test the end float and inspect the balls for any signs of indentation or pitting. Change the bearings if they are not up to the required standard. Pack the bearings with grease before replacing to the hub.

ASSEMBLING THE REAR BRAKE ANCHOR PLATE

Brake Shoe Cam. Grease the spindle of the cam and insert it into the housing from the inside of the brake anchor plate. Place the return spring in position (long end away from the anchor plate) and tap the lever arm onto the square shoulder at right angles to the flat side of the cam. Fit the lever nut and tighten.

Brake Shoes. Place the two shoes side by side in the positions which they will occupy in the drum. Fit the return springs to the retaining hooks, then, taking a shoe in each hand and at the same time holding the springs in tension, position the shoes to the anchor plate. By turning the top of the shoes inwards, the assembly can be placed over the cam and the fulcrum pin and snapped down into position by pressing on the outside of the shoes. Wind the brake lever arm anti-clockwise to engage the return spring.

ASSEMBLING THE REAR WHEEL

Brake Drum. If the brake drum and sprocket has been removed for rectification, it should be secured in position with the eight locking nuts. Ensure that four locking washers are used both on the inside and the outside of the brake drum. Tap the locking tabs up the sides of the bolts to lock them.

Bearing, Brake Drum Side. Place the locking ring into the hub from the brake drum side until it contacts the small shoulder inside the hub. Press the bearing in, up to the backing ring, and secure in position by tightening the ring nut. Lock the nut with the grub screw.

Grease. Put about an egg-cupful of grease into the hub.

Bearing, R.H. Side. Turn the wheel brake drum downwards and insert the bearing distance piece into the hub until it contacts the brake drum side bearing. Press the R.H. side bearing into the hub, followed by the dust cover.

Spindle. Insert the spindle through the bearings and secure the spindle (opposite brake drum) in the vice. Do not forget to protect the spindle threads against damage by fitting soft clamps over the vice jaws.

Anchor Plate Assembly. Fit the distance piece (shouldered end towards the operator) and, holding the brake lever slightly towards the "ON" position to overcome the tension of the return spring, fit the anchor plate over the spindle and to the brake drum. Replace the anchor plate securing nut to the spindle and securely tighten.

Shouldered Spindle Nut. Remove the wheel from the vice and replace with the brake anchor plate downwards, this time holding the spindle nut. Fit and screw down the shouldered nut until it is hard against the bearing.
The wheel is now ready for assembly to the frame.

Rear Wheel (Quickly Detachable)

FITTING THE REAR WHEEL TO THE FRAME

Wheel. Tilt the machine to the left as in dismantling and position the wheel between the swinging fork. Ensure that the anchor plate stud is correctly located in the brake torque stay hole.

Brake Rod. Re-position to the brake lever.

Chain Adjusters. Fit the adjusters to the spindle and position the end plates.

Chain. Re-fit the chain to the sprocket and replace the connecting link. Check the chain tension and adjust if necessary.

Spindle Nuts. Screw the nuts onto the spindle and securely tighten.

Brake Torque Stays. Fit the rear nut and securely tighten both nuts.

Brake Adjustment. Spin the wheel and check the operation of the brake pedal. Adjust if necessary.

REAR WHEEL (QUICKLY DETACHABLE)
(Fitted to Swinging Fork Frame only)

This wheel is mounted on three bearings, two roller bearings being situated in the hub and one journal ball bearing in the brake drum centre. The wheel is made quickly detachable by the simple method of splining the hub into the brake drum, thus eliminating the necessity of removing the rear chain and disconnecting the rear brake. All other details are as the rigid frame rear wheel.

REMOVING THE Q.D. REAR WHEEL FROM THE FRAME

Spindle. Fit a spanner on, or insert a suitable bar through the hexagon shaped spindle end (R.H. side) and unscrew until the spindle can be withdrawn.

Distance piece. Remove from between the R.H. fork and the wheel.

INDEX TO FIG. 50. QUICKLY DETACHABLE REAR WHEEL (T100 & T110)

Index No.	Description.	Index No.	Description.
1	Nut, L.H. side sleeve.	20	Spindle.
2	Nut, cam lever.	21	Adjuster, chain.
3	Plate, anchor.	22	End plate, adjuster.
4	Shoe c/w lining.	23	Nut.
5	Lining, shoe.	24	Lever, brake cam.
6	Rivet, lining.	25	Spring, cam lever return.
7	Brake drum and sprocket.	26	Spring, shoe return.
8	Felt washer.	27	Cam, brake operating.
9	Retainer, brake drum bearing.	28	Bearing, brake drum.
10	Rim, wheel.	29	Sleeve, brake drum.
11	Bearing, taper roller.	30	Circlip, bearing retaining.
12	Sleeve, bearing.	31	Cap, dust.
13	Hub.	32	Ring, bearing backing.
14	Spoke, 76° head.	33	Seal, hub to drum, dust.
15	Spoke, 100° head.	34	Nipple, spoke.
16	Cap, dust.	35	Ring, bearing backing.
17	Locknut, bearing.	36	Felt washer.
18	Collar, spindle distance.	37	Distance piece, R.H. bearing.
19	Collar, spindle.	38	Grease retainer.

Rear Wheel (Quickly Detachable)

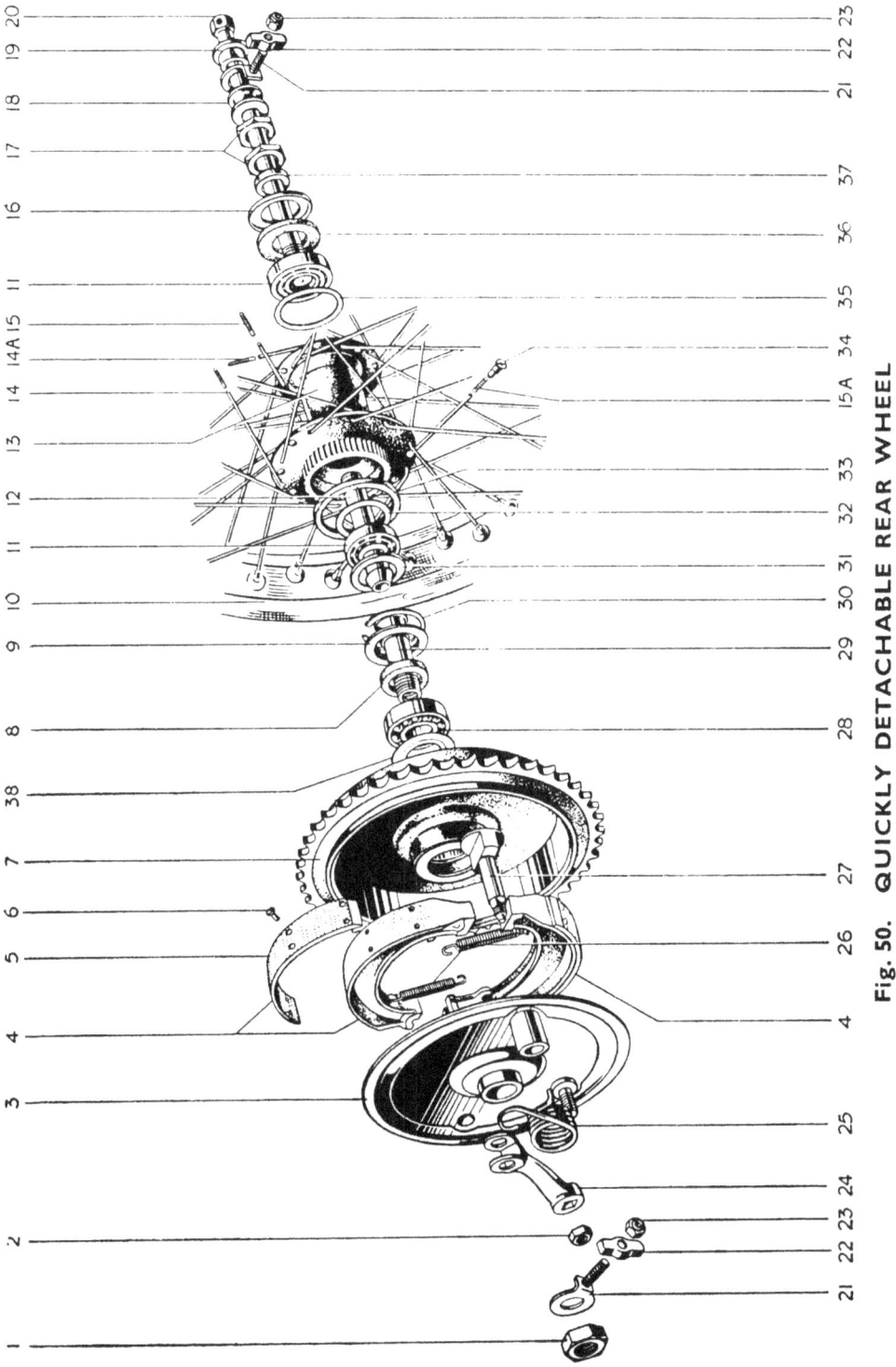

Fig. 50. QUICKLY DETACHABLE REAR WHEEL

Dismantling Rear Wheel (Quickly Detachable)

Wheel. Ease the wheel to the R.H. side until the hub splines are clear of the brake drum splines. Tilt the machine to the left (if a prop. stand is fitted, pull out and use as a steady) when the wheel can be removed from the R.H. side. See Fig. 49 on page 124 which clearly shows the method to adopt.

DISMANTLING THE Q.D. REAR WHEEL

Spindle Sleeve. Unscrew the two locknuts on the right hand end of the spindle sleeve and push the sleeve out of the hub from the right hand side.

Bearings. Extract the inner roller races and dust cover. The outer races are a press fit in the hub and should be tapped out from the opposite side with a soft drift. Care should be taken not to damage the bearing backing rings if there are no replacement rings available.

REMOVAL OF BRAKE DRUM AND SPROCKET

Chain. Engage a gear and remove the spring link; clear the chain from the sprocket.

Brake Adjusting Nut. Unscrew this nut and remove the brake rod from the lever arm.

Brake Torque Stay. Remove the rear nut.

Spindle Sleeve Nut. Unscrew this nut and remove the brake drum assembly from the frame.

DISMANTLING THE BRAKE DRUM AND SPROCKET ASSEMBLY

Anchor Plate Assembly. Hold the lever arm against the tension of the spring to prevent the brake shoes from binding and lift the anchor plate assembly away from the brake drum.

Brake Drum Spindle Sleeve. Push this sleeve out of the brake drum, applying pressure on the threaded end.

Bearing. Remove the bearing retaining circlip with a pair of thin nosed circlip pliers and tap out the bearing, dust cap and felt washer.

DISMANTLING THE ANCHOR PLATE ASSEMBLY

Brake Shoes. Take off both brake shoe return springs and remove the brake shoes.

Brake Shoe Cam. Remove the nut and washer securing the lever arm to the cam spindle and take off the lever arm. Withdraw the cam from the plate.

INSPECTION AND REPLACEMENT OF WORN PARTS

The examination of the wheel parts is exactly as described on page 118, for the rigid frame wheel, except for the following differences.

Brake Drum and Hub Splines. These should be a push fit into one another, slackness at this point would cause the wheel to chatter.

Assembling Rear Wheel (Quickly Detachable)

Brake Drum Bearing. Wash in petrol and when dry, check for pitting and indentation of the balls or race tracks and end float. Scrap if this is in evidence.

Sleeves. Examine the threads and the cone fittings on both. Also check the fit of the bearings as any slackness would cause a certain amount of wheel shake.

Felt Washer and Hub to Brake Drum Rubber Seal. When overhauling the wheel, the washers and seal should be replaced to ensure against loss of grease and grease penetration into the brake drum.

ASSEMBLING THE REAR BRAKE ANCHOR PLATE

Brake Shoe Cam. Grease the spindle of the cam and insert it into the housing from the inside of the brake anchor plate. Place the return spring in position (long end away from the anchor plate) and tap the lever arm onto the square shoulder at right angles to the flat side of the cam. Fit the lower nut and tighten.

Brake Shoes. Place the two shoes side by side in the positions which they will occupy in the drum. Fit the return springs to the retaining hooks, then, taking a shoe in each hand and at the same time holding the springs in tension, position the shoes to the anchor plate. By turning the top of the shoe inwards the assembly can be placed over the cam and the fulcrum pin and snapped down into position by pressing on the outside of the shoe. Wind the brake lever arm anti-clockwise to engage the return spring.

ASSEMBLING THE BRAKE DRUM AND SPROCKET ASSEMBLY

Bearing. Press the bearing into the brake drum and fit the felt dust excluder and washer on top. Secure in position with the circlip.

Spindle Sleeve (Short). Slide the spindle sleeve, threaded end first, through the dust cover, bearing and brake drum.

Anchor Plate Assembly. Hold the brake lever arm towards the "ON" position and slide the anchor plate assembly over the spindle sleeve and into the brake drum.

REPLACING THE BRAKE DRUM AND SPROCKET IN THE FRAME

Brake Drum and Sprocket. Position to the swinging fork and ensure that the stud on the anchor plate is located in the brake torque stay hole and screw the nut in position.

Rear Brake Rod. Engage the rod in the lever trunnion and screw on the adjuster nut.

Chain Adjuster. Fit over the sleeve and engage the end plate to the fork end. Screw on the adjuster nut to hold the adjuster in position.

Fitting Rear Wheel (Quickly Detachable)

Sleeve Nut. Screw onto the spindle sleeve and lightly tighten.

Chain. Fit the chain to the sprocket and fit the connecting link.
Do not make any adjustments or tighten the wheel nut until the wheel is fitted.

ASSEMBLING THE Q.D. REAR WHEEL

Bearings. Press the backing rings into the hub up to the small shoulder and press in the outer races up to them. Fill the hub with about an egg-cupful of grease and place the inner roller races in position.

Spindle Sleeve. Enter the threaded end of the spindle sleeve into the hub from the brake drum side and press through both bearings.

Dust Covers. The brake drum side dust cover is a press fit and should be pushed in up to the bearing. The dust cover on the opposite side has a felt washer insert which should be fitted before the cover is pressed into the hub.

Locking Nuts. Place the small spacing washer over the threaded end of the spindle sleeve and press it into the space between the dust cover and the spindle sleeve. Screw one of the locknuts onto the sleeve until a "nip" is felt, and then slacken back a $\frac{1}{4}$ of a turn so that the sleeve will rotate freely. Tighten the other nut up to it and lock into position. Again test the rotation of the sleeve.

FITTING THE WHEEL TO THE FRAME AND BRAKE DRUM

Hub Rubber Seal. Fit the new rubber seal over the hub splines.

Wheel. Tilt the machine over as in dismantling and enter the wheel between the forks. Right the machine and then locate the hub splines into the brake drum splines.

Spindle. To the spindle, first fit the collar with the cone shaped end towards the hexagon, then the chain adjuster with the stud inwards. Fit the distance piece between the fork and wheel and insert the spindle through the wheel; screw into the hub sleeve.

Chain Adjuster End Plate. Fit to the R.H. adjuster stud and fork end and secure with the nut.

Adjustments. Check the chain and brake adjustments, and finally the wheel alignment. When correct, tighten the L.H. wheel nut and then place a bar or spanner to the spindle hexagon and turn until the spindle is tight. Check the brake torque stay nuts for tightness.

Spring Wheel

SPRING WHEEL—Mk. 2

This wheel has been designed to operate over long periods without maintenance. It will be noted that there is no provision for greasing, as before the wheel is assembled, the bearings and other working surfaces are fully loaded with grease sufficient for 20,000 miles (30,000 kms.).

In view of the above and the special equipment required to dismantle the spring wheel for rectification, owners are strongly advised to return the wheel to their dealer, or direct to our Service Department, when attention is needed.

The following instructions are given however, for owners who wish to carry out their own maintenance and repairs. No attempt should be made to dismantle the plunger guide box without the aid of the special jig illustrated on page 136.

REMOVAL OF THE WHEEL FROM THE FRAME

Mudguard. Disconnect the rear light leads under the saddle. Remove the bolts connecting the rear section mudguard to the frame and lift the mudguard away. It is unnecessary to disturb the mudguard of the TR5 model in order to remove the wheel.

Chain. Disconnect the spring link from the rear chain and disengage from the sprocket. Engage a gear to prevent the chain rolling off the sprocket.

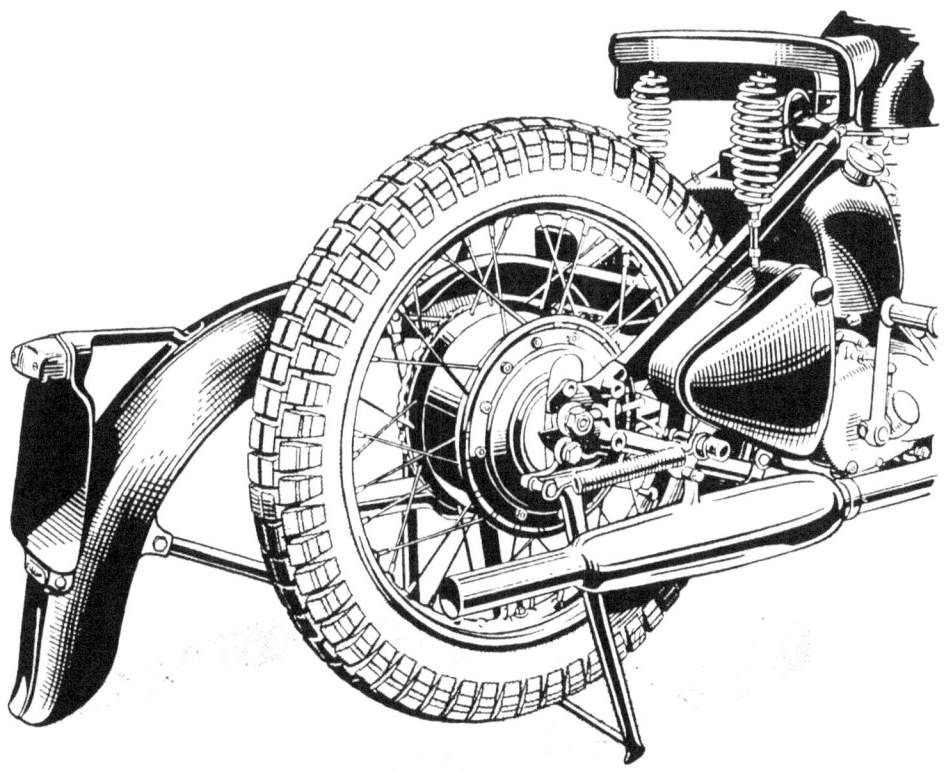

Fig. 51. REAR MUDGUARD SECTION REMOVED FOR TYRE REPAIR OR WHEEL REMOVAL

Spring Wheel

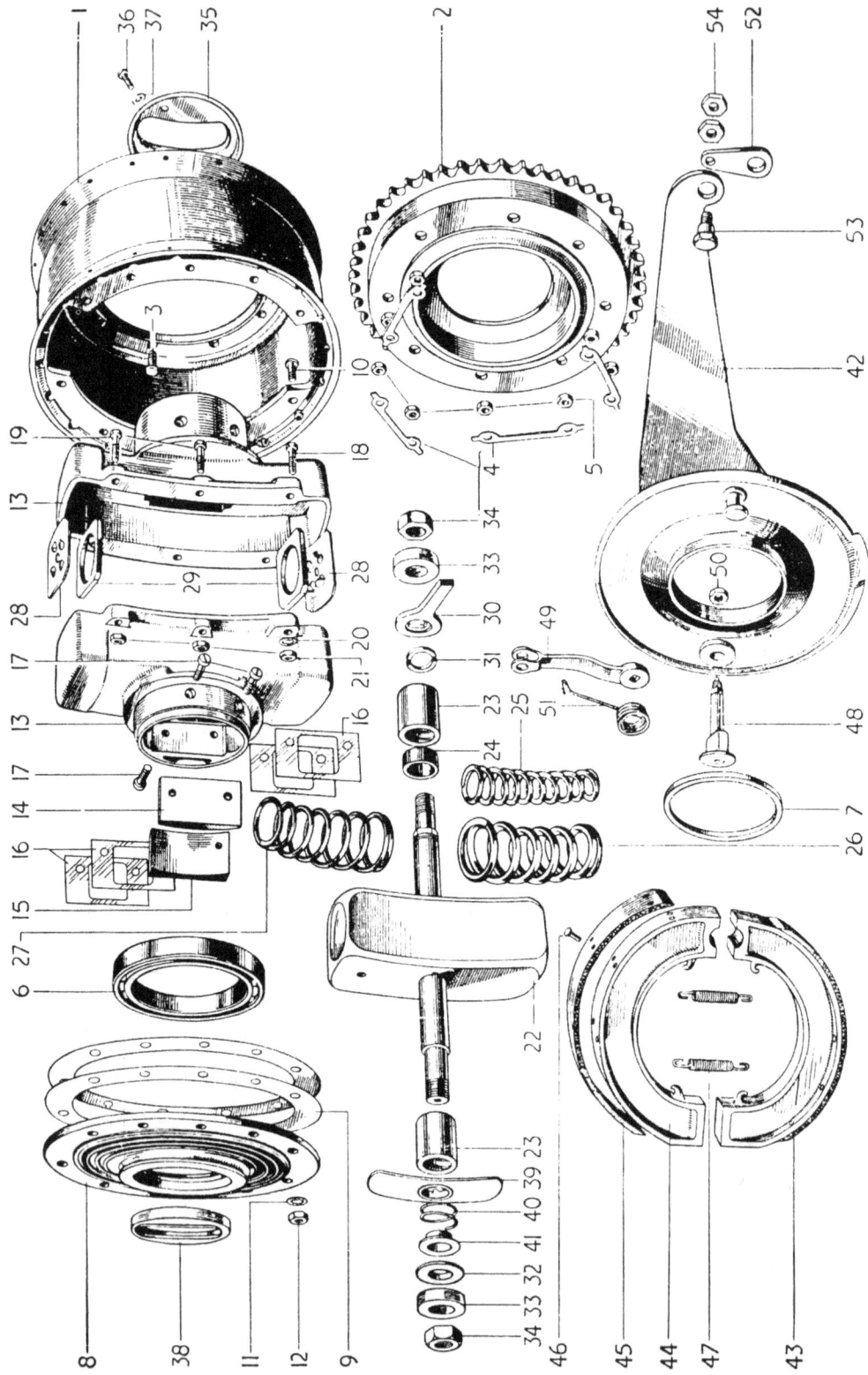

Fig. 52. REAR SPRING WHEEL (COMPONENT PARTS)

INDEX TO FIG. 52.

REAR SPRING WHEEL (COMPONENT PARTS)

Index No.	Description.	Index No.	Description.
1	Hub.	28	Plate, spring locator.
2	Brake drum and sprocket.	29	Buffer, spring (rubber).
3	Bolt, brake drum to hub.	30	Lever, axle shaft anchorage.
4	Lockplate.	31	Circlip, split.
5	Nut.	32	Collar, R.H. distance.
6	Bearing, wheel.	33	Collar, outer distance.
7	Ring, spacer L.H. bearing.	34	Nut, axle shaft.
8	End plate, hub.	35	Cover, L.H. dust.
9	Shim, end plate.	36	Screw.
10	Bolt, end plate to hub.	37	Washer.
11	Washer.	38	Cover, R.H. dust.
12	Nut.	39	Plate, dust.
13	Box, plunger guide.	40	Spring, dust plate.
14	Pad, front slipper (Convex).	41	Sleeve, dust plate centre.
15	Pad, rear slipper (Concave).	42	Plate, anchor.
16	Shim, slipper pad.	43	Shoe, c/w lining.
17	Screw, slipper pad.	44	Shoe, brake.
18	Bolt, high tensile (top rear and bottom front).	45	Lining, shoe.
19	Bolt.	46	Rivet, lining to shoe.
20	Washer.	47	Spring, shoe return.
21	Nut.	48	Cam, brake operating.
22	Assembly, axle and guide.	49	Lever, brake cam.
23	Roller, slipper.	50	Nut.
24	Sleeve, L.H. distance.	51	Spring, cam lever return.
25	Spring, inner main.	52	Link, anchorage.
26	Spring, outer main.	53	Bolt.
27	Spring, rebound.	54	Locknut.

Brake Pedal Adjuster. Unscrew the adjuster and depress the brake pedal to clear the brake rod from the brake lever arm.

Anchor Plate Pivot. Unscrew the two locknuts at the top of the anchor plate pivot and remove the pivot bolt.

Spindle Nuts. Remove the two spindle nuts and distance collars and withdraw the wheel from the frame.

Dismantling Spring Wheel

Brake Anchor Plate. Place the wheel on the bench, brake side uppermost. Prise off the spindle to frame anchorage lever and remove the two split collars underneath. Withdraw the dust excluder centre sleeve and sliding portion. Unscrew the dust excluder securing screws and ease the cover away. Lift the brake anchor plate. Remove the cast-iron ring.

Slipper Roller. Before removing the brake drum side slipper roller, test for freedom of rotation and clearance at each side. If the roller rotates freely and the clearance is not more than 0.002" (0.05 mm.) EACH SIDE, it will be in order to proceed with the dismantling. Should the clearance be above the limit, make a note of the dimensions to assist rectification on assembly. After checking, remove the slipper roller. Turn the wheel over and remove the chamfered collar and dust excluder assembly. Remove the slipper roller, after checking, as described above.

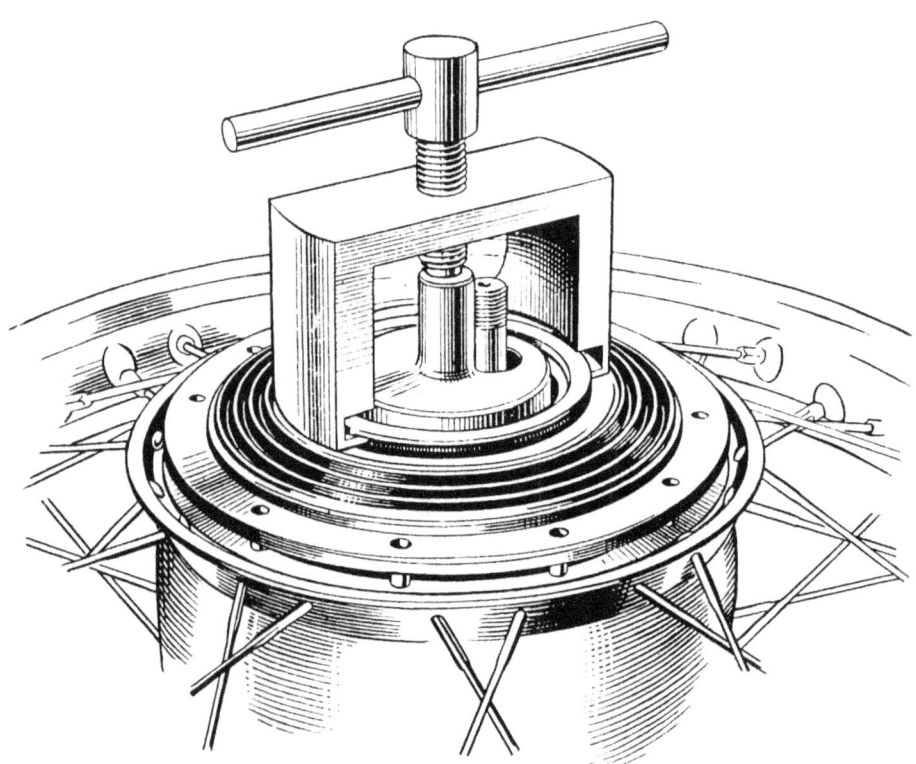

Fig. 53. **SPRING WHEEL END PLATE REMOVAL**

End Plate. Remove the ten nuts securing the end plates to the hub and, using the special jig No. Z.66 (See Fig. 53) withdraw the end plate from the hub by tightening the centre screw of the jig.

Aluminium Shims. These shims are fitted beneath the end plate and should be counted on removal to ensure correct clearance on re-assembly.

Dismantling Spring Wheel

Plunger Guide Box Assembly. Withdraw the assembly from the hub.

Brake Drum and Sprocket. Bend back the four locking tabs and remove the eight nuts securing the brake drum to the hub. Remove the brake drum and sprocket and, using a suitably shaped piece of hard wood, drift out the brake drum side bearing.

End Plate Bearing. Tap out this bearing using a suitable soft drift. Removal can be facilitated by heating the back plate to approximately 100° C.

DISMANTLING THE ANCHOR PLATE ASSEMBLY

Brake Shoes. Remove the two springs and lift the brake shoes away.

Brake Cam. Remove the brake lever arm retaining nut and drift the cam spindle out, when the lever arm and spring will also be released.

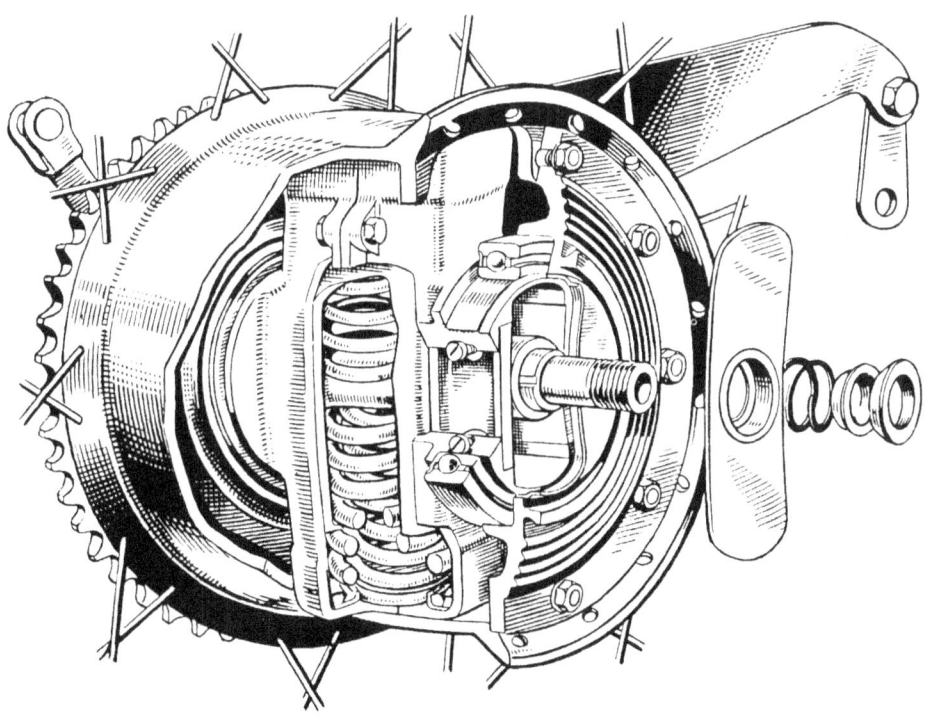

Fig. 54. REAR SPRING WHEEL (SECTIONED)

DISMANTLING THE PLUNGER GUIDE BOX ASSEMBLY

Plunger Guide Box. Remove the four outside bolts from the plunger guide box and unscrew the two centre bolts sufficiently to enable the cases to be parted about ⅜" (1.0 cm.). Using the jig illustrated below, place the plunger guide box assembly into the jaws with the concave side of the box towards the inside of the jig.

Tighten the jaws of the jig until the springs are sufficiently tensioned. Remove the last two bolts and take off the cases. Release the jig until the tension of the springs is released and remove the springs from the plunger guide.

Slipper Pads. If these pads show no sign of wear, it is unnecessary to remove them. Wear is generally noticed on the thrust side only. (Front pad on the chain side and Rear pad on the opposite). To remove, unscrew the two screws holding the pad in position.

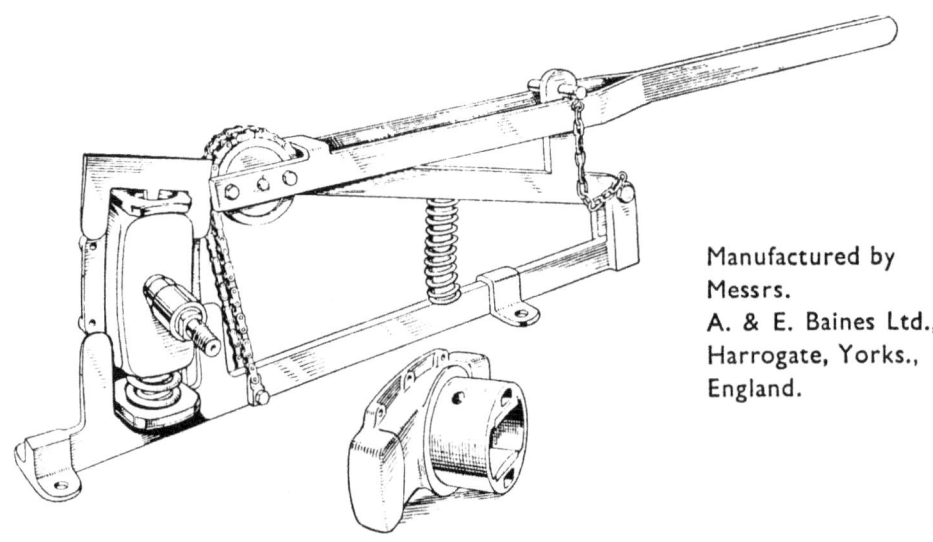

Manufactured by Messrs.
A. & E. Baines Ltd.,
Harrogate, Yorks.,
England.

Fig. 55. JIG FOR COMPRESSING PLUNGER GUIDE BOX SPRINGS

RE-ASSEMBLING THE PLUNGER GUIDE BOX ASSEMBLY

Roller and Slipper Pads. If the steel slipper pads have been removed for replacement or adjustment purposes, it will be necessary to assemble the plunger box, less the springs, plates and rubber buffers. Between the roller and slipper pad there must be an equal clearance of .002" (0.05 mm.) on each side, to allow for any deformation of the box after the springs have been fitted. To enable the fitter to obtain the correct clearance, aluminium shims of .002" and .003" (0.050 and 0.075 mm.) are available. When the pads are in position, ensure that the screws securing them to the case are well tightened.

Springs. When the pads have been fitted correctly the case should be split again and re-assembled with the springs. Place the axle and guide on the bench, with the longer side of the axle to the left and the convex side uppermost. Lubricate and insert the heavy and light springs in the bottom hole, with the curvature of the springs conforming to the guide. Place the other spring in the top hole in the same way. Fit the rubber buffers and spring plates to the springs, with the plate curve conforming to the guide. Fit the assembly into the jig, the two springs being in the lower position. Depress the jig sufficiently to allow the cases to be fitted.

Casings. Grease and fit the casings, then release the jig and remove the assembly. Fill with lubricant through the gap in the cases and tap the cases together with a hide hammer. Fit and tighten the six nuts and bolts. NOTE: the top rear bolt and the bottom front bolt are made from H.T. steel: colour blue-black.

RE-ASSEMBLING THE ANCHOR PLATE ASSEMBLY

Brake Cam Spindle. Grease the spindle and fit to the anchor plate. Fit the return spring and lever arm, making certain that the lever arm is in the correct position. Fit the remaining nut and tighten.

Brake Shoes. Place the brake shoes on the bench in the position they will occupy in the brake plate. Fit the springs and holding them in tension, place the shoes over the cam and pivot.
Press down and snap into position.

RE-ASSEMBLING THE REAR SPRING WHEEL

Bearings. Fully load the bearings with grease (See Recommended Lubricants) and assemble to the back plate and brake drum. Ensure that the bearing chip shield in each case, faces towards the hub centre.

Hub Shell Bolts. Fit all the bolts to each side of the hub shell.

Brake Drum. Assemble the brake drum to the hub and lock the nuts with new locking plates.

Spring Box Assembly. Fit the assembly into the hub and press well home into the brake drum side bearings.

Shims. Fit the shims to the hub, making sure that as many shims are replaced, as were removed.

End Plate. Replace the end plate and bearing and tighten up the nuts securely.

Slipper Roller, R.H. Grease the slipper pads and spindle on the back plate side and fit the slipper roller.

Fitting Spring Wheel

Dust Excluder Assembly, R.H. Fit the dust excluder with the concave side facing forwards. Assemble the centre sleeve spring, sliding portion and chamfered collar. The chamfer on the collar should be towards the hub centre.

Slipper Roller, L.H. Turn the wheel over and fit the distance piece over the spindle. Grease the slipper pads and fit the slipper collar.

Large Cast Iron Ring. This ring should be fitted over the guide box case, so that it abuts against the inner ring of the bearing.

Brake Anchor Plate Assembly. Hold the brake slightly towards the "ON" position by turning the brake lever, and fit the anchor plate assembly to the brake drum.

Dust Excluder Assembly, L.H. Replace the dust excluder assembly with the concave side to the front and secure with the two screws. Ensure that the wheel spindle is in its topmost position and the brake anchor arm facing forward. Fit the split cotters into the groove and the frame anchorage lever onto the spindle.

RE-FITTING THE WHEEL TO THE FRAME

The re-fitting procedure is exactly the reverse of the removal, but the fitter should ensure that the anchorage lever fits into the channel on the left side chain stay lug. Due to the close proximity of the wheel drum, it is not possible to assemble the spring link with the two ends of the chain on the rear sprocket. To overcome this difficulty, join the ends with a spare link inserted from the outside. Now turn the wheel so that the spring link can be pressed in from the inside of the chain, pressing out the spare link in the process.

TYRES

The Dunlop Motor Cycle Tyres as fitted to all models, are of the wire bead type and are fitted into a well-base rim. The wire bead ensures that there will be no stretch in the tyre and in combination with the well-base rim, provides for easy fitting and removal of the tyres and the safe use of air pressures.

TYRE PRESSURE

Tyre pressure should always be carefully maintained as an insufficiently inflated tyre is a prevalent cause of failure of the tyre walls. The actual pressure at which the tyres should be maintained, is a matter for experiment and depends on the rider's weight and also the weight of a passenger and luggage if carried.

DUNLOP RECOMMENDED TYRE PRESSURES (SOLO)

MODEL.		TYRE SIZE.	INFLATION PRESSURE.	
			P.S.I.	Kgms/sqr.cm.
5T, 6T & T110 SWINGING FORK	FRONT	3.25-19	18	1.3
	REAR	3.50-19	19	1.35
T.100 SWINGING FORK ...	FRONT	3.25-19	17	1.2
	REAR	3.50-19	19	1.35
TR.5 SWINGING FORK ...	FRONT	3.00-20	21	1.5
	REAR	4.00-18	16	1.1

These inflation pressures are based on a rider's weight of 170 lb.

When additional weight is added, reference should be made to the Dunlop Booklet which advises the necessary increased inflation pressure.

EXAMINATION

Especially during the period when the roads are being tarred and gritted, the tyres should be examined periodically and any sharp pieces of stone removed from the treads. If they are allowed to remain, no immediate damage may be done but they will later work right through the cover and puncture the tube.

PUNCTURED REAR TYRE (RIGID FRAME MODELS)

In the event of a rear tyre puncture, it is not necessary to remove the wheel to carry out the repair. As shown in Fig. 51, Page 131, with the mudguard rear section removed a large circumference of the wheel is exposed, which makes it easy for the rider to remove one side of the tyre from the rim.

For the other models, the wheel must first be removed.

REMOVING THE TYRE

Valve Cap and Core. Unscrew the valve cap and use the specially shaped end to unscrew the valve core and deflate the tyre. Unscrew the knurled nut and with the valve cap and core, place the parts where they will be free from dirt and grit.

Preparation of Tyre and Levers. It is advisable to lubricate the cover beads with a little soapy water before commencing to remove the tyre. Levers should be dipped in this solution before each insertion.

Tyres

Removing the First Bead. Insert a lever AT THE VALVE POSITION and while pulling on this lever, press the bead into the well of the rim diametrically opposite the valve position. Insert a second lever close to the first and prise the bead over the rim flange. Remove the first lever and re-insert a little further away from the second lever. Continue round the bead in steps of 2-3 inches (5 to 8 cms.) until the bead is away from the rim.

Inner Tube. Push the valve out of the rim and remove the inner tube.

Removing the Second Bead. Stand the wheel upright and insert a lever between the remaining bead and the rim. Pull the cover away from the rim.

FITTING THE TYRE

Rim Band. Make sure that the rough side of the rubber rim band is fitted against the rim and that the band is central in the well.

Fig. 56. ILLUSTRATION SHOWING THE POSITION OF THE VALVE IF THE TYRE HAS CREPT ROUND ON THE RIM

Inner Tube. Inflate the inner tube just sufficiently to round it out without stretch, dust it with french chalk and insert it into the cover, leaving it protruding beyond the beads for about 4 inches either side of the valve.

Lubrication. Here again it is a wise precaution to lubricate the beads and levers with soapy water.

First Bead. Squeeze the beads together at the valve position to prevent the tube from slipping back inside the cover and push the cover towards the rim, threading the valve through the valve holes in the rim band and rim. Allow the first bead to enter the well of the rim and the other bead to lie above the level of the rim flange. Working from the valve, press the first bead over the rim flange by hand, moving forward in small steps and making sure that the part of the bead already dealt with lies in the well of the rim. If necessary, use a tyre lever for the last few inches.

Second Bead. Press the second bead into the well of the rim diametrically opposite the valve. Insert a lever as close as possible to the point where the bead passes over the flange and lever the bead into the flange, at the same time pressing the fitted part of the bead into the well of the rim. Repeat until the bead is completely over the flange, finishing at the valve position.

Valve. Push the valve inwards to make sure that the tube near the valve is not trapped under the bead. Pull the valve back and inflate the tyre. Check that the fitting line on the cover is concentric with the top of the rim flange and that the valve protrudes squarely through the valve hole. Fit the knurled rim nut and valve cap.

SECURITY BOLT

The rear tyre is fitted with a security bolt and although the basic procedure for fitting and removing the tyre is the same, the following additional instructions should be followed.

REMOVING THE TYRE

Valve Cap and Core. Remove as described and deflate the tyre.

Security Bolt and Nut. Unscrew the nut and push the bolt through the inside of the cover.

First Bead. Remove as described.

Security Bolt. Remove from rim.

Inner Tube. Remove as described.

Second Bead. Remove as described.

FITTING THE TYRE

Rim Band. Fit as described.

First Bead. Fit as described but without the inner tube inside.

Security Bolt. Fit to the rim.

Inner Tube. Inflate as described and fit into the cover.

Second Bead. Fit as described but as the security bolt and valve position is reached, push the security bolt well into the cover and make sure that the inner tube is resting on the canvas flap of the security bolt and not overlapping the sides.

Valve. Fit the valve and inflate the tyre. Bounce the wheel at the point where the security bolt is fitted and tighten the security bolt nut.

FRAME

SWINGING FORK

The swinging fork is pivoted to the main frame by a ground, hollow spindle. Two phosphor bronze bushes are pressed into the fork bridge lug to provide a bearing surface for the fork to swing on. The spindle is a drive fit into the frame lug and a working fit in the fork bushes. To retain the spindle in position, a rod is passed through the hollow in the spindle and at each end a retainer cap is made captive, by a nut screwed on the rod end. Between the bridge lug and frame lug on the R.H. side, a spacing washer is fitted in order to obtain the clearance which should be between .0005"-0.0065" (0.013-0.16 mm.). A grease nipple is fitted to the frame to provide access for grease to the bearing by means of a grease gun. (See Routine Maintenance.).

Under average conditions the life of the bearing bushes is approximately 20,000 miles (30,000 kms.). The operation required to replace the bushes is of a major type which calls for the removal of the primary chaincase assembly, gearbox covers, rear wheel and mudguard assembly. If the private owner attempts this work, he should ensure that he has sufficient tools available to complete the work. Details of removing the above mentioned parts will be found by referring to the index on page 210.

GIRLING SUSPENSION DAMPER UNITS

These units are completely self-contained and are known under the type number S/MDA/4/4, which should always be referred to in any correspondence.

During the normal life of the unit the maintenance is negligible; such parts as the main spring and rubber bushes can be easily changed by the owner, but should the hydraulic unit be suspected, no attempt should be made to dismantle it. The complete units should be returned to a Lucas-Girling Depot or the manufacturers, where a service unit can be obtained, or the fault in the suspected unit rectified.

Girling Spring Units

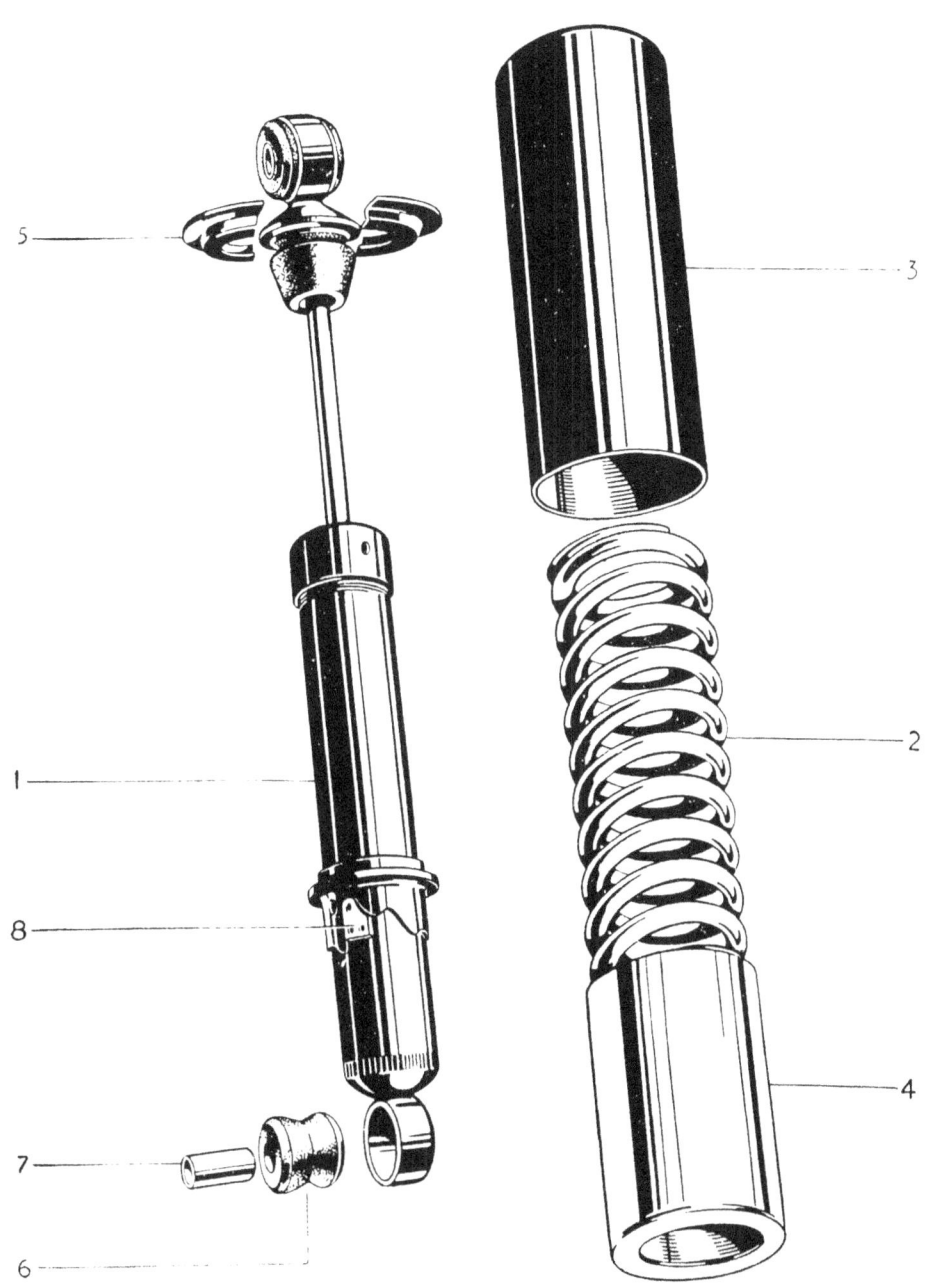

Fig. 57. GIRLING HYDRAULIC SUSPENSION UNIT

INDEX TO FIG. 57. GIRLING HYDRAULIC SUSPENSION UNIT.

Index No.	Description.	Index No.	Description.
1	Damper unit.	5	Retainer, spring.
2	Spring, suspension.	6	Bush, rubber bearing.
3	Dirt shield, upper.	7	Sleeve, bearing bush.
4	Dirt shield, lower.	8	Cam, spring abutment.

Changing Girling Spring Units

TO INCREASE THE STATIC SPRING RATE

If additional weight is added to the rear of the machine such as a heavy pillion passenger and pannier equipment with luggage, the swinging fork member will position itself above the horizontal. This condition will reduce the springing effect and to overcome it, the main spring poundage in the damper unit can be increased by turning the spring abutment cam (see Fig. 57) with the 'C' spanner (supplied in the toolkit) to engage the second position, or, if necessary the third position.

CHANGING THE SPRINGS

DISMANTLING

Unit Fixing Bolts. Remove the top and bottom bolts when the unit can be detached.

Dust Cover. Secure the bottom eye between vice jaws on the side faces (protect the jaws with aluminium clamps). Grip and depress the cover sufficiently to enable the removal of the split spring retainer collars.

Spring. Remove the dust cover and spring.

ASSEMBLY

The assembly is carried out in exactly the reverse order to the dismantling sequence but the following observations should be carefully noted.

Springs. Before replacing, lubricate with high melting point grease.

Dust Covers. Ensure that these are not damaged and are completely free from any foreign matter. Either would cause noisy operation of the unit.

Unit Piston Rod. Do not lubricate with either oil or grease but ensure that the rod is perfectly clean.

Checking Unit Operation. The piston rod should not be operated with the unit in the upside down position. The movement must be checked in the working position, otherwise air will pass into the pressure tube causing the oil to emulsify, resulting in inefficient damping until the unit rectifies itself.

MAXIMUM MOVEMENT

The stroke of the units is $3\frac{7}{8}''$ (9.84 cms.) and this allows for approximately $\frac{5}{16}''$ (8.0 mm.) compression of the bump rubber.

TWISTGRIP CONTROL

Two types of twistgrip are employed, one having the normal quick action and the other (which is fitted to the TR5 only), a progressive action which gives the competition rider more throttle control at low speeds. In each case the damping of the rotor is controlled by a knurled adjuster nut fitted in the twistgrip. To increase the damping, screw in the adjuster until the friction is sufficient to hold the rotor sleeve in any position. Remember that the twistgrip will close immediately the hand is removed to give a road signal if the damping device is not sufficiently adjusted. Maintenance of the twistgrip calls only for light grease lubrication when assembled.

DISMANTLING (5T, 6T, T100 & T110)

Cable Thimble. Unscrew the thimble from the twistgrip head. This is usually made easier by pulling on the cable adjacent to the twistgrip. When unscrewed, the cable simply pulls out of the twistgrip.

Rotor Sleeve. Pull back the twistgrip rubber using a pair of thin, round nosed pliers. Remove the circlip from the head when the rotor sleeve assembly can be withdrawn.

Head. Slacken the grub screw which secures the head to the handlebar and withdraw the head.

ASSEMBLY

Rotor Sleeve to Head. These can be replaced before assembling to the handlebar. Lightly grease rotor end ring and fit the rotor sleeve into the head with the nipple housing adjacent to the cable hole.

Slide the retaining plate into position and assemble the circlip to the head. Roll back the rubber grip. If a new rubber is to be fitted, first wet the inside with petrol and then push it smartly over the sleeve. This job is done better after the twistgrip has been fitted to the handlebar.

Twistgrip to Handlebar. Grease the swaged portion of the handlebar and slide on the twistgrip; lock in the desired position with the grub screw.

Throttle Cable. Holding the outer casing, pull the inner wire, gripping it close to the cable ferrule with a pair of soft nosed pliers. With the other hand rotate the twistgrip sleeve to the closed position, thread the nipple end of the wire into the head and slowly rotate the sleeve when the nipple housing will locate the nipple. When located, replace the thimble cable over the wire and screw into the head.

DISMANTLING (TR5)

Head Clamp Screws. Remove the two screws when the two halves of the head can be taken away.

Rotor Sleeve. Disconnect the cable nipple and withdraw the sleeve from the handlebar.

Twistgrip

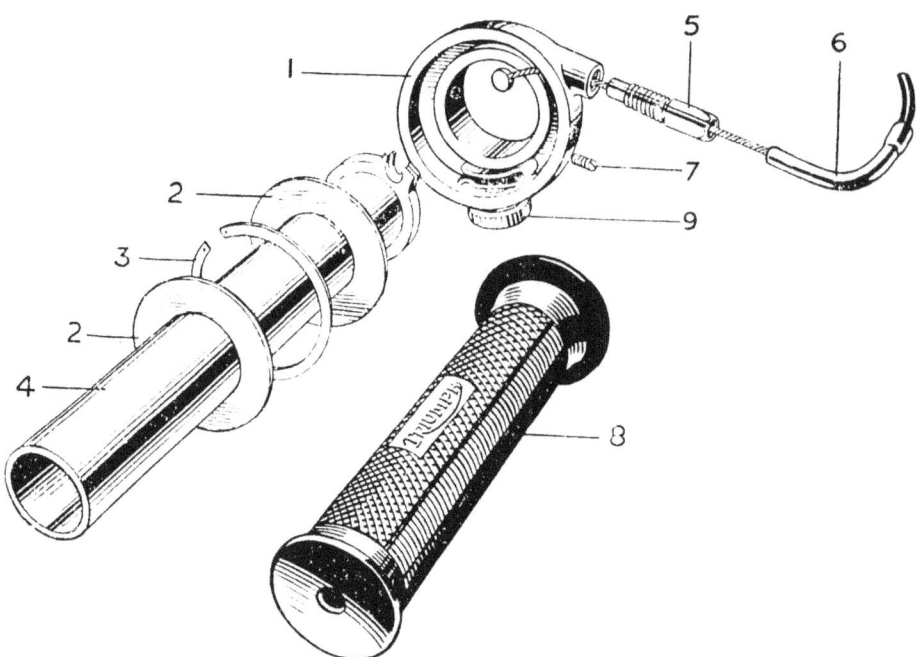

Fig. 58. TWISTGRIP (5T, 6T, T100 & T110)

INDEX TO FIG. 58. TWISTGRIP (5T, 6T, T100 & T110)

Index No.	Description.	Index No.	Description.
1	Head assembly.	6	Guide tube.
2	Plate, retaining.	7	Grub screw.
3	Circlip.	8	Grip, rubber.
4	Sleeve assembly.	9	Screw, friction adjuster.
5	Thimble, cable.		

ASSEMBLY

Rotor Sleeve. Grease the handlebar and slide on the rotor sleeve.

Throttle Cable. Fit the wire nipple to the rotor sleeve.

Head. Assemble top and bottom halves to the handlebar and rotor sleeve. Enter the clamp screws and position the cable guide tube into the recessed portion of the twistgrip halves; fully tighten the two clamp screws.

Twistgrip

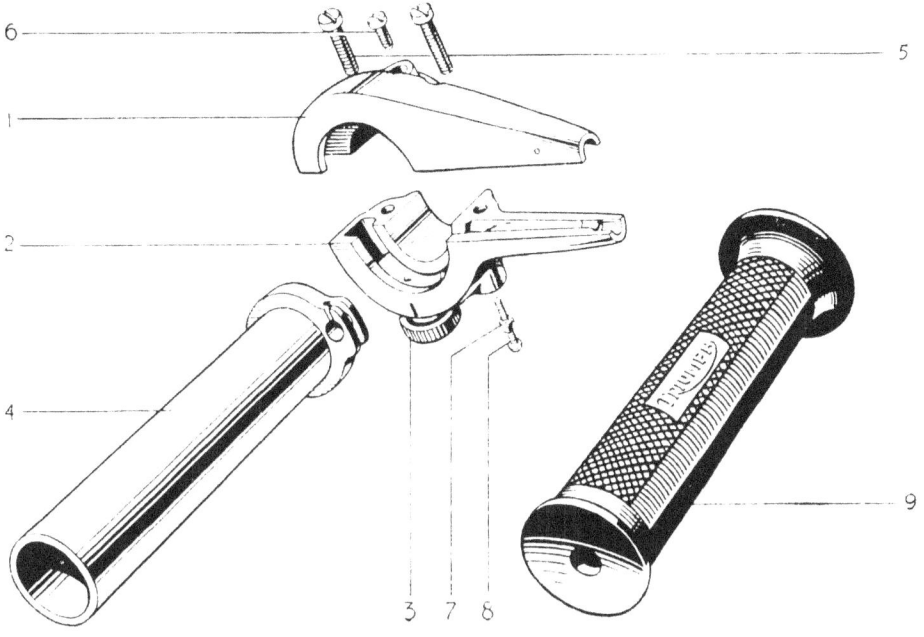

Fig. 59. TWISTGRIP (TR5)

INDEX TO FIG. 59.   TWISTGRIP (TR5)

Index No.	Description.	Index No.	Description.
1	Head assembly, plain half.	5	Screw, head clamp.
2	Head assembly, threaded half.	6	Grub screw.
3	Screw, friction adjuster.	7	Locknut.
4	Sleeve, assembly.	8	Screw, stop.
		9	Grip, rubber.

Grub Screw. Lock the twistgrip in the desired position by screwing down the grub screw between the two clamp screws.

Rotor Sleeve Stop. Adjacent to the knurled damper screw is a small screw and nut and by slackening the nut and screwing in the screw the rotor is arrested earlier when in the closed position, thus leaving the throttle valve slightly open.

PETROL TAP ADJUSTMENT

To make an adjustment, replacement or repair to either type of petrol tap the petrol must be drained from the tank.

Push-pull Type. To adjust a leaking tap, first remove the grub screw locking the plunger to the body, when the plunger assembly can be removed. Grip the plunger end in a suitable tool and turn the plunger knob in a clockwise direction; this expands the cork washer and will make a petrol tight fit when replaced in the petrol tap body. If the cork has deteriorated to any degree, a new cork can be fitted at a very low cost.

Taper Type. Remove the faulty tap and dismantle; take out the split pin, remove the washer, spring back plate and withdraw the spindle and lever assembly. Clean the body and spindle and then apply a smear of fine grinding-in paste to the spindle, add a little oil and rotate the spindle in the tap body using the same motion as when grinding-in the valves. When a true surface is obtained, wash the parts thoroughly in petrol and apply tallow fat to the spindle before assembly. Check the tension of the spring and if insufficient stretch slightly.

FITTING A SIDECAR
(RIGID FRAME MODELS)
(also see Supplement)

First the motorcycle must be prepared for sidecar use. Fork springs of the heavier type must be fitted to counteract the additional load placed on the forks. The extra load will make it necessary to reduce the gear ratios to obtain maximum performance. To carry out this modification the engine sprocket should be changed for one giving the gear ratios required (see Technical Data, pages 6 to 9). Two sidecar fittings only are supplied by us, one fitting on the rear chain stays immediately in front of the rear wheel spindle and the other at the front engine plate to frame bolts. These fittings are adaptable for nearly all sidecars; all other fittings are obtainable from the sidecar manufacturers.

When the machine is prepared, attach the sidecar to the front and rear lugs and tighten up the universal joints, but not the clip pinch bolts. Adjust the sliding tubes through the lugs so that the sidecar is as close to the machine as possible; this prevents excessive drag. Keep the front and rear tubes of the sidecar parallel to the ground and the nose elevated sufficiently to overcome any tendency to drag when the outfit is taken round a right-hand bend at speed. The next point to check is the amount of toe-in. To do this, two parallel aligning sticks are required of sufficient length to extend beyond front and rear wheels of the machine. Place one stick along the off-side of the machine allowing it to touch the wall of the rear tyre, allowance being made at the front tyre for the difference in size. Now place the other stick alongside the sidecar wheel in similar fashion. Measure the distance between the sticks immediately at the rear of the motorcycle rear wheel. Check the measurement at the front and adjust until the reading is $\frac{3}{8}''$ less than the rear measurement. Tighten up the clip connections. It is now time to attach the third, and if fitted, the fourth point connection.

Here again leave the clip pinch bolts loose. Set the machine slightly out of the vertical, leaning away from the sidecar about 5 degrees, then tighten all fittings. Test the outfit on the road with a passenger in the sidecar or an equivalent load and ascertain its steering qualities. If possible use a road with a flat surface; if not available use the crown of the road. If the outfit pulls to one side of the road or the other, check the amount of toe-in again and make sure that the sidecar wheel is as near as possible in alignment with the rear wheel of the machine. Should the sidecar have a tendency to lift easily on left-hand bends, lean the machine more to the vertical.

If these few precautions are taken during fitting, the rider will be amply repaid in comfort and a reduction in general wear and tear.

CLEANING MOTORCYCLE

A clean motorcycle not only gives pride of ownership, but also assists the owner in maintaining his machine in first class condition.

There are on the market extremely good cleaning solvents for removing oil and road dirt from the exterior of the machine, and they can be obtained from most accessory dealers. The preparation should be applied with a 1" paint brush to the machine which must be dry and about 5 minutes allowed to elapse in order that it can penetrate the oily surfaces. It should then be washed off with water from a watering can; the reason the latter is used is to enable the operator to direct a controlled stream of water thus avoiding trouble such as water in the brakes and ignition faults. If the air cleaner is disconnected the carburetter should be suitably covered to stop any ingress of water. After completion of this work the surplus moisture should be removed with a chamois leather, and when all surfaces are dry a good polish should be applied. For a quick finish a liquid cleaner called "FLAZPOL" gives excellent results and is also a good preservative. For a lasting finish a good wax polish should be used and at each stage of the cleaning, always use soft dusters.

AMAL CARBURETTER
(Models 5T, TR5, T100 & T110)

The AMAL needle jet carburetter is fitted to all the above mentioned models and, unless the machine is to be used for some special purpose, we strongly recommend that the settings are not interfered with. The settings are arrived at after careful experiment and it is unlikely that a different setting will improve the fuel consumption, or increase the maximum power output. Alternative settings are however listed for the models T100 & T110 when the air filter is disconnected.

During the early life of the machine it is advisable to remove the float bowl and clean it out occasionally to prevent the jets becoming blocked. A common cause of erratic running at low speeds, explosions in the silencers and poor pick-up when accelerating is a CHOKED SLOW RUNNING ORIFICE IN THE JET BLOCK. To remedy this fault, the carburetter mixing chamber must be completely dismantled and the jet block withdrawn to gain access to the orifice. To clear, push a thin strand of wire through the hole to dislodge any foreign matter. Wash the jet block in petrol and dry off with pressure air to ensure that all passage ways are perfectly clear.

OPERATION OF CARBURETTER PARTS

Throttle Stop Screw. This screw should be set to open the throttle sufficiently to keep the engine running at a low tick over when the twistgrip is shut off.

Pilot Air Screw. To set the idling mixture, this screw should be set in or out to enrich or weaken, normal number of turns out is about $2\frac{1}{2}$. The screw controls the suction on the pilot petrol jet by metering the amount of air which mixes with the petrol.

Needle and Needle Jet. A tapered needle is attached to the throttle and either allows more or less petrol to pass through the needle jet as the throttle is opened or closed throughout the range, except when idling or nearly full throttle.

The taper needle position in relation to the throttle opening can be set according to the mixture required by fixing it to the throttle with the needle clip spring in a certain groove, thus either raising or lowering it. Raising the needle enriches the mixture; lowering it weakens the mixture at throttle openings from a quarter to three quarters open. Machines are delivered from the factory with the needle in the fourth notch from the top, and the needle should be lowered to the middle notch after 1,000 miles (1,500 Kms.).

Throttle Valve Cut-Away. The atmospheric side of the throttle is cut away to influence the depression on the main fuel supply and thus gives a means of tuning between the pilot and needle jet range of throttle opening. The amount of cut-away is recorded by a number marked on the throttle viz., 6/3 means throttle type 6 with No. 3 cut-away; larger cut-aways, say 4 and 5 give weaker mixture and 2 and 1 richer mixtures.

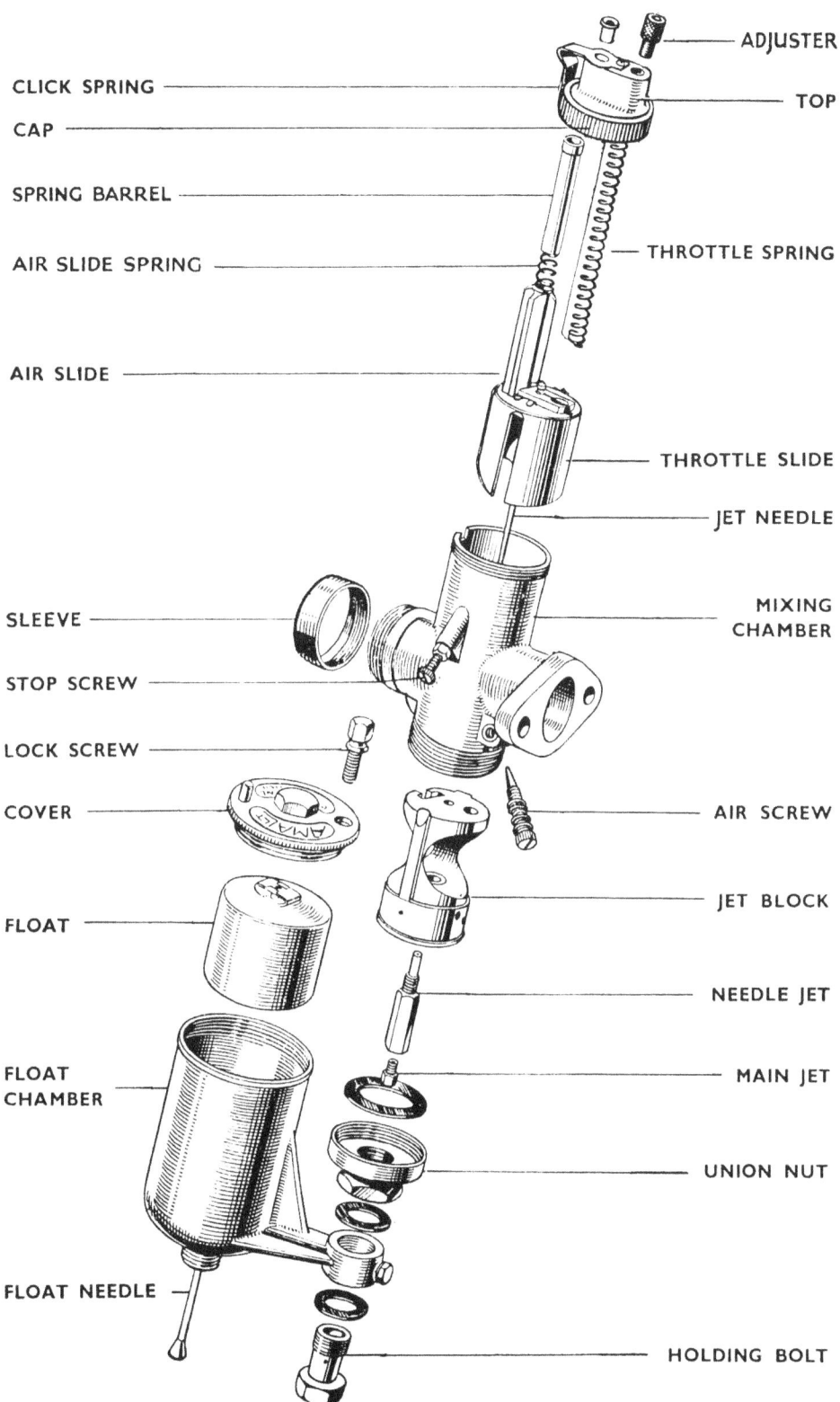

Fig. 60. AMAL CARBURETTER

Amal Carburetter

Air Valve. Is only used for starting and running when cold, and for experimenting with, otherwise, run with it wide open.

Tickler. A small plunger spring loaded in the float chamber lid. When pressed down on the float, the needle valve is dislodged from its seat and so "flooding" is achieved. Flooding temporarily enriches the mixture until the level of the petrol subsides to normal.

GENERAL

Erratic running at low speeds can be due to distortion of the carburetter flange; this fault is generally caused by uneven tightening of the flange nuts. To rectify, first place a straight edge across the flange face to ascertain the amount of bow; if the bow is only slight, rub the flange surfaces over with a piece of emery cloth which has been tacked to a flat surface. If the flange cannot be trued up in this way it should be filed with a 6" (15 cms.) flat smooth file, and then finished off as stated above.

If the silencers are removed or replaced by the megaphone type for the machine to be raced, it is essential that the carburetter is given a richer setting and a larger main jet.

BASIC CARBURETTER SETTING FOR RACING

	Valve.	Needle.	Needle Jet.	Main Jet.
Petrol	4	2	109	200
50/50 Petrol/ Benzole	4	2	109	220
*Alcohol Fuel	4	2	113	660

*The standard Jet Block can be modified by drilling out the Pilot Jet orifice to 0.031" (No. 68 Morse drill).

JOINT GASKETS

On the 5T and T110 Models the joint gaskets between the induction manifold and the cylinder head should be coated with a jointing compound. This prevents the thin paper washers weaving between the two dissimilar metals and partially obstructing the induction apertures.

For further information see AMAL leaflet.

AIR FILTER

Two types of air filters are fitted, the "D" shaped type, and the flat type. See Figs. 61 and 62.

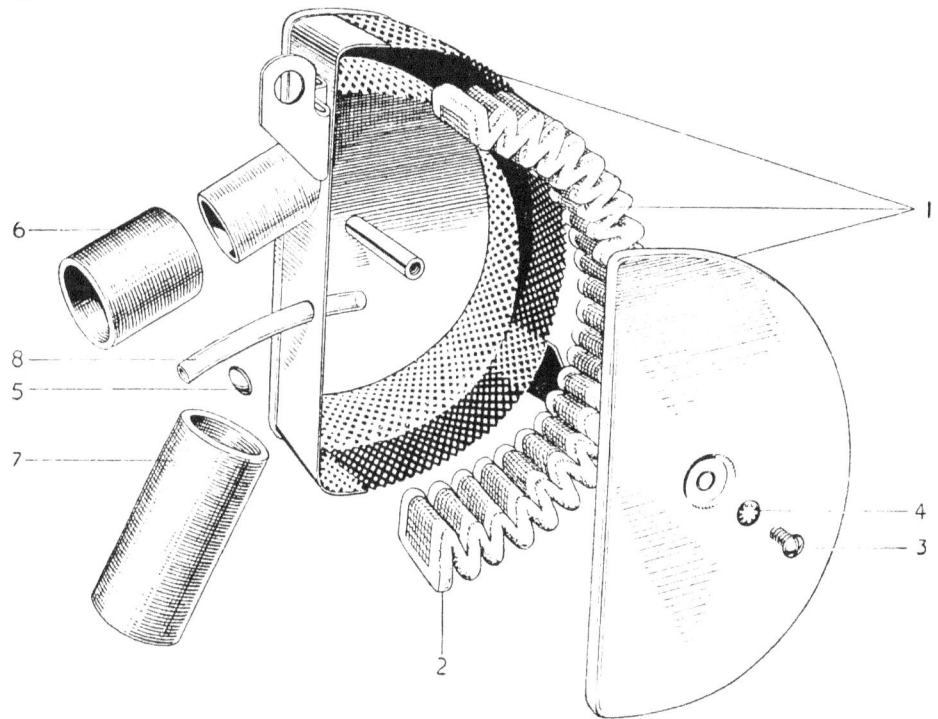

Fig. 61. AIR FILTER

INDEX TO FIG. 61. AIR FILTER

Index No.	Description.	Index No.	Description.
1	Filter assembly.	6	Connection, sleeve to filter (rubber) 5T.
2	Element, filter.	7	Connection, sleeve to filter (rubber) 6T.
3	Screw, cover.	8	Vent pipe, carburetter to filter, 6T.
4	Washer, shakeproof.		
5	Grommet, air filter vent hole.		

SERVICING THE FILTER

Rigid Frame Models. To remove the filter for servicing, the battery and battery carrier must first be removed. Disconnect the rubber sleeve and remove the air filter.

Air Filter

Swinging Arm Frame Models. To service the filter on these models, the oil tank must first be detached. This operation necessitates the removal of the three fixing bolts and disconnection of the oil pipes. Disconnect the rubber sleeve and remove the air filter.

To remove the element on the "D" shaped filter, unscrew the two screws securing the cover, when the latter can be removed and the element extracted. The "flat" type, simply remove the cover to which the element is attached.

Every 2,000 miles (3,000 kms.), the filter element should be removed and washed in petrol until all road dust is extracted. Put the element in a convenient place to dry off. In extreme conditions (dust, sand, etc.) this servicing should be at more frequent intervals. When dry, re-oil the element with "Vokes Trifiltrene" filter oil. If this is unobtainable SAE 20 grade oil may be used.

The filter element should be changed every 10,000 miles (15,000 kms.) and in countries where dusty conditions prevail the change should be made at more frequent intervals. This procedure is most important as a choked filter will cause loss of performance and heavy petrol consumption.

The maximum power output with the air filter attached, is very little affected, but if the absolute maximum is required for the T100 & T110 models, remove the rubber sleeve and increase the main jet as follows:—

        T100 & TR5 ... Replace 220 with 240
        T110 ... ... Replace 250 with 270

DO NOT remove the filter sleeve from the S.U. carburetter (See page 155 for further information).

INDEX TO FIG. 62. AIR FILTER

Index No.	Description.
1	Filter assembly.
2	Element with cover.
3	Connection, sleeve to filter (rubber).

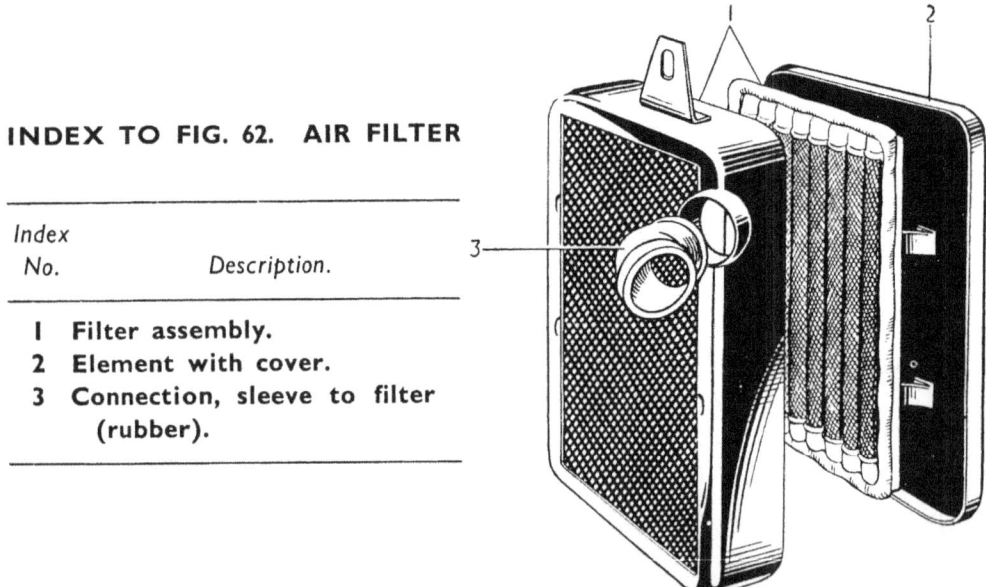

Fig. 62. AIR FILTER

THE S.U. M.C.2. CARBURETTER *

ADJUSTMENT AND TUNING

The S.U. Carburetter is of the automatically expanding type in which the cross sectional area of the air passage, and the effective orifice of the jet are variable.

The choice of the needle which governs the effective orifice of the jet is settled for a particular engine after considerable testing, both on the engine test bed and afterwards on Road Test, with Premium Grade Petrols, and it is not, therefore, a common requirement that the needle type should be changed from the maker's original specification. Low grade and alcohol blended petrols may require the substitution of a richer than standard needle.

If any doubt arises as to the correctness of the type fitted, this can be checked by first removing the suction chamber and then slackening the side needle screw when the needle can be pulled out and its markings by numbers or letters checked. These identifying letters and numbers may be rolled round the shank, or stamped on the flat end of it. If, therefore, an alteration to the mixture strength is required this needle alone should be changed, as all jets are of standard size and as THE JET ADJUSTING NUT IS FOR SETTING THE IDLING ONLY.

It is most important that the needle is fitted with its shoulder FLUSH WITH THE FACE OF THE PISTON, as shown in the diagram.

When detaching the suction chamber and piston assembly from the main carburetter body (necessary when checking or changing the needle) it will be necessary to remove the OIL CAP. After the two side screws have been removed lift the assembly off the carburetter body. This will call for a certain amount of manual dexterity, as the suction chamber can only be lifted a limited amount. One hand is required to lift the suction piston upwards inside the chamber against the piston spring, whilst the other steadies the suction chamber. The complete unit can then be moved sideways, clear of the main instrument, but great care must be taken to see that the JET NEEDLE IS NOT BENT.

When re-fitting the suction chamber and piston the procedure is, of course, reversed, and the piston should be held as high up as possible inside the suction chamber whilst the assembly is guided carefully into the piston bore and jet in the main body. A slot in the small piston diameter registers with a riveted brass guide in the body.

Tuning the carburetter, which should only be carried out after the engine has reached its normal running temperature, is confined to correct idling adjustment by means of the throttle stop screw, which governs the amount of throttle opening for IDLING SPEED, and the jet adjusting nut (18) which controls the IDLING MIXTURE. Screwing this nut up weakens the mixture and down enriches it.

NOTE. This nut must not be forced, as this may set the jet off centre.

All references to numbers in the script apply to Fig. 64 only.

S.U. Carburetter

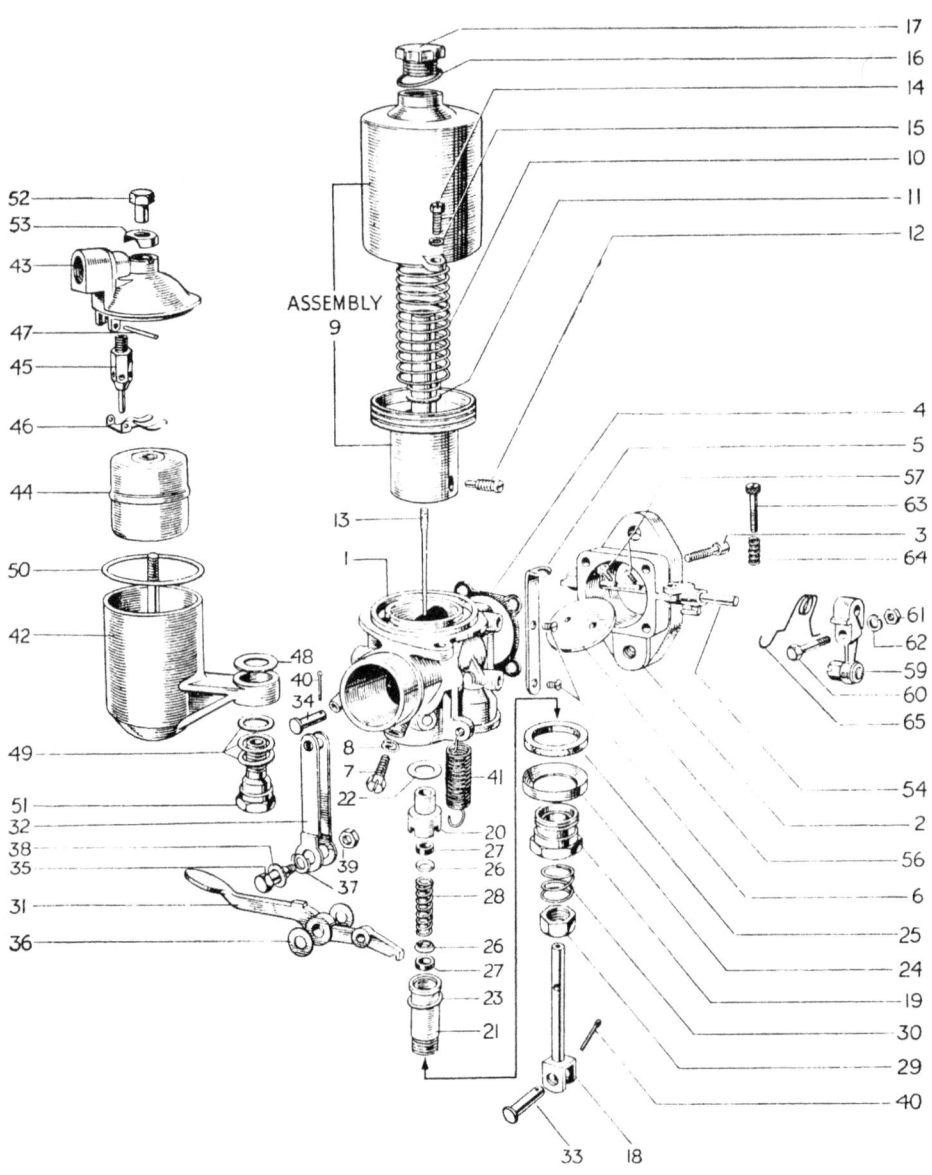

Fig. 63. S.U. CARBURETTER (COMPONENT PARTS)

INDEX TO FIG. 63. S.U. CARBURETTER (COMPONENT PARTS)

Index No.	Description.	Index No.	Description.
1	Body.	33	Pivot pin, long.
2	Adaptor, throttle barrel.	34	Pivot pin, short.
3	Screw, adaptor to body.	35	Bolt.
4	Gasket, adaptor to body.	36	Washer, fibre.
5	Abutment, throttle cable.	37	Washer, spring.
6	Screw.	38	Washer.
7	Screw, plug 2 B.A.	39	Nut.
8	Washer.	40	Split pin.
9	Chamber, suction complete.	41	Spring, return.
10	Spring, piston.	42	Chamber, float.
11	Washer, thrust.	43	Lid, float chamber.
12	Screw, needle.	44	Float.
13	Needle, jet.	45	Needle and seat.
14	Screw.	46	Lever, hinged.
15	Washer, spring.	47	Pin, hinge.
16	Washer, oil cap.	48	Washer, fibre.
17	Oil cap, octagonal.	49	Washers, 2-fibre, 1-brass.
18	Jet.	50	Washer, float chamber lid.
19	Screw, jet.	51	Bolt, holding.
20	Bearing, jet top half.	52	Nut, float chamber lid.
21	Bearing, jet bottom half.	53	Cap, brass.
22	Washer, copper.	54	Throttle spindle.
23	Washer, copper.	56	Disc throttle.
24	Ring, sealing (Brass).	57	Screw.
25	Ring, sealing (Cork).	59	Lever, throttle.
26	Washer, gland (Brass).	60	Bolt.
27	Washer, gland (Cork).	61	Nut.
28	Spring.	62	Washer.
29	Nut, adjusting.	63	Screw, adjusting.
30	Spring.	64	Spring, adjusting screw lock.
31	Lever, jet.	65	Spring, lever return.
32	Link, jet.		

WARNING. Move one "flat" of the nut round at a time and remember to apply slight downward pressure on the jet lever to ensure that the jet follows the adjusting nut, as the jet lever spring (Pt. No. 4872/1) is not strong enough to do this itself (as in car practice), its sole purpose being to retain the jet against vibration in the position set by the rider. Three "flats" in either direction should be sufficient to identify progress; excess movement would indicate an air leak in the induction system or an ignition fault.

A correct idling mixture gives an even beat with a colourless exhaust—too rich a mixture gives a trace of black in the exhaust with a rhythmical or regular misfire—too weak a mixture gives a splashy irregular type of misfire with a marked tendency to stop.

S.U. Carburetter

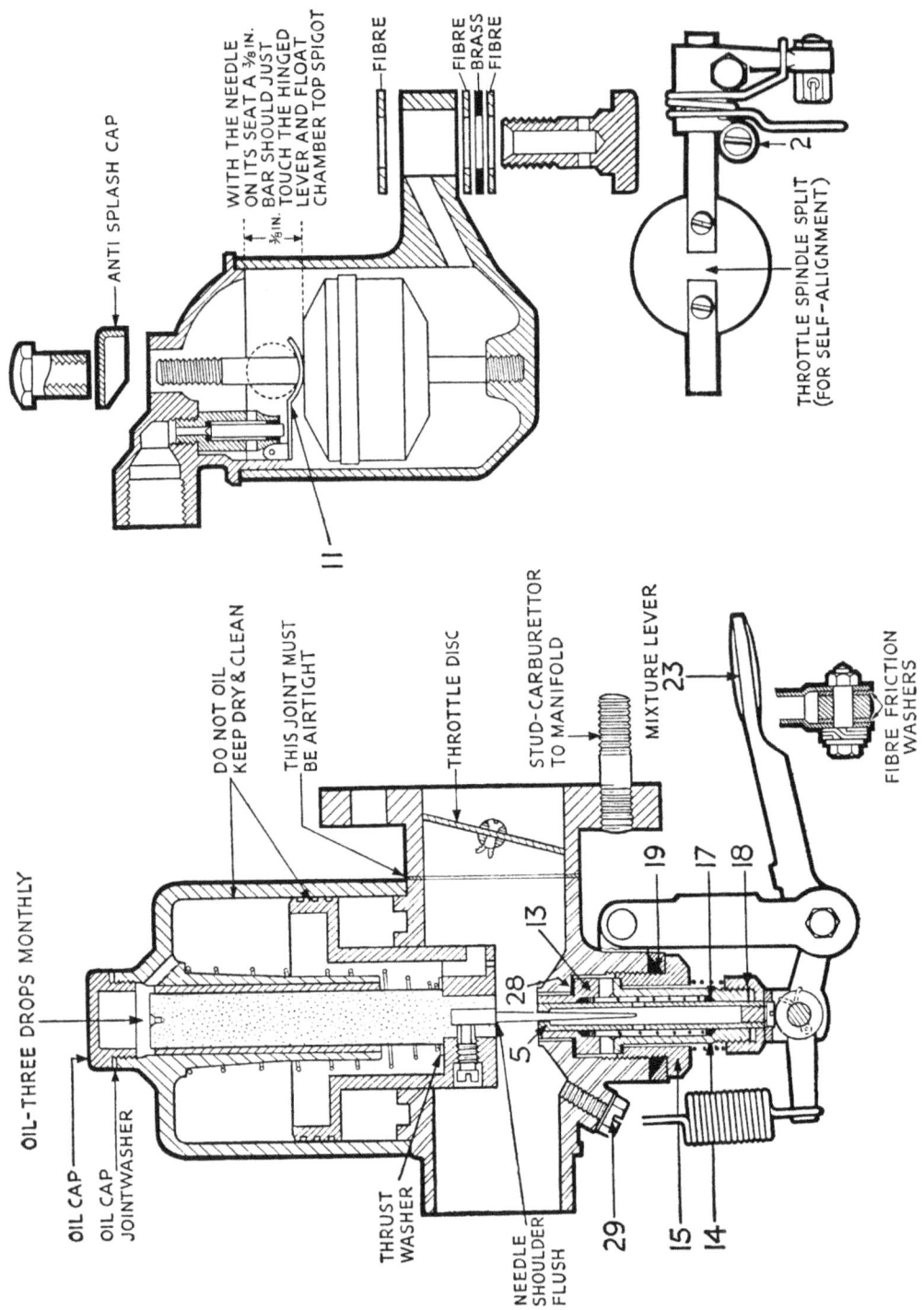

Fig. 64. S.U. CARBURETTER (DIAGRAM)

Maintenance S.U. Carburetter

DEFECTS IN OPERATION

When an engine runs erratically, faults other than carburation can be contributory causes. Before interfering with the carburetter, the following possibilities should be considered:—

(a) Compression—Equal pressure in both cylinders; check tappet clearances.
(b) Moisture condensation (water)—Examine float chamber and H.T. cables.
(c) Ignition System—Inspect the distributor points, clean and adjust if necessary.

Contact breaker and condenser condition is most important. Sparking plugs should be cleaned and re-gapped (See Technical Data) and pressure tested. Correct timing is vital to good idling, in particular excessive advance and faulty operation of the automatic mechanism must be rectified.

(d) Check for air leaks:—
  (i) Between the MANIFOLD and CYLINDER HEAD.
  (ii) Between the MANIFOLD and CARBURETTER.
  (iii) Between the TWO HALVES of the CARBURETTER.
  (iv) At the SUCTION CHAMBER CAP.

If, however, the engine and ignition are found to be faultless the following points should be checked on the carburetter:—

STICKING OF PISTON

The symptoms here are either stalling and a refusal of the engine to run slowly or, alternatively, lack of power accompanied by excessive fuel consumption. This defect is easily detectable. When the engine is not running the piston should rest upon the bridge (28). When raised by the hand through the air intake, the piston should drop freely and strike the bridge sharply and distinctly. To do this the filter rubber connection must first be removed.

If it becomes prematurely arrested in its downward movement, or appears unduly reluctant to break away from its position of rest on the bridge when an attempt is made to raise it from this position, the jet should be lowered by means of its lever, and the test repeated.

If the symptoms persist, it can be assumed that either the large diameter of the piston is making contact with the bore of the suction chamber, or the small diameter with the carburetter body, or that the piston rod is not sliding freely within its bush. When, on the other hand, sticking has been eliminated by the act of lowering the jet, the indication is that the needle is binding on the jet either due to its being bent or to the latter being out of centre. Normally the needle should never touch the jet orifice when correctly assembled.

(If visual evidence clearly indicates needle wear and jet ovality, both should be renewed).

Rectification should be conducted as follows according to the diagnosis:—

DIRT OR CONTACT BETWEEN THE PISTON AND SUCTION CHAMBER, OR STICKING OF THE PISTON ROD IN ITS BUSH.

Maintenance S.U. Carburetter

If dirt or corrosion of the suction chamber, piston or piston rod is responsible then the parts should be cleaned with a solvent such as petrol, thinners, degreasing fluid or alcohol, but no abrasive material should be used. They should be re-assembled dry and clean with OIL ON THE PISTON ROD ONLY. If, on the other hand, there is metallic contact the high spot may be removed with a scraper PROVIDED THAT THE GREATEST CARE IS TAKEN; INDISCRIMINATE SCRAPING WILL RENDER THE PARTS SCRAP.

Bent Needle or incorrectly centred Jet
A bent needle should be replaced as straightening is seldom satisfactory, and an incorrectly centred jet should be re-centred according to the instructions given below. In either case contact between these two parts is likely to have caused wear and both may have to be replaced.

LUBRICATION
EVERY MONTH, or as frequently as may be found necessary, remove the plastic oil cap from the top of the suction chamber and thoroughly oil the piston rod and guide bush assembly with thin machine oil.

When the oil cap and joint washer have been replaced, ensure that the cap is FIRMLY SCREWED DOWN. An air leak at this point would upset the automatic operation of the piston in the suction chamber, causing a rich setting and loss of speed.

ECCENTRICITY
Re-centring of the jet in relation to the needle will be necessary should the jet have become laterally displaced in service due to inadequate tightening of the locking screw (15), or any other cause. This operation will of course, also be necessary if the jet and its associated parts have been removed for any reason. Before proceeding as described in the next paragraph, first try turning the jet round 180° as, if the jet head has been connected to the mixture lever in a different place to that at which it was originally "centred" the action of the piston will be restricted.

The procedure for re-centring the jet is as follows:—
The jet adjusting nut (18) should first be screwed upwards to its fullest extent, THE JET HEAD THEN BEING RAISED TO CONTACT IT so that the jet assumes its highest possible position. The locking screw (15) should now be loosened sufficiently to release the jet and the jet bush assembly (5), (13), (14), etc., and permit this to be moved laterally.

A moderate side loading applied to the lower protruding part of the lower jet bush (14) will indicate whether or not the assembly has been sufficiently freed. The piston should now be raised and, maintaining the jet in its highest position, allowed to drop. This will cause the needle to move the jet gradually but positively into position, and thus bring about the required centralisation.

The locking screw should now be tightened and the jet returned to its former position. Should any indication of contact between the needle and the jet persist, which may sometimes occur due to further displacement of the assembly on finally tightening the locking screw, this must again be slackened off and the operation repeated.

S.U. Carburetter

FLOODING FROM FLOAT CHAMBER OR MOUTH OF JET

Flooding may occur due to a punctured float, or to dirt between the float chamber needle valve and its seating. To remedy either defect, the float chamber lid should be removed and the necessary cleaning, float replacement or repair effected. The needle and seating unit number is T2, to identify which two ring grooves are machined around the seating.

Flooding may also occur if the original manufacturer's setting of the hinged fork lever (11) in the top of the float chamber has been disturbed, possibly causing the petrol level to be higher than normal, this higher level giving a slow petrol bleed over the jet bridge. The setting figure for this fork is that with the fork pressing the needle home on its seating, a $\frac{3}{8}''$ (9.5 mm.) diameter test bar should just slide easily between the curve of the fork and the circular facing of the float lid casting.

Flooding may also be caused by a bad seal between the float needle and its seating, and which may sometimes be restored by giving the needle a few light taps with a delicate instrument such as the handle of a screwdriver:

ROUGH HANDLING WILL RENDER THE PARTS SCRAP.

Leakage from bottom of Jet

If persistent slow leakage is observed in the neighbourhood of the jet head, it is probable that the jet gland washer (7) and its lower counterpart, together with the locking screw washer (19) require replacement. The jet lever (23) should first be detached from the jet head, the locking screw (15) removed, and the entire jet and jet bush assembly withdrawn. On re-assembly, great care should be taken to replace all parts in their correct situations, as shown in the diagram. Re-centring of the jet, as previously described, will of course be necessary after this operation.

HINTS AND TIPS

These are a few of the points to which the Owner should pay particular attention in order to maintain minimum fuel consumption and maximum power.

1. The Float Chamber. If rough running and poor idling are suddenly experienced, the internal float chamber condition is usually responsible. To overcome this trouble remove the float chamber every two months and thoroughly clean. When replacing, do not overtighten the lid sleeve nut as this will cause distortion and leakage of fuel at the joint between lid and float chamber.

2. Air Leaks. Leakage at the manifold to engine and carburetter to manifold will completely upset the smooth performance of the engine.

3. Sticking Piston. Dirt, corrosion or malalignment of the jet will cause the piston to stick. Make sure that the suction chamber and piston are perfectly dry and clean, and that the PISTON ROD, which must move freely in its bush, IS OILED. Before attempting to re-centre the jet try the effect of turning it through 180°. It may have been replaced in the opposite position, in the mixture lever.

4. Throttle Spindle. Overstressing the throttle spindle torsion return spring is a common fault. This causes the coils to bind before full throttle is attained, and may disturb the whole mechanism. Incorrect positioning of the movable throttle lever may do the same.

S.U. Carburetter

LUBRICATE THROTTLE CABLE TO ENSURE SMOOTH AND POSITIVE THROTTLE OPERATION.

5. Plastic Cap. Do not forget to fit the washer, as the spindle can foul the cap before full lift occurs, resulting in restricted power. Always use the correct part, a car type (with a hole in) will **NOT** do.

6. Piston Spring. Do not mutilate the spring by stretching, otherwise the performance and fuel consumption of the motorcycle will be adversely affected. If in doubt regarding the spring pressure a new one of the correct type should be fitted.

Make sure that the ignition control is working properly, that the timing is correct and, in particular, that it is not over advanced—**especially** at idling.

AIR FILTER

THE AIR FILTER SHOULD NOT BE DISCONNECTED IN AN ATTEMPT TO INCREASE THE MAXIMUM SPEED OF THE MACHINE. THE CARBURETTER AND AIR FILTER ARE DESIGNED TO GIVE MAXIMUM EFFICIENCY AND, IN FACT, THE REMOVAL OF THE FILTER WILL IMPAIR GENERAL PERFORMANCE AS THE CARBURETTER IS EXPOSED TO ROAD DUST AND OTHER FOREIGN MATTER. IF THE AIR FILTER IS NOT CONNECTED THERE IS A LIKELIHOOD THAT THE FREEDOM OF THE PISTON IN THE SUCTION CHAMBER WILL BE RESTRICTED. **ITS FREE MOVEMENT IS VITAL TO THE SATISFACTORY OPERATION OF THE CARBURETTER, OF THE ENGINE AND, THEREFORE, OF THE WHOLE MOTORCYCLE.**

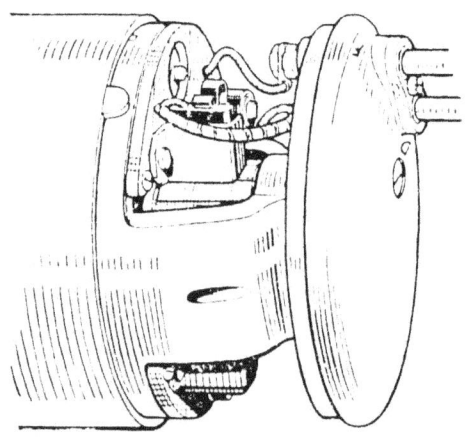

Fig. 65. DYNAMO (Model E3L).

LUCAS ELECTRICAL EQUIPMENT
DYNAMO LIGHTING AND MAGNETO IGNITION

DYNAMO

Output Control. The dynamo works in conjunction with a regulator unit to give compensated voltage control. Although combined structurally, the regulator and cut-out are electrically separate. Both are accurately adjusted during manufacture and should not be tampered with.

The regulator provides a completely automatic control. It causes the dynamo to give an output which varies according to the load on the battery and its state of charge. When the battery is discharged, the dynamo gives a high output, but if the battery is fully charged then the dynamo gives only a trickle charge so as to keep the battery in good condition. In addition to controlling the output of the dynamo according to the condition of the battery, the regulator provides for an increase of output to balance the current taken by the lamps when in use.

The cut-out is an automatic switch which connects the dynamo to the battery only when the dynamo voltage exceeds the battery voltage, or conversely, which disconnects to prevent the battery discharging through the dynamo windings.

The dynamo output is accurately set to suit the requirements of the motorcycle and in normal service the battery will be kept in a good condition. If due to special running conditions it is found that the battery is not kept in a charged condition or is being overcharged, the regulator should be re-set by a Lucas Service Depot or Agent. Accurate measuring equipment is required to set the regulator correctly.

Ammeter Readings. Normally, during day time running when the battery is in good condition, the dynamo gives only a trickle charge so that the ammeter needle should show only a small deflection to the "+" side of the scale.

A discharge reading should be observed immediately after switching on the headlamp. This usually happens after a long run when the battery voltage is high. After a short time the battery voltage will drop and the regulator will respond, causing the dynamo output to balance the lamp load.

Lubrication. No lubrication is required to these models as ball bearings are fitted at both ends. These bearings are packed with grease during assembly and will last until the machine is taken down for a general overhaul.

Inspection of Brushgear and Commutator. Every six months, remove the commutator cover and inspect the brushgear and commutator. The brushes, which are held in boxes by means of springs, must make firm contact with the commutator. Move each brush to see that it is free to slide in its holder; if it sticks, remove it and clean with a cloth moistened with petrol. Care must be taken to replace the brushes in their original position, otherwise they will not "bed" properly on the commutator. If after long service the brushes have become worn to such an extent that they will not bear properly on the commutator they must be replaced. Always use genuine Lucas brushes, which should be fitted by a Service Agent so that they can be properly bedded to the commutator.

Dynamo Wiring Diagram

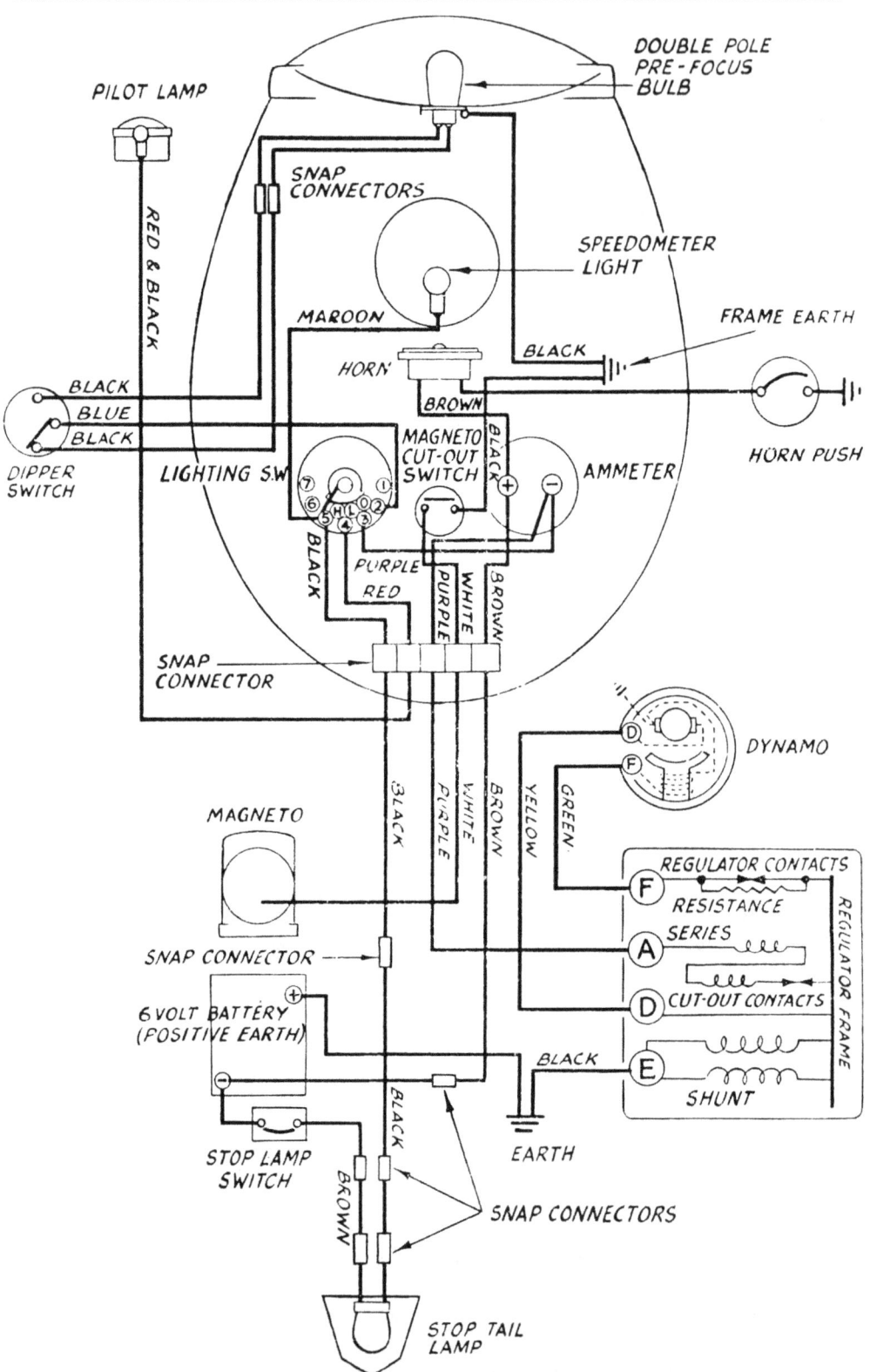

Fig. 66. **WIRING DIAGRAM (T100 & T110)**

Examine the commutator, which should be free from any trace of oil or dirt and should have a highly polished appearance. Clean a dirty or blackened commutator by pressing a clean dry cloth against it whilst the engine is slowly turned over by means of the kickstarter crank. (It is an advantage to remove the sparking plugs before doing this). If the commutator is very dirty, moisten the cloth with petrol.

MAGNETO

The magneto is of rotating armtuare pattern, having its magnet cast into the body, so eliminating joints and improving the weatherproof properties of the magneto. The ignition timing is controlled by a manual lever situated on the handlebar.

Lubrication—Every 3,000 miles (5,000 kms.). The cam is supplied with lubricant from a felt pad contained in a pocket in the contact breaker housing. A small hole in the cam fitted with a wick, enables the oil to find its way to the surface of the cam. Remove the contact breaker cover, turn the engine over until the hole in the cam can be clearly seen and then carefully add a few drops of thin machine oil. Do not allow any oil to get on or near the contacts. If the cam ring is removed, the wick should be taken out and soaked in thin machine oil. Wipe the wick to remove surplus oil, before replacing.

The contact breaker rocker arm pivot also requires lubrication and the complete contact breaker must be removed for this purpose. Take out the hexagon-headed screw from the centre of the contact breaker and carefully lever the contact breaker off the tapered shaft on which it fits. Push aside the rocker arm retaining spring, lift off the rocker arm and lightly smear the pivot with Mobilgrease No. 2 or an equivalent grease.

Remove the cam ring, which is a sliding fit in its housing, and lightly smear inside and outside surfaces with Mobilgrease No. 2. Removal and re-fitting of the cam can be made easier if the handlebar control lever is half retarded, thus taking the cam away from its stop pin. Allow one or two drops of thin machine oil to the felt cam lubricator in the housing. Re-fit the cam, taking care that the stop peg in the housing and the timing control plunger engage with their respective slots.

If an earthing brush is fitted at the back of the contact breaker base, see that it is clean and can move freely in its holder, before re-fitting to the contact breaker. When replacing the contact breaker, take care to ensure that the projecting key on the tapered portion of the contact breaker base engages with the keyway cut in the magneto spindle, otherwise the timing of the magneto will be affected. Replace the contact breaker securing screw and tighten with care.

The armature bearings are packed with grease during assembly and will not need attention until the motorcycle is dismantled for general overhaul, when it is advisable to have the magneto inspected by a Lucas Service Depot or Agent.

Magneto Maintenance

Adjustment of Contact Breaker Setting. The setting of the contact breaker must be checked every 3,000 miles (5,000 kms.). To do this, remove the contact breaker cover and turn the engine until the contacts are seen to be fully open. Check the gap with a feeler gauge having a thickness of 0.012"-0.015" (0.30 to 0.40 mm.), a gauge for this purpose is provided on the spanner usually supplied with each magneto. If the setting is correct, the gauge should be a sliding fit, but if the gap width varies appreciably from the gauge thickness it must be adjusted. Keep the engine in the position giving maximum separation of the contacts, slacken the locknut and turn the contact screw by its hexagon head until the gap is set to the gauge. Tighten the locknut and re-check the setting.

Cleaning Contacts. Every 6,000 miles (10,000 kms.), take off the contact breaker cover and examine the contact breaker. Dirty or pitted contacts can be cleaned with a fine carborundum stone, or, if this is not available, very fine emery cloth can be used.

Wipe away any dirt or metal dust with a cloth moistened with petrol. Contact breaker springs should be examined and any rust removed. To render the contacts accessible for cleaning, proceed as outlined below.

After cleaning, check the contact breaker setting.

Removal of Contacts for Cleaning. Unscrew the contact breaker securing screw. Carefully lever the contact breaker off the tapered shaft on which it fits. Push aside the locating spring and lift the rocker arm off its pivot, when it will be possible to clean the contacts. When replacing the contact breaker, check that the projecting key, on the tapered portion of the contact breaker base, engages with the keyway cut in the armature spindle, otherwise the timing of the magneto will be affected. Replace the contact breaker securing screw and tighten with care.

High Tension Pick-up. About every 6,000 miles (10,000 kms.), remove the high tension pick-up. Wipe the moulding with a clean dry cloth. Check that the carbon brush moves freely in its holder, but take care not to stretch the brush spring unduly. If the brush is dirty, clean it with a cloth moistened with petrol. If the brush is worn to within $\frac{1}{8}$" (3.0 mm.) of the shoulder it must be renewed.

Before re-fitting the high tension pick-up, clean the slip ring track and flanges by pressing a soft dry cloth on the ring with a suitably shaped piece of wood, while the engine is slowly turned.

Renewing High Tension Cables. When high tension cables show signs of cracking or perishing, they must be replaced, using 7 mm. rubber covered ignition cable.

To replace a high tension cable proceed as follows:—

Remove the metal washer and moulded terminal from the defective cable. Thread the new cable through the moulded terminal and cut back the insulation for about $\frac{1}{4}$" (6.0 mm.). Pass the exposed strands through the metal washer and bend them back radially. Screw the terminal into the pick-up moulding.

LUCAS RM 14 A.C.

LIGHTING AND IGNITION

GENERAL DESCRIPTION

Under NORMAL running conditions, electrical energy in the form of rectified A.C. passes through the battery from the alternator—the rate of charge depending on the position of the lighting switch. When no lights are in use, the alternator output is sufficient only to supply the ignition coil and to trickle-charge the battery. When the lighting switch is turned to the "PILOT" or "HEAD" positions, the output increases proportionately.

Under EMERGENCY starting conditions, trickle-charging continues whilst an ignition performance similar to that from a magneto is obtained. AFTER THE ENGINE HAS BEEN STARTED, NORMAL RUNNING IS RESUMED BY TURNING THE IGNITION KEY FROM "EMG" to "IGN". IF THE BATTERY MUST BE REMOVED, THE ENGINE CAN BE RUN WITH THE IGNITION SWITCH IN THE "EMG" POSITION PROVIDING THAT THE BATTERY NEGATIVE CABLE (BROWN) IS EARTHED TO THE FRAME. UNDER THESE CONDITIONS NO LIGHTS ARE AVAILABLE.

CIRCUIT DETAILS

The alternator stator carries three pairs of series-connected coils, one pair being permanently connected across the rectifier bridge network. The purpose of this latter pair is to provide some degree of charging current for the battery whenever the engine is running.

Connections to the remaining coils vary according to the positions of the lighting and ignition switch controls. When no lights are in use, the alternator output from the battery charging coils is regulated to a minimum by interaction of the rotor flux set up by current flowing in the short circuited coils.

In the "PILOT" positions these latter coils are disconnected and the regulating fluxes are consequently reduced. The alternator output therefore increases and compensates for the additional parking light load. In the "HEAD" position, the alternator output is further increased by the connection of all three pairs of coils in parallel.

EMERGENCY STARTING (IGNITION SWITCH AT EMG.)

With this circuit the contact breaker is arranged to open when the alternating current in the windings reaches a maximum. The ignition coil primary winding and the contact breaker are connected in series. When the contacts separate H.T. current is induced in the coil secondary windings, thus producing a spark at the plug.

A.C. Generator

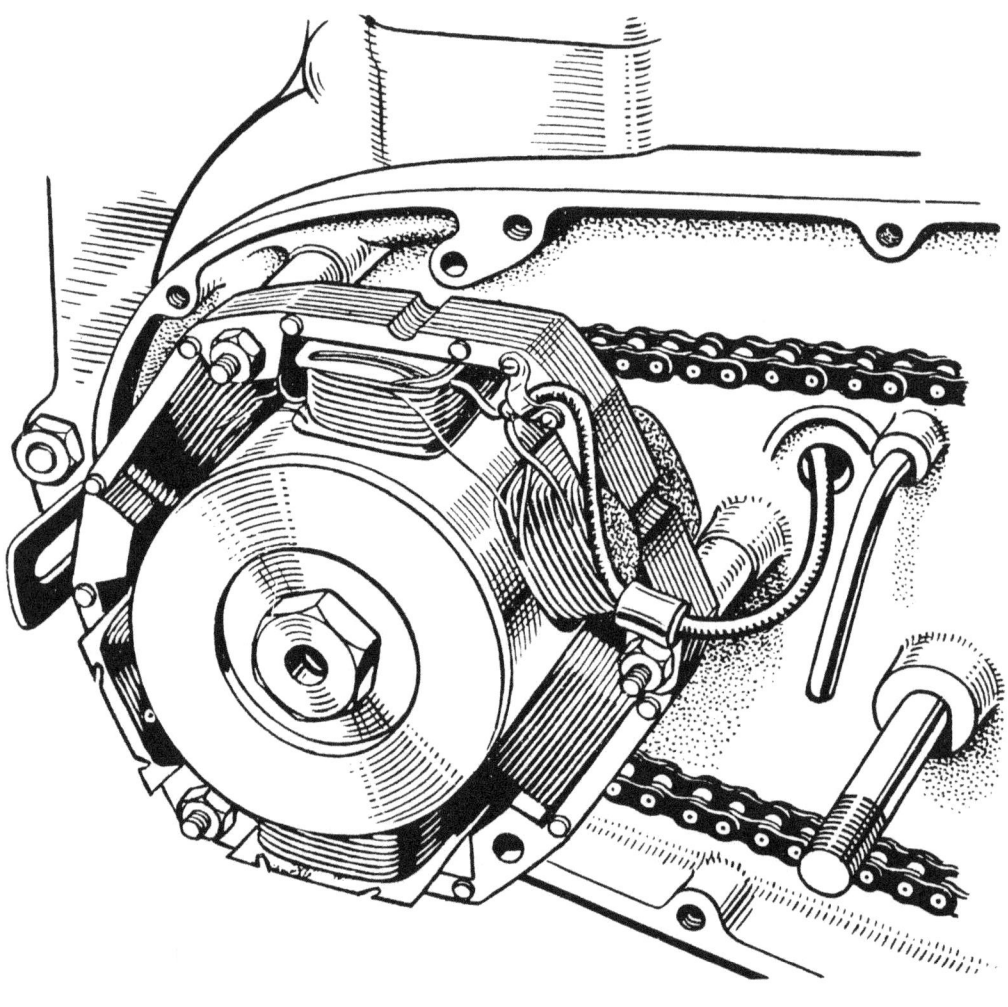

Fig. 67. **PRIMARY CHAINCASE COVER REMOVED TO SHOW ROTOR AND STATOR**

A.C. Generator Wiring Diagram

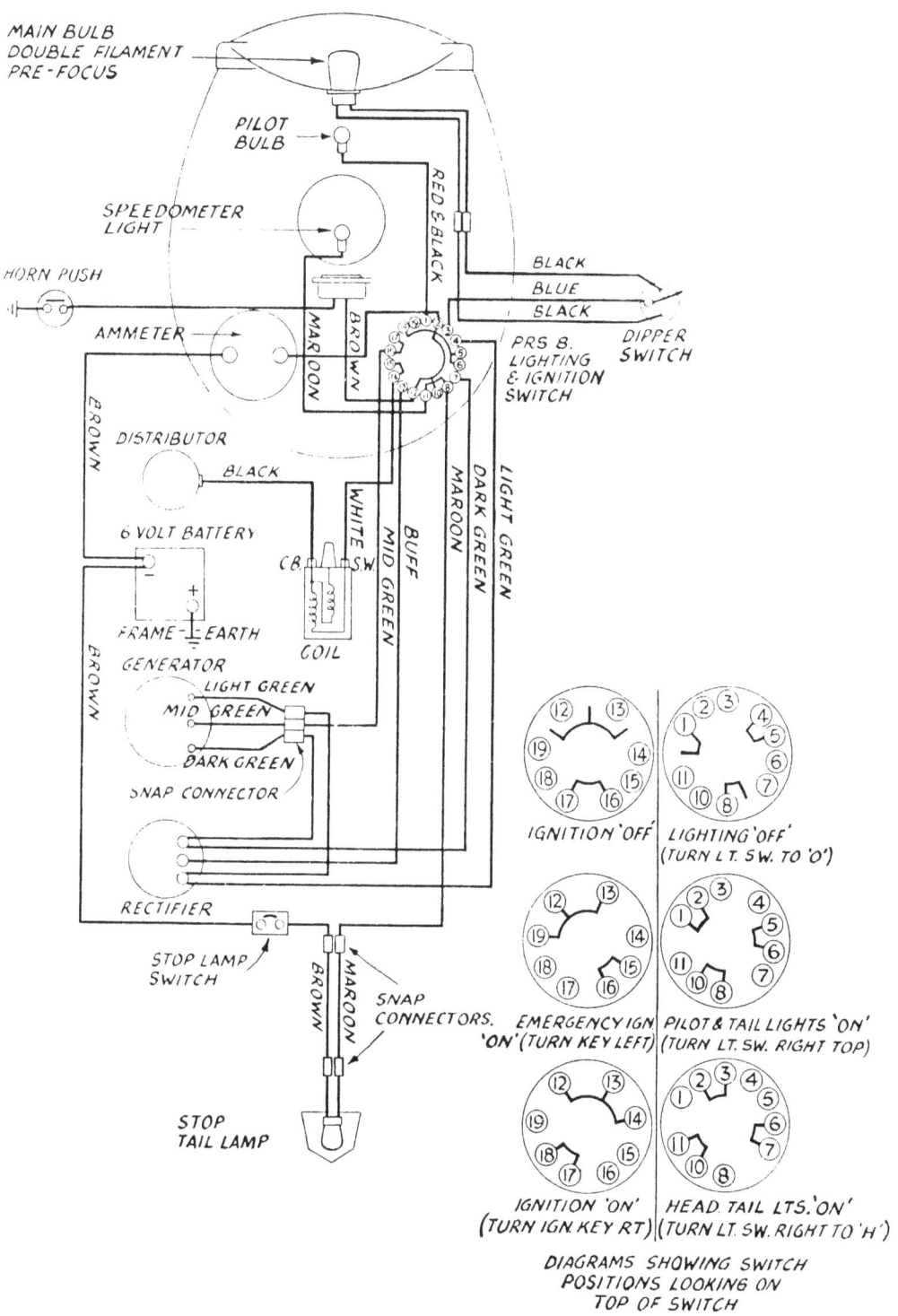

Fig. 68. WIRING DIAGRAM (5T & 6T)

A.C. Generator

Since, with the ignition switch at "EMG" and the engine running, the battery receives a charging current, the battery voltage soon begins to rise. The rising voltage opposes the alternator voltage, gradually effecting a reduction in the energy available for transfer to the coil. In the event of a rider omitting to return the ignition key from position "EMG" to position "IGN" this reduction in spark energy will cause misfiring to occur and will remind the rider to switch over to normal running.

As previously mentioned, continuous running without a battery is readily arranged by earthing the cable normally connected to the battery negative terminal.

CONSTRUCTION

The alternator consists essentially of a spigot-mounted and bolted 6-coil laminated stator with the centre-bored rotor carried on, and driven by, an extension to the crankshaft. The rotor has an hexagonal steel core, each face of which carries a high energy permanent magnet keyed to a laminated pole tip. The pole tips are riveted circumferentially to brass side plates, the assembly being cast in aluminium and machined to give a smooth external finish. The stator and rotor can be separated without any need to fit magnet keepers to the rotor poles.

RATING

The alternator is designed for use with headlamp bulbs not exceeding 30-watts rating (or equivalent Continental touring bulbs which, although of higher wattage rating, are yet suitable due to the generally higher average road speeds encountered abroad).

THE ALTERNATOR

Except for an occasional inspection of the snap-connectors in the three green output cables—these connectors must be clean and tight—the alternator requires no maintenance.

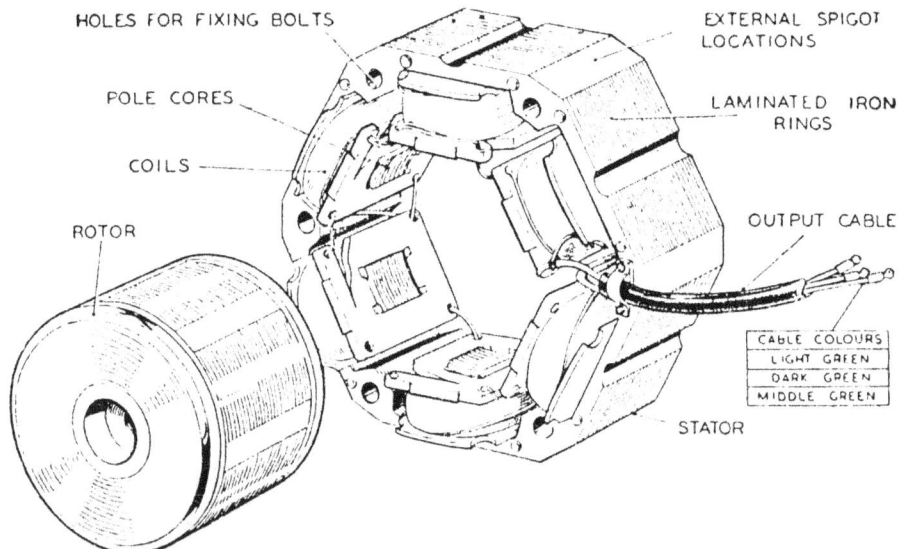

Fig. 69. ALTERNATOR (Model RM14).

Distributor

IGNITION COIL

The ignition coil should be kept clean, particularly between the terminals, and the terminal connections kept tight.

CONTACT BREAKER UNIT

Lubrication every 3,000 miles (5,000 kms.)

(i) Remove the metal cover and lightly smear the face of the cam with one of the greases recommended for the grease gun use in the "Recommended Lubricants" chart in the Instruction Book. If this is not available, clean engine oil may be used.

WARNING

When carrying out the above lubrication, no oil or grease must be allowed to get onto or near the contacts.

(ii) Lubricate the automatic timing control mechanism, using thin machine oil.

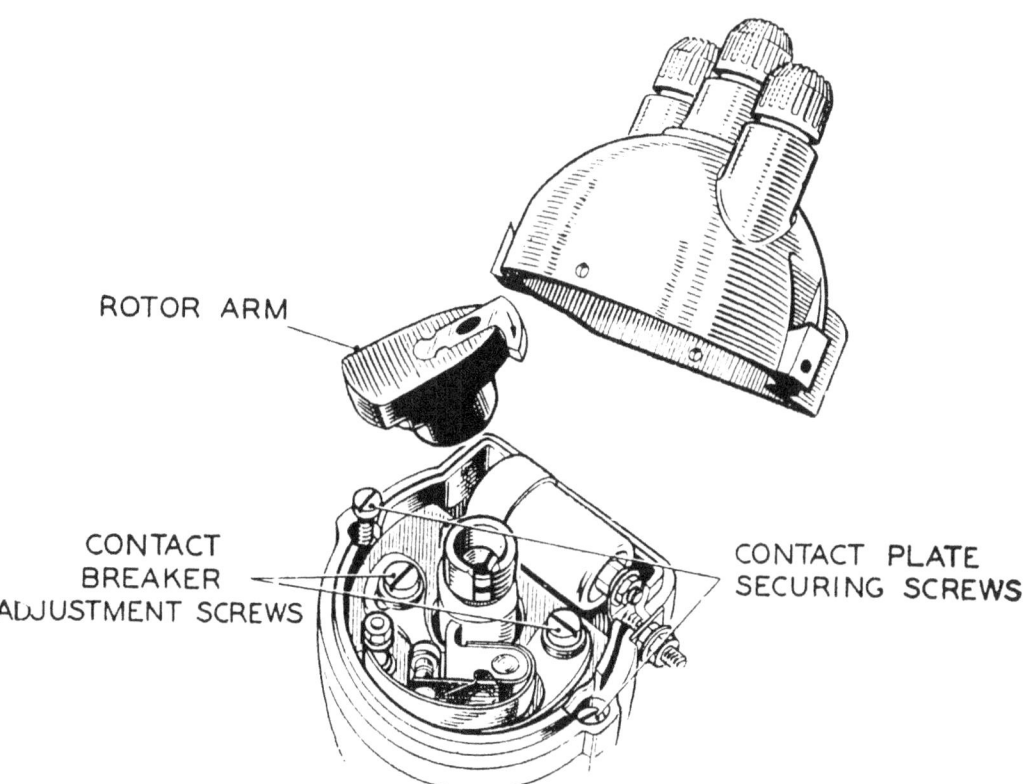

Fig. 70. DISTRIBUTOR MODEL DKX2A WITH COVER REMOVED

Distributor

Cleaning: Every 6,000 miles (10,000 kms.)

Remove the distributor cover and wipe it inside and outside with a clean dry fluffless cloth.

Examine the contact breaker. The contacts must be free from grease or oil. If they are burned or blackened, clean with fine carborundum stone or very fine emery cloth, afterwards wiping away any dirt or metal dust with a clean petrol moistened cloth.

CONTACT BREAKER SETTING

The contact breaker setting should be checked after the first 500 miles (800 kms.) running and subsequently every 6,000 miles (10,000 kms.). To check the gap, turn the engine over slowly until the contacts are seen to be fully open and insert a 0.014"-0.016" (0.36 to 0.4 mm.) feeler gauge between the contacts.

If the gap width is correct, the gauge will be a sliding fit. If the gap width varies appreciably from the gauge thickness, the setting must be adjusted. To do this, keep the engine in the position giving the maximum contact opening and slacken the screw at the side of the unit body. Slide the fixed contact carrier into its slotted hole until the correct gap is obtained. Re-tighten the screw.

HIGH TENSION

If the high tension cables show signs of perishing or cracking, they should be replaced using a 7 mm. rubber covered ignition cable. To do this, remove the metal washer and moulded nut from the defective cable. Thread the new cable through the moulded nut and bare the conductor for about a $\frac{1}{4}$ inch (6 mm.). Pass the exposed strands through the metal washer and bend back the strands radially. Re-fit the moulded nut into the H.T. terminal. On the models 5T & 6T the H.T. cable for the coil to distributor should also be treated in a similar manner.

A.C. Ignition Fault Finding

BEFORE SEARCHING FOR AN IGNITION FAULT, ALWAYS CHECK OVER ALL ELECTRICAL CONNECTIONS; CLEAN AND TIGHTEN IF NECESSARY.

ENGINE WILL NOT START.   NO SPARK AT PLUGS

Note. To check, remove the plugs and place them on the cylinder head after re-fitting the connector. Turn the ignition switch to "IGN" (clockwise) and kick over the engine. The plugs should fire with a blue spark. If there is no spark, turn switch to "EMG" (anti-clockwise) and test again.

Plug Oily, Fouled or Faulty. Clean thoroughly, preferably in a plug cleaning machine, re-set the points gap to 0.020" (0.50 mm.) and re-fit. Replace with correct grade plug if faulty.

Distributor, Coil or Condenser Faulty

Distributor. See that the cover is properly fitted and the clips secure. Check the gap of the contact breaker points and clean and adjust if necessary (see page 172).

Coil. First clean the coil, particularly between the cable connections. To check the low tension circuit, connect a volt meter between the coil terminal marked "SW" and earth. If there is no reading with the ignition switched on there is a fault in the switch or the lead to the coil. Next connect the volt meter between the coil terminal marked "C.B." and earth. No reading here with the ignition switched on indicates a fault in the coil primary winding. If these tests show that the low tension primary circuit is in order, remove the coil H.T. lead from the distributor cover. Remove the cover and rotate the engine until the contact points are closed. Switch on the ignition and hold the end of the coil H.T. lead about $\frac{1}{4}$" (6 mm.) from the cylinder block. Flick the contact points open with the finger and a spark should pass to the cylinder block. No spark indicates a fault in the coil H.T. winding. Any fault in a coil can only be corrected by fitting a new unit.

Condenser. To test the condenser, switch on the ignition and connect a volt meter across the open contacts. If there is no reading, remove the condenser and re-test. If a reading on the meter is then obtained, the condenser is faulty and should be changed.

ENGINE WILL NOT START WITH SWITCH ON "IGN" BUT STARTS ON "EMG".

Battery discharged due to short circuit, poor condition due to age or damage, prolonged use for parking or low rate of charge from alternator. Have battery charged from external source and equipment checked by an authorised Lucas Agent or Triumph Dealer as soon as possible.

Lamps

ENGINE RUNS WITH SWITCH ON "IGN" BUT NOT ON "EMG".

Examine leads and connections from ignition switch to coil, and from coil to distributor. Check distributor contacts and ignition timing (See pages 70 and 172). If the machine will not run in "EMG" switch position, have the equipment checked by an authorised Lucas Agent or Triumph Dealer.

ROUGH RUNNING AND MISFIRING WITH SWITCH AT "IGN".

Check earth connection for battery and rectifier and wiring of switch and rectifier.

LAMPS

HEADLAMPS FITTED TO MACHINES INTENDED FOR THE HOME MARKET AND FOR EXPORT, EXCLUDING EUROPE

These lamps have a double filament pre-focus 6 volt 30/24 watt Lucas No. 312 bulb.

HEADLAMPS FITTED TO MACHINES INTENDED FOR EXPORT TO EUROPE

These lamps have a double filament pre-focus 6 volt 35/35 watt Lucas No. 403 bulb.

HEADLAMPS FITTED TO MACHINES INTENDED FOR EXPORT TO FRANCE ONLY

These lamps have a double filament pre-focus 6 volt 36/36 watt bulb (yellow) with a three point connection to the lamp.

Basically the above lamps are identical, the difference occurring only with the method of attachment of the bulb in the French type headlamp and in the power of the bulbs.

HEADLAMPS FITTED TO THE TR5 MODELS

These lamps are fitted with a double filament 6 volt 30/30 watt Lucas bulb (Not Pre-focused) and a pilot bulb 6 volt 3 watt.

REPLACING THE HEADLAMP BULB

Nacelle Type. To gain access to the headlamp bulb, slacken the front rim retaining screw situated at the top of the lamp fixing ring. Disengage and withdraw the front rim and light unit assembly, removing the upper edge first. With the exception of the French headlamp, press the moulded adaptor inwards and turn it to the left. Lift off the adaptor and withdraw the defective bulb. When inserting a replacement bulb, locate the slot in the bulb flange with the projection in the bulb holder. Re-fit the adaptor, engaging its moulded recesses with corresponding projections on the bulb holder. Press inwards and secure by turning the adaptor to the right.

Lamps

On the French headlamp, release the two clips securing the adaptor and remove the adaptor. Take out the defective bulb by pressing it in and turning to the left. When replacing the bulb, engage the three points on the bulb in the slots of the adaptor, press in and turn to the right to secure. Replace the adaptor with the projection on the adaptor engaging in the slot on the headlamp and secure by re-fastening the clips. Re-fit the rim to the nacelle, locating the bottom of the rim first. Tighten the securing screw and check the beam setting.

TR5. To gain access to the bulbs, release the fastener catch at the base of the lamp when the rim and reflector assembly can be removed from the shell. The focusing of the main bulb is made by slackening the holder clip screw and moving the bulb holder in or out as desired. When replacing the reflector rim assembly, first fit the reflector to the shell and locate with the rubber head; assemble the rim and glass, engaging the tongue into the top of the shell and the fastener catch into the rim.

SETTING THE HEADLAMP BEAM

To check the headlamp beam setting, place the motorcycle in front of a light coloured wall at a distance of about 25 feet (8 metres). The machine should be carrying its normal load during this check, since the weight of the rider (and pillion passenger) may affect the setting. Switch on the main beam. This should be directed straight ahead and parallel with the ground. If it is not, loosen the two small screws on either side of the lamp fixing ring, and raise or lower the beam by pulling out or pressing in, the bottom of the ring. When the required adjustment has been obtained, re-tighten the two screws.

With the Lucas pre-focus type bulb fitted in these lamps, the filament is correctly positioned during manufacture in relation to the focal point of the reflector. No further focusing is necessary.

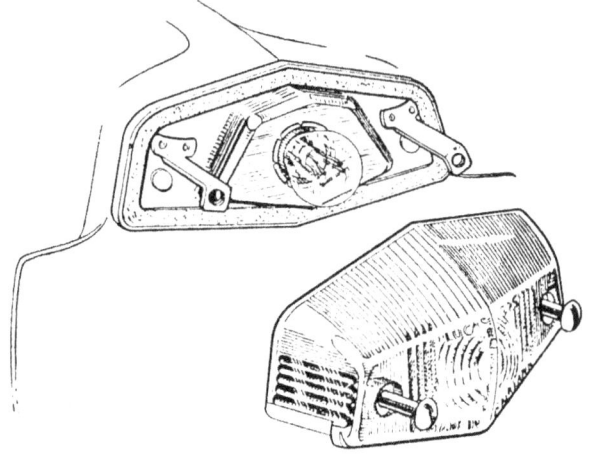

Fig. 71. MODEL 525 STOP-TAIL LAMP

PARKING LAMP

These lights are fitted with a 6 volt 3 watt Lucas No. 988 bulb, for all markets. To replace the bulb, unscrew the two screws on either side of the rim and remove the rim and glass. The bulb can then be detached by pressing it in and turning to the left. Replace the bulb and the rim and glass in the reverse order to the removal.

REAR LAMP

Access to rear light bulbs is gained by removing the two moulded cover retaining screws. The correct replacement for the stop tail lamp is Lucas No. 384 6 volt 6/18 watt bulb. This bulb has offset securing pins to prevent incorrect insertion into the bulb holder and to ensure that the higher wattage filament is illuminated when the brake pedal is depressed. In the event of failure of the 6 watt filament do not change the cables over to obtain rear lighting from the 18 watt filament as the heat generated will probably burn the plastic lens.

HEADLAMP AND TOP NACELLE UNIT

REMOVAL (Dynamo Equipped Models)

Battery. Disconnect the battery positive lead.

Steering Damper. Unscrew and remove.

Headlamp. Unscrew the retaining screw at the top of the headlamp retaining ring and ease the headlamp away from the ring, pulling from the top. Disconnect the earth wire (black) from the bulb holder frame, and the two headlight leads (black) at the snap connectors.

Retaining Ring. Remove by unscrewing the two small screws at the sides of the ring.

Motifs. Unscrew the four screws and two nuts securing the motifs and remove.

Rear Nacelle Retaining Screws. Remove the two small screws and nuts holding the rear of the top unit to the fork covers, being careful not to lose the nuts.

Five Point Connector. Disconnect all leads at the connector. If the top unit only is being removed, leave the connector in position on the stanchion. If however, it is intended to remove the fork assembly, remove the connector from the stanchion and disconnect the leads so that the connector remains with the top unit.

Speedometer. Unscrew the speedometer drive cable at the head.

Removing Headlamp and Nacelle

Horn. Disconnect both leads.

Dipswitch Lead to Light Switch. Disconnect at the light switch (No. 2 position).

Assembly. Re-assemble in the reverse manner.

REMOVAL (A.C. Equipped Models)

Dismantle as for T100 & T110 to "Rear Nacelle Retaining Screws" and proceed as follows:

Lighting and Ignition Switch. Unscrew the small grub screw at the side of the plastic switch lever and pull the lever away from the switch. Unscrew the brass nut around the switch body and remove the name disc. Unscrew the two switch to nacelle retaining screws and push the switch through into the nacelle.

Horn. Disconnect the black lead from the horn terminal.

Speedometer. Unscrew the speedometer drive cable at the head and detach the speedometer light.

Ammeter. Disconnect the brown leads at the ammeter; one from the L.H. terminal and two from the R.H. terminal.

NOTE

If it is intended to remove the top unit only, it is unnecessary to proceed any further. If the forks are to be removed however, it will be necessary to disconnect the blue lead from the dipper switch to switch position number 3 and also the red and black pilot light lead. Both these leads are fitted with snap connectors.

Assembly. Re-assemble in the reverse manner.

BATTERY

Topping Up

During charging, water is lost by gassing and evaporation and this must be replaced to maintain the battery in a healthy condition. Once a month or more often in warm climates, the level of the electrolyte in the cells of the battery must be examined; if necessary, distilled water must be added to bring the electrolyte just level with the top of the separators.

Never use a naked light when examining the condition of the cells, as there is a danger of igniting the gas coming from the active materials.

The correct acid level device consists of a central tube with a perforated flange which rests on a ledge in the filling orifice. When topping-up a battery fitted with these devices, pour distilled water around the flange (not down the tube) until no

Battery Maintenance

more drains through into the cells. This will happen when the electrolyte level reaches the bottom of the central tube and prevents further escape of air displaced by the topping up water. By lifting the tube slightly, the small amount of water in the flange will drain into the cell and the electrolyte level will then be correct.

Checking the Condition of the Battery

Occasionally check the condition of the battery by taking measurements of the specific gravity of the electrolyte in each of the cells. A small volume hydrometer is required for this purpose—this instrument resembles a syringe containing a graduated float which indicates the specific gravity of the acid in the cell from which the sample has been taken.

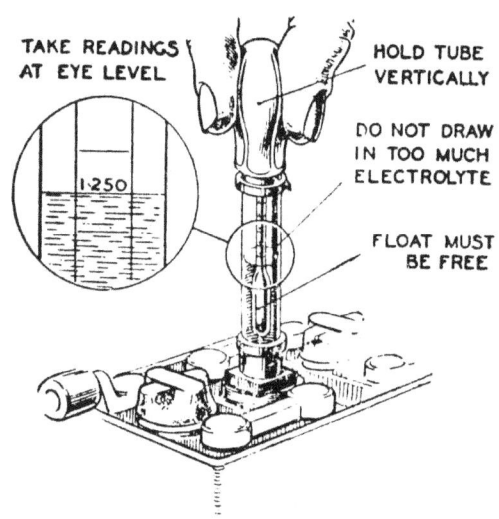

Fig. 72. **TAKING HYDROMETER READINGS**

Measurements should not be taken immediately after the cells have been "topped-up" as the electrolyte will not be thoroughly mixed.

The space between each separator is not wide enough to permit the nozzle of a hydrometer to be inserted. Before taking a sample, tilt the battery to bring sufficient electrolyte above the separators.

Specific gravity readings and their indications are as follows:—
    1.280-1.300   ...   .   Cell fully charged.
    About 1.210   ...   .   Cell about half discharged.
    Below 1.150   ...   .   Cell fully discharged.
The reading for each of the cells should be approximately the same.

If one cell gives a value very different from the rest, it may be that acid has spilled or has leaked from that particular cell, or there may be a short circuit between the plates. In this case the battery should be examined by a Lucas Service Depot or Agent.

Battery Maintenance

Never leave the battery in a discharged condition. If the motorcycle is to be out of use for any length of time have the battery fully charged and every fortnight, give it a short refreshing charge to prevent any tendency for the plates to become permanently sulphated.

Detachable Cable Connectors

When connecting the battery, unscrew the knurled nut and withdraw the collet or cone shaped insert, noting that it is not interchangeable with the collet in the other terminal. Bare the end of the cable for about one inch and thread one bared end through the knurled nut and collet. Bend back the cable strands over the narrow end of the collet and insert the collet and cable into the terminal block. Secure the connection by tightening the knurled nut.

Battery Earth

The A.C. Lighting-Ignition Unit and dynamo unit have been designed for positive (+ve) earth systems. If the battery connections are reversed the equipment will be damaged.

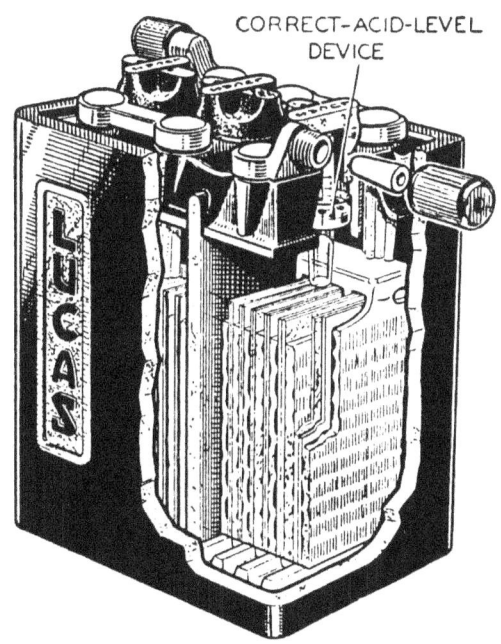

Fig. 73. **BATTERY MODEL PU7E/9**
Showing correct-acid-level device and detachable cable connectors.

ELECTRIC HORNS

These horns, before being passed out of the Works, are adjusted to give their best performance, and will give a long period of service without any attention.

Electric Horn

If the horn becomes uncertain in its action, giving only a choking sound, or does not vibrate, it does not follow that the horn has broken down. First ascertain that the trouble is not due to some outside source, e.g. a discharged battery, a loose connection, or short circuit in the wiring of the horn. In particular, ascertain that the horn push bracket is in good electrical contact with the handlebars.

It is also possible that the performance of a horn may be upset by its mounting becoming loose.

Adjustment

The following adjustment will not alter the tone of the horn. It will take up any wear of the moving parts which, if not corrected, may result in loss of power and roughness of note.

Accurate adjustment requires the use of a 0-10 amp. D.C. ammeter—the maximum permissible current consumption being 6 amperes at 6 volts—but the owner rider, who may not possess one of these instruments can carry out the following procedure if the horn note is considered to have deteriorated:—

Operate the horn push and turn the adjustment screw anti-clockwise until the horn just fails to sound. Release the horn push and turn the adjustment screw clockwise for six notches, i.e. a quarter of a turn, when the original performance should be restored. If further adjustment is necessary, turn the screw one notch at a time.

If the original performance cannot be restored by adjustment do not attempt to dismantle the horn, but return it to a Lucas Service Depot for examination.

SPARKING PLUGS

The sparking plug is of great importance in satisfactory engine performance and every care should be taken to fit the correct type when replacements are necessary.

There is little to be gained by experimenting with different types of plugs as the type fitted to standard equipment, are best suited to your particular engine. (See Technical Data for your Machine). Sparking plugs required for racing purposes are much "harder" and advice on such matters should be obtained from the manufacturers.

The correct gap setting of the sparking plug is .018" (0.45 mm.) (Magneto Ignition) and 0.020" (0.50 mm.) (Coil Ignition). Do not guess this distance but use a feeler gauge which can be supplied by the plug manufacturer at a very reasonable cost.

When re-setting, bend the side electrode only. Never bend the centre electrode as this may split the insulator tip.

The TR5 and T100 are fitted with long reach plugs which are screwed directly into the alloy cylinder head. If either plug indicates tightness when removing, pour a little penetrating oil around the base of the plug and allow it to seep around the threads. By doing this the plug will be more easily removed and the cylinder head plug threads will not be damaged. Smear the threads with graphite grease before replacing.

Sparking Plug

When the sparking plug is removed for examination, the insulator will show one of the following conditions:

ASH WHiTE. This is a sign that the plug is over-heating. Usual cause is the mixture strength too weak (a common cause being a faulty carburetter to cylinder head joint washer) or the ignition too far retarded.

DULL BLACK. This indicates that the plug is running too cold or, in other words the insulator is insufficiently hot to burn off the carbon. This is caused by too rich a mixture or the engine left running with a generous slow running setting (quality screw).

LIGHT BROWN. This shows that the mixture strength is correct and the engine is running at the right temperature.

Before re-fitting the plugs, make sure that the copper washers are not defective in any way. If they have become worn and flattened, fit new ones to ensure that a gastight joint is obtained.

When installing plugs, first screw the plugs down by hand as far as possible, then use spanner for tightening only. Always use a tubular box spanner to avoid possible fracture to the insulator, but do not under any circumstances use a movable wrench. Paint splashes, accumulation of grime and dust etc., on the top half of the insulator are often responsible for poor plug performance. Plugs should be wiped frequently with a clean rag.

To save petrol and prevent difficult starting, plugs should be cleaned and tested at regular intervals, and it is suggested that this service be performed at your garage on a special "Air Blast" service unit. Plugs which are allowed to remain oily and dirty with corroded electrodes will seriously impair the efficient running of the motor and waste precious petrol.

To obtain maximum efficiency from the engine and also to maintain good petrol consumption which the motorcycle has when new, plugs should be changed at regular intervals as old plugs are wasteful and cause poor and sluggish running. We recommend inspection, cleaning and testing every 3,000 miles (5,000 kms.), and it will be found economical to replace with new ones annually.

Toolkit

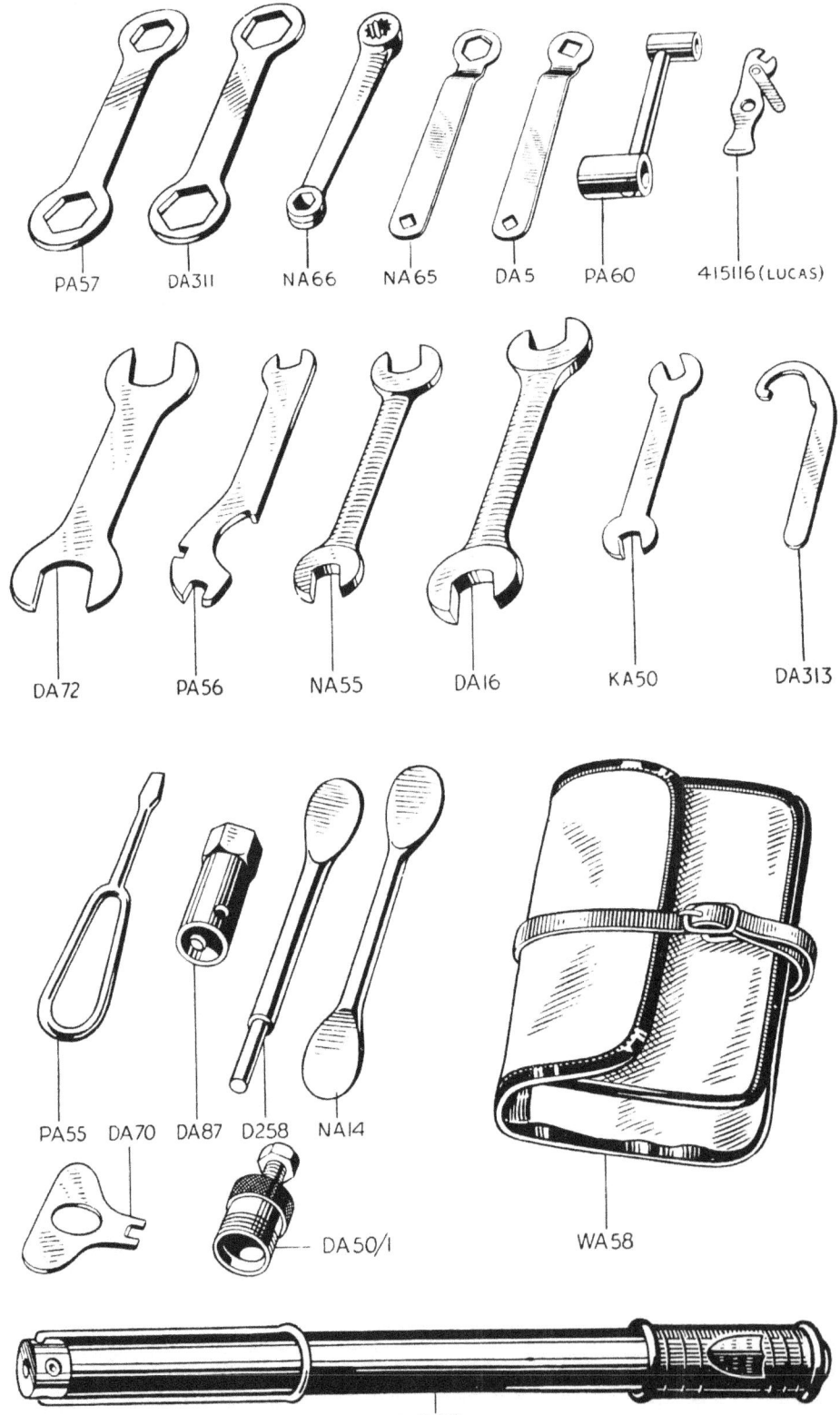

Fig. 74. TOOLKIT

TOOLKIT

Part No.	Description.	Purpose.
PA.57	Spanner closed $\frac{1}{2}'' \times \frac{9}{16}''$ Whit.	Wheel nuts
DA.311	Spanner closed $\frac{5}{8}'' \times \frac{11}{16}''$ Whit.	,, ,,
NA.66	Spanner closed $\frac{3}{16}'' \times \frac{5}{16}''$ Whit.	General
NA.65	Spanner closed $0.218'' \times \frac{3}{16}''$ Whit.	Adjusting tappets
DA.5	Spanner closed $0.218'' \times 0.338''$ sq.	,, ,,
PA.60	Spanner, box $\frac{1}{4}'' \times \frac{5}{32}''$ Whit.	Cyl. head bolts
415116	Spanner	Magneto points
DA.72	Spanner open $\frac{1}{2}'' \times \frac{9}{16}''$ Whit.	Wheel bearing nuts
PA.56	Spanner combination	General
NA.55	Spanner open $\frac{1}{4}'' \times \frac{5}{16}''$ Whit.	,,
DA.16	Spanner open $\frac{3}{8}'' \times \frac{7}{16}''$ Whit.	,,
KA.50	Spanner open $0.375'' \times \frac{1}{8}''$ Whit.	,,
DA.313	Spanner open "C"	Adjusting Girling units
PA.55	Screwdriver	General
DA.87	Spanner, box	Sparking plug
D.258	Tyre lever-cum-tommy bar	—
NA.14	Tyre lever—double ended	—
NA.12	Grease gun	—
WA.58	Tool bag	—
DA.70	Key	Clutch adjustment
DA.50/1	Extractor	Clutch centre
D.49	Tyre inflator	—

SUPPLEMENTARY INSTRUCTIONS

With the exception of the 3T engine, which will be referred to separately, the instructions in the main body of the instruction manual may be applied to all machines from 1945 to the present day. With the aid of this supplement and the accompanying data sheet, no difficulty will be found in selecting the instructions for any individual machine.

Some of the more important changes during this time are as follows: The Mk. 1 spring wheel was introduced in 1948 and together with the Mk. 2 wheel, which was introduced in 1951, may be fitted to any of the rigid frame machines. A modified gearbox was introduced in 1950, with the speedometer drive taken from the timing side end of the layshaft, and although similar in construction the parts of the gearbox are not interchangeable with the previous model. Where earlier models are fitted with a spring hub the speedometer drive is taken from a pinion behind the final drive sprocket.

Models previous to 1949 have the orthodox telescopic fork, for which the servicing instructions are the same as the Trophy fork in the accompanying instruction manual, but in 1949 the nacelle was introduced containing a 6" diameter headlamp. Also in 1949 the oil pressure gauge was dispensed with, as the instrument panel in the fuel tank was no longer fitted, and an oil pressure indicator button on the timing cover substituted. The return of the oil from the overhead rocker gear on the earlier models is by internal oil ways in the cylinder head and block, but in 1949 external oil drain pipes were fitted from the cylinder head to the push rod cover tubes.

An S.U. Carburetter was fitted to the Thunderbird for 1952, and this necessitated an eye in the saddle tube for the air filter connection, this frame being used on all models up to the introduction of the swinging arm frame. In 1952 the nacelle was changed to accommodate a 7" diameter headlamp, incorporating a prefocus light unit. At the same time (from engine number 19706 NA) the electrical system was changed to POSITIVE EARTH wiring.

Tappet Adjustment. All machines with cast iron cylinder heads and barrels previous to engine number 37560 should be used with a tappet clearance of .001" (see page 37, para. a.), and machines with alloy cylinder heads and barrels previous to engine number 37560 should be used with a tappet clearance of .002" inlet and .004" exhaust.

In 1953 quietening ramps were added to the camshafts, and all machines from engine number 37560 with an identification mark on the drive side crankcase next to the engine number, must be used with tappet clearance of .010". Use of a smaller tappet clearance with these particular camshafts will result in the valves being burnt out.

A major change took place in 1953 when the Speed Twin was fitted with the Lucas RM.12 AC/DC lighting equipment. Following the experience gained with this generator the improved RM.14 type was fitted to the Speed Twin and also the Thunderbird for the 1954 season.

A rubber buffer shock absorber is incorporated in the clutch hub from the engine number 32303. All models previous to this number have a spring loaded cam type shock absorber on the engine mainshaft. To remove the engine sprocket nut engage top gear and use a well fitting box spanner. The tommy-bar should be struck several sharp blows with a suitable hammer or mallet when it will be found to unscrew quite easily.

The order of assembly is as follows: Sleeve, engine sprocket, slider, spring, collar and nut. The nut should be screwed home with the box spanner in the same manner as when unscrewing, finishing with several sharp hammer blows to lock the nut up tight.

The frame with swinging arm suspension was first fitted to the Tiger models in 1954, and extended to the rest of the range in 1955. In addition to the other changes this frame also employs a different method of gearbox mounting, but the actual shafts and gears are identical. A stronger crankshaft and larger timing side main bearing were fitted to all models except the Speed Twin for 1954 and extended to the Speed Twin for 1955. The Amal Monobloc carburetter was introduced during the 1955 season and is now fitted to all models except the Thunderbird.

The 1955 5T and 6T swinging arm models differ from the earlier A.C. equipped models, in that the alternator stator is mounted on the inner half of the chaincase. Therefore it is unnecessary to disconnect the alternator lead when removing the outer half of the primary chaincase. The 6T is also fitted with a different distributor giving a smaller range of movement, and note of this should be taken when timing the ignition.

Cylinder Head Bolts. The cylinder head torque stay bolts are fitted in the front position on all rigid frame machines and in the rear position on all swinging arm frame machines.

FITTING A SIDECAR
SWINGING ARM FRAME MODELS

The machine should be prepared in the usual manner by fitting stronger fork springs, a smaller engine sprocket and stronger springs and bump stops to the Girling rear suspension units.

It is somewhat difficult to compress the stronger suspension unit springs, and it is suggested that if there is a local Girling agent, he should be entrusted with the job.

For the guidance of those who do not live within easy reach of a Girling agent, the procedure is as follows: Depress the top dust cover and remove the spring retainers. The top dust cover, main spring and bottom dust cover may now be lifted off. Slide the rubber bump stop down the damper piston rod and fit the halves of the bump stop with the point of the cone facing upwards, taking care to tighten the four Allen screws evenly. Smear the new spring with high melting point grease, fit to the unit and replace the split spring retainer.

The Amal Monobloc Carburetter

There are available three fixing points on the frame of the swinging arm machine; one at the bottom of the seat tube, one at the top of the seat tube and a lug, which is fixed to the front engine plates to provide the third point.

The fourth point connection is supplied by the sidecar manufacturers and should be fitted to the front down tube. Care should be taken to ensure that the front mudguard and stand remain clear of the fitting when the front fork is fully compressed.

For best results the sidecar wheel spindle should be 6" ahead of the rear wheel spindle, and the wheel should toe in $\frac{3}{8}$" (see page 148). The machine should be set so that it leans in slightly when the outfit is unladen, i.e. it should be approximately vertical when the rider is on the machine.

THE AMAL MONOBLOC CARBURETTER

HOW IT OPERATES

When the engine is idling, mixture is supplied from the pilot jet system, then as the throttle slide is raised, via the pilot by-pass. The mixture is then controlled by the tapered needle working in the needle jet and finally by the size of the main jet. The pilot system is supplied by a pilot jet, which is detachable, for cleaning purposes and which when assembled into the carburetter body is sealed by a cover. The main jet does not spray directly into the mixing chamber, but discharges through the needle jet into the primary air chamber, and the fuel goes from there as a rich petrol-air mixture through the primary air choke into the main air choke.

This primary air choke has a compensating action in conjunction with bleed holes in the needle jet, which serve the double purpose of air-compensating the mixture from the needle jet and allowing the fuel to provide a well, outside and around the needle jet, which is available for snap acceleration.

The carburetter is provided with an air control lever for use when starting from cold or experimenting. At all other times the control should be kept fully opened.

ADJUSTMENT

The carburetter should be adjusted when the engine is thoroughly warm but a long period of stationary running should be avoided as this will over-heat the engine and false settings may be obtained.

The throttle stop screw should be adjusted to give the slowest possible tick-over and the pilot air adjusting screw then screwed in or out to make the engine run regularly and faster. The throttle stop screw should be lowered to the new slowest tick-over position and the process repeated. When no further improvement can be made the response to the throttle should be checked; if there is any spitting as the throttle moves away from the stop try enriching the pilot mixture by screwing the pilot air screw in one half turn. Finally adjust the throttle cable so that there is no unnecessary backlash in the cable and then lock the adjuster.

FAULT FINDING AND MAINTENANCE

Occasionally remove and clean the petrol filter gauze from inside the banjo connection. If flooding occurs check this gauze to see that it is in good condition and then remove the float chamber cover, float and float needle. Examine for dirt or damage on the needle and the needle seating. When replacing the float see that the narrow hinge leg is uppermost, as this operates the needle, and do not forget to replace the float spindle bush. Make sure that the cover plate and washer are clean and in good condition before re-assembling.

Erratic slow running may be caused by air leaks at the flange and the flange should be checked with a straight edge, and if necessary very carefully trued up with a fine file or emery cloth used on a flat surface such as plate glass. When refitting the carburetter always use a new paper joint washer and then tighten the fixing nuts evenly.

For more detailed instructions on tuning see the Amal leaflet number 502.

SPECIAL INSTRUCTIONS

T.110 MODEL

When using the T.110 model at speeds below 40 m.p.h. the ignition should be partly retarded by moving the ignition control lever, on the left handlebar, approximately 1/5 of its travel away from the stop. ("Fully Advanced" position).

Whilst it is advisable to use premium grade fuel in all Triumph motorcycles, its use is essential in the T.110. Premium grade fuel may be unobtainable in certain territories overseas and in such cases lower compression ratio pistons should be fitted.

If the machine is used exclusively for long, fast runs, it is advisable to fit Champion L.A.11 sparking plugs.

350 c.c. TWIN-MODEL 3T DE LUXE

ENGINE

Dry sump lubrication is used on the 3T model. The oil from the tank is fed through a pipe to the pressure side of the oil pump. From there the oil, under pressure, is fed to the timing side plain bearing, where it is picked up by the crankshaft annular groove and forced through drilled oilways to the big end assemblies. It then issues from the big ends in the form of an oil fog, which lubricates the internal parts of the engine. The pressure is regulated by means of a release valve situated in the front offside crankcase. The valve consists of a piston and spring and, should the oil pressure become excessive, the piston is forced back on its spring, allowing surplus oil to pass through the uncovered hole in the release valve body to the crankcase. It will be seen that the strength of the oil pressure release valve spring regulates the poundage of the oil pressure.

The rocker gear, push rods and tappets, are lubricated by scavenge oil which, after being used, returns to the crankcase by way of the push rod tubes.

TAPPET ADJUSTMENT (3T)

Tappet adjustment is made on the rocker arms after removing the two tappet inspection covers on the rocker boxes. Method of adjustment is described in the Workshop Manual.

CLUTCH

The clutch on the 3T model has three corked and four steel plates. All other details as Workshop Manual.

TYRES

Dunlop recommended tyre pressure for the 3T model:
                Front 16 lbs.   Rear 18 lbs.

3T DE LUXE CRANKCASE ASSEMBLY

The lower half of the 3T de Luxe engine is fundamentally similar to the larger engine but differs in the construction of the crankshaft assembly and has a white metal timing side main bearing.

When dismantling the 3T crankcase assembly the same procedure should be followed as for the larger machines. The only difference being that the crankshaft timing pinion has a thread on its end portion and may be removed by the use of the ordinary cam wheel removal tool part number Z.89. Replacing the timing side main bearing is a skilled task, and the bearing should preferably be line reamed or broached after fitting in the crankcase. It should be noted that the fit of this bearing controls the oil pressure at the big ends, and if this bearing is slack the oil pressure will be low.

Crankcase Assembly (3T De Luxe)

Unlike the larger models the big ends on the 3T are not split and it is necessary to dismantle the flywheel assembly to remove the connecting rods. The lower part of the flywheel should be held in a vice and the pinch bolts and nuts removed. Place a soft metal drift through the flywheel against the opposite crank and carefully drive out the crank by using a hammer on the drift. Drive out the other crank in the same manner. Do not lose or damage the small tube connecting the two cranks, as this maintains the oil seal at this point.

If the big ends are worn it will be found necessary to fit reconditioned connecting rods and have the crank journals reground. If the crank journals have to be reground it is necessary to regrind the parts of the crank journal which mate with the flywheel and fit a new flywheel with a smaller hole. Three undersizes of rods are supplied, minus .010", minus .020" and minus .030". All cranks which are returned to the works for re-grinding of the journals have the timing side main bearing journal reground at the same time, this bearing also being available in the same three undersizes.

To Assemble the 3T Crankshaft

Thoroughly wash all parts in petrol or paraffin before commencing to assemble. Fit the oil seal tube to the drive side crank and lightly oil the bearing portion of the crank journal. Care should be taken to allow no oil to reach the portion which mates with the flywheel hole. Fit the connecting rod to the drive side crank with the marking "Flywheel Side" in its correct position. To align the assembly during the fitting of the crank a round bar ($\frac{1}{2}$"-.003" + .000") should be passed through the datum hole drilled in the lower part of the flywheel and the crank threaded over this same bar by means of its own datum hole. Press the drive side crank into the flywheel until the connecting rod is just free to move, then repeat the sequence for the timing side crank. The correct side play for the rods is .015" to .020", and if the clearance at one side is greater than this the offending crank should be pressed in until the play is equalised. Now insert and lightly tighten the pinch bolts. The final alignment of the assembly should be carried out by placing a ball race over each main bearing journal and spinning the assembly in a jig. The assembly should be checked for truth at 3 points, the drive side mainshaft, the timing side mainshaft and the flywheel rim; if the assembly does not run true it should be taken out of the jig and the offending crank web tapped with a lead or hide hammer and then re-checked. The maximum permissible out of truth is .0005" on the end of the drive side mainshaft. Finally tighten the pinch bolt and re-check.

New crank journal diameter = 1.3730"-1.3735"
New T.S. bearing journal ,, = 1.2485"-1.2490"
New T.S. bearing I.D. = 1.2495"-1.2500"

Crankcase Assembly (3T De Luxe)

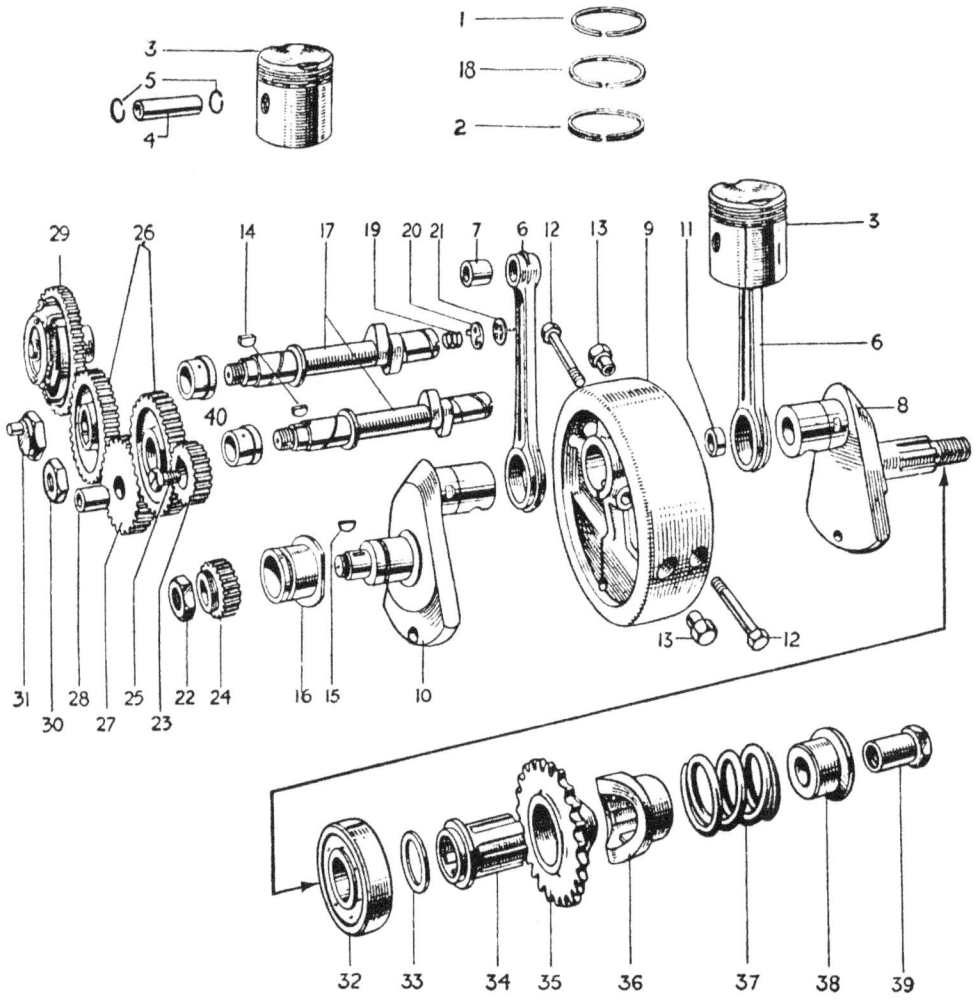

ENGINE 3T—CRANKSHAFT, CONNECTING RODS, PISTONS, TIMING GEARS, ETC.

1. Top piston ring.
2. Scraper ring.
3. Piston.
4. Gudgeon pin.
5. Circlip.
6. Connecting rod.
7. Little end bush.
8. D. S. crank.
9. Flywheel.
10. T. S. crank.
11. Oil seal tube.
12. Pinch bolt.
13. Nut, pinch bolt.
14. Key, camshaft.
15. Key timing pinion.
16. T. S. main bearing.
17. Camshaft.
18. Taper piston ring.
19. Spring, breather valve.
20. Valve, crankcase breather.
21. Disc, breather valve.
22. Nut, timing pinion.
23. Dynamo pinion.
24. Timing pinion.
25. Screw, dynamo pinion.
26. Camshaft pinion.
27. Intermediate pinion.
28. Bush, intermediate pinion.
29. Automatic timing device.
30. Nut, exhaust camshaft.
31. Nut, inlet camshaft.
32. D.S. main bearing.
33. Distance washer.
34. Sleeve, shock absorber.
35. Engine sprocket.
36. Slider, shock absorber.
37. Spring, shock absorber.
38. Collar, shock absorber.
39. Nut, sleeve.

DECARBONISING

The early 3T models have long studs fitted to the crankcase, the cylinder block and head being held down by eight bolts screwing into these studs.

DISMANTLING THE 3T ENGINE

(1) Disconnect exhaust pipes, carburetter, engine steady bracket, H.T. cables, and remove plugs.

(2) Take off the rocker gear feed pipe by removing the two banjo unions at the rocker spindles.

(3) To remove the cylinder head, unscrew the eight holding down bolts. Lift the cylinder head vertically and detach the push rods and cover tubes, when the head can be lifted clear of the cylinder block.

(4) To remove the valves from the cylinder head, a valve spring compressor tool is required. When the valve springs are in a compressed state the valve spring cotters can easily be detached with the use of a screwdriver. Carefully mark the valve to aid replacement.

(5) If the rocker arms are quite free on their spindles, it is undesirable to strip the rocker gear. Should it be necessary, the spindles can be tapped out from the threaded end, using a soft tool, and the rocker arms extracted from the rocker box.

(6) To remove the cylinder block on early models, it is only necessary to raise it clear of the crankcase studs. On later models, first remove the holding down nuts. Before lifting the cylinder block, care should be taken to prevent the tappets falling into the crankcase. This can be overcome by placing a short $\frac{1}{4}''$ bolt between the tappet grooves.

(7) Pistons can be taken off by removing two circlips and tapping out gudgeon pins clear of the connecting rod with a soft drift. Care must be taken to support the opposite side of the piston adequately whilst carrying out this operation. Suitably mark the pistons so that correct re-assembly may be assured.

ASSEMBLING THE 3T ENGINE

(1) Replace pistons—ensure correct positioning of circlips and the gaps in the piston rings are not in line.

(2) Prepare cylinder block—grease base washer and fit to block. Fit the four tappets and secure them against falling into the crankcase. The block must be installed with the "DS" mark, which will be found on the base flange, to the drive side of the engine.

Decarbonising

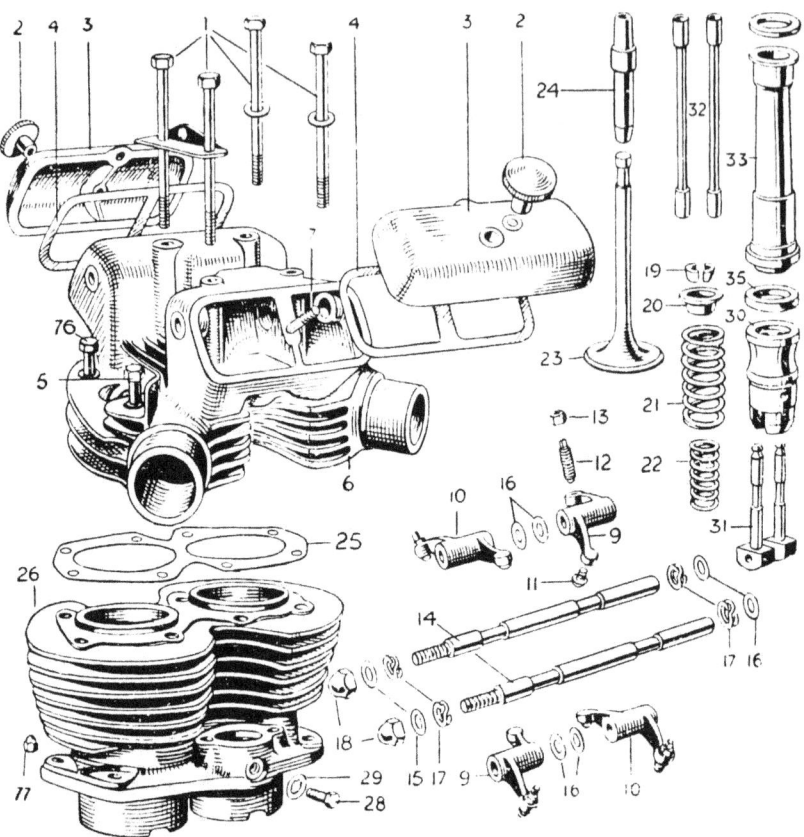

3T ENGINE

Exploded view of top portion

1. Bolt, cylinder head.
2. Knurled nut.
3. Cover, inspection.
4. Washer, inspection cover.
5. Bolt, cylinder head.
6. Head, cylinder.
7. Stud, inspection cover.
8. Washer, fibre.
9. Rocker, R.H.
10. Rocker, L.H.
11. Pin, ball.
12. Pin, adjusting.
13. Nut, lock.
14. Spindle, rocker.
15. Washer.
16. Washer, plain.
17. Washer, spring.
18. Nut, spindle.
19. Collar, split.
20. Collar, spring.
21. Spring, outer.
22. Spring, inner.
23. Valve.
24. Guide, valve.
25. Gasket, cylinder head.
26. Block, cylinder.
28. Screw, tappet block.
29. Washer, shakeproof.
30. Block, tappet.
31. Tappet.
32. Rod, push.
33. Cover, push rod.
34. Washer, fibre.
35. Washer, oil seal.
76. Bolt, cylinder head.
77. Nut, cylinder to crankcase.

(3) Fit rubber seal washers to push rod tubes. Grease upper push rod tube washers, cylinder head gasket and fit to the cylinder head.

(4) Assemble inlet push rods and tubes to cylinder head. To aid assembly the lower push rod cover tube cups are marked with a vertical line. This must be centralised and placed facing the magneto and dynamo respectively. Fit the four centre holding down bolts and torque bracket to cylinder head and place in position on the cylinder block.

(5) To fit the exhaust push rods, the cylinder head should be raised about 1". This can be done by placing a piece of wood either side between the cylinder head fin and the block fin. Position both inlet and exhaust push rods on the tappets, remove the wood pieces and gently lower cylinder head to block. Inspect the rocker balls for correct assembly to push rod cups. Now lightly tighten the four centre bolts down.

(6) Fit the four remaining bolts and evenly tighten the cylinder head down.

(7) Adjust tappets and replace covers.

(8) Refit torque brackets to frame clip, carburetter, sparking plugs, H.T. cable, rocker oil feed pipe and exhaust pipes.

(9) Run engine and carry out stationary tests. After stopping re-tighten all nuts and bolts.

SPRING WHEEL Mk. I

The following instructions are given for the benefit of dealers or owners wishing to maintain the early type of Spring Wheel. However, should there be a large number of parts in need of replacement, we would strongly recommend that the wheel is modified to Mk. II specification. For further details, please contact the Service Department, Triumph Engineering Co. Ltd., or the local Triumph Dealer.

DISMANTLING

(1) Remove spindle to frame locator. To remove the dust excluder, withdraw the distance collars, then centre sleeve, spring and dust plate. To extract the dust cover from the hub, gently prise it away. On early models a rubber gaiter is fitted; this can be removed in exactly the same manner.

(2) Place the wheel spindle in the vice, having the back plate uppermost and remove the 10 nuts. The back plate can now be removed and the shims carefully eased off the studs.

(3) Turn the wheel over and unscrew the brake anchor plate in an anti-clockwise direction. When unscrewing, either remove the brake lever spring or hold the lever in such a position as to prevent the brake shoes binding on the brake drum.

Spring Wheel Mk. I

(4) Remove the spring box assembly from the hub.

(5) To remove the outer race from the drive side, a suitable piece of hardwood should be employed. The race is removed by driving from the outside of the hub.

(6) The offside outer race which is situated in the back plate should be removed by a special tool, or the plate heated sufficiently to allow the race to drop out. Great care must be taken if the latter operation is carried out, as excessive heat will destroy hardening of the race.

LUBRICATION OF PARTS
Liberally smear all working parts with graphite grease before assembly.

ASSEMBLY

(1) Replace the drive side outer race to the hub and ensure that it is fully home.

(2) Fit the inner race to the spring box and grease before assembly. Note that the ball cage assembly should be fitted with the cage towards the wheel centre.

(3) Insert the spring box into the hub.

(4) Assemble the race to the off-side with the balls facing towards the back plate.

(5) Fit the shims to the hub and assemble the back plate. Screw up the nuts securing the back plate and test the rotation of the spring box for freedom during the tightening. Failure to do this after new parts have been fitted may result in indentation of the outer ball race or fracture of the hub parts. Any tightness can be obviated by fitting extra shims, allowing the spring box to rotate and at the same time allowing no lateral movement.

(6) Place the wheel in the vice or a suitable jig with the drive side uppermost and screw on the brake anchor plate. Turn back the anchor plate after fully tightening until the wheel turns freely. The brake cam lever bush should then be lined up with the wheel spindle for assembly purposes.

(7) Fit the dust cover and then locate the dust plate, ensuring that the spigot is positioned. Place the spring over the spindle and assemble centre sleeve. Fit spindle to frame locator on the near side and bevel washer to the off side, bevel facing inwards. Where the rubber gaiter is fitted it is advisable to centralise the spindle, here a rig will have to be made to overcome the spring tension.

Spring Wheel Mk. I

View of Spring Wheel Mk. I showing hub mechanism.

MODEL	3T 1946-51		6T 1950-51	6T 1952-53	6T 1954	6T 1955	TR5 1949-54	TR5 1955	T.110 1954	T.110 1955
ENGINE. Br. & Stk. mm	55 × 73.4		71 × 82	71 × 82	71 × 82	71 × 82	63 × 80	63 × 80	71 × 82	71 × 82
Capacity—c.c.	349		649	649	649	649	498	498	649	649
Compression—Ratio	6.3 : 1	7 : 1	7 : 1	7 : 1	7 : 1	7 : 1	6 : 1	8 : 1	8.5 : 1	8.5 : 1
Power Output r.p.m.	17 at 6,000	19 at 6,500	34 at 6,300	34 at 6,300	34 at 6,300	34 at 6,300	25 at 6,000	33 at 6,500	42 at 6,500	42 at 6,500
Tappet Clearance ins.	.001		*.001	.010	.010	.010	.002 in .004 ex	.002 in .004 ex	.002 in .004 ex	.002 in .004 ex
Valve Timing in Degrees	22 66 63 25		26½ 69½ 61½ 35½	26½ 69½ 61½ 35½	26½ 69½ 61½ 35½	26½ 69½ 61½ 35½	26½ 69½ 61½ 35½	51½ 72½ 72½ 51½	51½ 72½ 72½ 51½	51½ 72½ 72½ 51½
IGNITION. Type	Magneto		Magneto	Magneto	Coil	Coil	Magneto	Magneto	Magneto	Magneto
Contact Gap—ins.	.012		.012	.012	.014-.016	.014-.016	.012	.012	.012	.012
Timing (fully adv'd.)	$\frac{11}{32}''$		$\frac{3}{8}''$ or 37°	$\frac{3}{8}''$ or 37°	Re. at T.D.C.	Re. $\frac{1}{32}''$ or 6°	$\frac{3}{8}''$ or 37°	$\frac{15}{32}''$ or 41°	$\frac{23}{64}''$ or 35°	$\frac{23}{64}''$ or 35°
Sparking Plug (equiv.)	L.10.S		L.10.S	L.10.S	L.10.S	L.10.S	NA.10	NA.10	L.11.S	L.11.S
Plug Gap—ins.	.015-.018		.015-.018	.015-.018	.018-.022	.018-.022	.015-.018	.015-.018	.015-.018	.015-.018
CARBURETTER, Type	275		276	S.U.-M.C.2	S.U.-M.C.2	S.U.-M.C.2	376	376	289	376
Main Jet	120		⊙ 140	—	—	—	150	220	200	250
Needle Jet	107		107	—	—	—	107	.1065	107	.1065
Needle Type	5		6	M.9	M.9	M.9	6	C	29	C
Needle Position	2		2	—	—	—	3	3	3	3
Throttle Valve	5/4		6/3½	—	—	—	6/3½	376/3½	29/4	376/3½
Pilot Jet	—		—	—	—	—	—	25	—	25

GEAR RATIOS	Pre 1950							Pre 1950			
Top	5.8	5.8	4.57	4.57	4.57	4.57	5.24	5.24	5.24	4.57	4.57
3rd	6.95	6.90	5.45	5.45	5.45	5.45	7.46	7.60	6.24	5.45	5.45
2nd	10.00	9.80	7.75	7.75	7.75	7.75	11.58	12.02	8.85	7.75	7.75
Bottom	14.70	14.13	11.20	11.20	11.20	11.20	15.25	16.08	12.8	11.20	11.20
ENG. SPROCKET Solo	19		24	24	24	24	21	21	21	24	24
Sidecar	—		21	21	21	21	—	—	—	21	21
CHAIN LENGTH Primary ½" × .305"	74		80	80	80	70	76	76	70	70	70
Rear ⅝" × ⅜"	90		93	93	93	101	90	90	100	101	101
CAPACITY, Petrol, gls.	3		4	4	4	4	2½	2½	3	4	4
Oil, pints	6		6	6	6	6	6	6	6	6	6
Gearbox, pints	1		1	1	1	1	1	1	1	1	1
Prim. Chaincase, pts.	1/3		1/3	1/3	1/3	1/3	1/3	1/3	1/3	1/3	1/3
TYRE SIZE. Front	3.25/19		3.25/19	3.25/19	3.25/19	3.25/19	3.00/20	3.00/20	3.00/20	3.25/19	3.25/19
Rear	3.25/19		3.50/19	3.50/19	3.50/19	3.50/19	4.00/19	4.00/19	4.00/18	3.50/19	3.50/19
BRAKE SIZE. Front ins.	7		7	7	7	7	7	7	7	8	8
Rear, ins.	†7		†7	7†	7†	7	7†	7†	7	7	7
REAR SUSPS'N. Type	R. or S.W.		R. or S.W.	R. or S.W.	R. or S.W.	Sw. Arm	R. or S.W.	R. or S.W.	Sw. Arm	Sw. Arm	Sw. Arm

R. Arm = Rigid
S.W. = Spring Wheel
Sw. Arm = Swinging Arm
† = 8 with Spring Wheel
⊙ = 170 for 1950 machines
* = Up to Engine No. 37560

MODEL	**5T** 1946-52	**5T** 1953-54	**5T** 1955	**T.100** 1946-50	**T.100** 1951-53	**T.100** 1954	**T.100** 1955	**T.100C** 1953
ENGINE. Bore & Stroke mm	63 × 80	63 × 80	63 × 80	63 × 80	63 × 80	63 × 80	63 × 80	63 × 80
Capacity c.c.	498	498	498	498	498	498	498	498
Compression Ratio	7 : 1	7 : 1	7 : 1	7.6 : 1	7.6 : 1	7.6 : 1	8 : 1	8 : 1
Power Output at r.p.m.	27 at 6,300	27 at 6,300	27 at 6,300	30 at 6,500	32 at 6,500	32 at 6,500	32 at 6,500	42 at 7,000
Tappet Clearance—ins.	* .001	.010	.010	.001	*.002 in. .004 ex.	.010	.010	.002 in. .004 ex.
Valve Timing in Deg.	$26\frac{1}{2}$ $69\frac{1}{2}$ $61\frac{1}{2}$ $35\frac{1}{2}$	$26\frac{1}{2}$ $69\frac{1}{2}$ $61\frac{1}{2}$ $35\frac{1}{2}$	$26\frac{1}{2}$ $69\frac{1}{2}$ $61\frac{1}{2}$ $35\frac{1}{2}$	$26\frac{1}{2}$ $69\frac{1}{2}$ $61\frac{1}{2}$ $35\frac{1}{2}$	$26\frac{1}{2}$ $69\frac{1}{2}$ $61\frac{1}{2}$ $35\frac{1}{2}$	$26\frac{1}{2}$ $69\frac{1}{2}$ $61\frac{1}{2}$ $35\frac{1}{2}$	$26\frac{1}{2}$ $69\frac{1}{2}$ $61\frac{1}{2}$ $35\frac{1}{2}$	$51\frac{1}{2}$ $72\frac{1}{2}$ $72\frac{1}{2}$ $51\frac{1}{2}$
IGNITION. Type	Magneto	Coil	Coil	Magneto	Magneto	Magneto	Magneto	Magneto
Contact Gap—ins.	.012	.014-.016	.014-.016	.012	.012	.012	.012	.012
Timing (fully advanced)	$\frac{3}{8}$" or 37°	Ret'd $\frac{1}{32}$" or 7°	Ret'd $\frac{1}{32}$" or 7°	$\frac{3}{8}$" or 37°	$\frac{3}{8}$" or 37°	$\frac{3}{8}$" or 37°	$\frac{3}{8}$" or 37°	$\frac{15}{32}$" or 42°
Sparking Plug (or equiv.)	L.10.S	L.10.S	L.10.S	L.10.S	NA.10	NA.10	NA.10	NA.12
Plug Gap—ins.	.015-.018	.018-.022	.018-.022	.015-.018	.015-.018	.015-.018	.015-.018	.015-.018
CARBURETTER. Type	276	276	376	276	276	276	376	276 (2)
Main Jet	140	140	200	160	150	150	220	150
Needle Jet	107	107	.1065	107	107	107	.1065	107
Needle—Type	6	6	C	6	6	6	C	6
Needle Position	2	2	3	3	3	3	3	2
Throttle Valve	$6/3\frac{1}{2}$	$6/3\frac{1}{2}$	$376/3\frac{1}{2}$	$6/3\frac{1}{2}$	$6/3\frac{1}{2}$	$6/3\frac{1}{2}$	$376/3\frac{1}{2}$	6/4
Pilot Jet	—	—	30	—	—	—	25	—

		Pre 1950			Pre 1950				
GEAR RATIOS	Top	5.0	5.0	5.0	5.0	5.0	5.0	5.0	5.0
	3rd	6.0	5.95	5.95	6.0	5.95	5.95	5.95	5.95
	2nd	8.65	8.45	8.45	8.65	8.45	8.45	8.45	8.45
	Bottom	12.70	12.20	12.20	12.70	12.20	12.20	12.20	12.20
ENG. SPROCKET.	Solo	22	22	22	22	22	22	22	22
	Sidecar	19	19	19	19	19	19	19	—
CHAIN LENGTH	Primary ½" × .305"	78	78	70	78	78	70	70	78
	Rear ⅝" × ⅜"	93	93	100	93	93	100	100	93
CAPACITY.	Petrol, galls.	4	4	4	4	4	4	4	4
	Oil—pints	6	6	6	6	6	6	6	8
	Gearbox—pints	1	1	1	1	1	1	1	1
	Prim. Chaincase—pints	1/3	1/3	1/3	1/3	1/3	1/3	1/3	1/3
TYRE SIZE.	Front	3.25/19	3.25/19	3.25/19	3.25/19	3.25/19	3.25/19	3.25/19	3.25/19
	Rear	3.50/19	3.50/19	3.50/19	3.50/19	3.50/19	3.50/19	3.50/19	3.50/19
BRAKE SIZE.	Front—ins.	7	7	7	7	7	8	8	7
	Rear—ins.	7†	7†	7	7†	7†	7	7	8
REAR SUSPS'N.	Type	R. or S.W.	R. or S.W.	Sw. Arm	R. or S.W.	R. or S.W.	Sw. Arm	Sw. Arm	S.W.

R. Arm = Rigid   Sw. Arm = Swinging Arm   ⊙ = 170 for 1950 machines
S.W. = Spring Wheel   † = 8 with Spring Wheel   * = Up to Engine No. 37560

Lubrication Chart

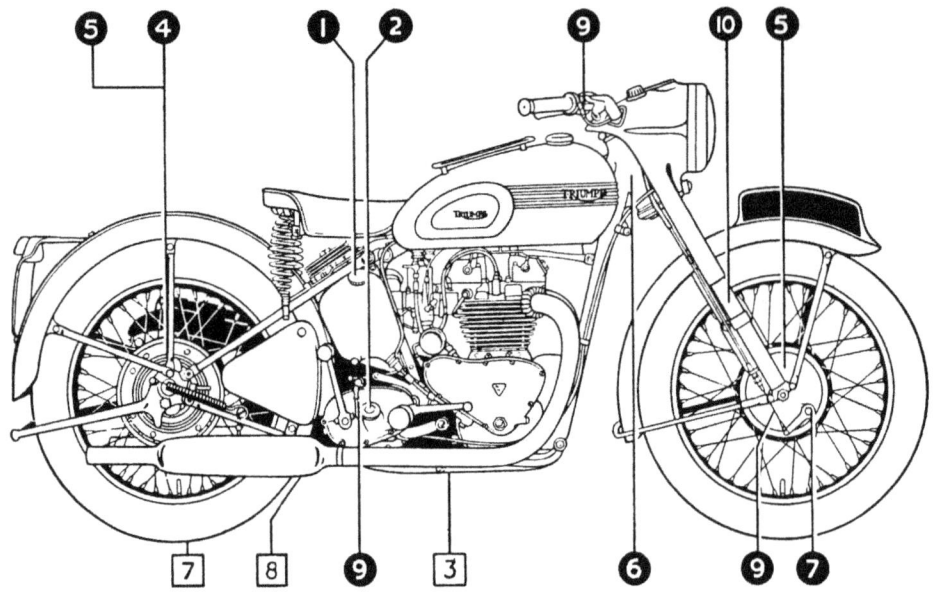

Fig. 75. LUBRICATION CHART

No.	Part.	S.A.E.	No.	Part.	S.A.E.
1	Engine Oil Tank	20 or 30	7	Brake Cam Spindle	Grease
2	Gearbox	50	8	Footbrake Pedal Spindle	Grease
3	Primary Chaincase	20	9	Exposed Cables	20
4	Spring Wheel	Grease	10	Fork (Hydraulic)	20
5	Wheel Hubs	Grease		OIL-CAN LUBRICATION	
6	Steering Head	Grease		All Brake Rod Joints and Pins	20

Lubrication Chart

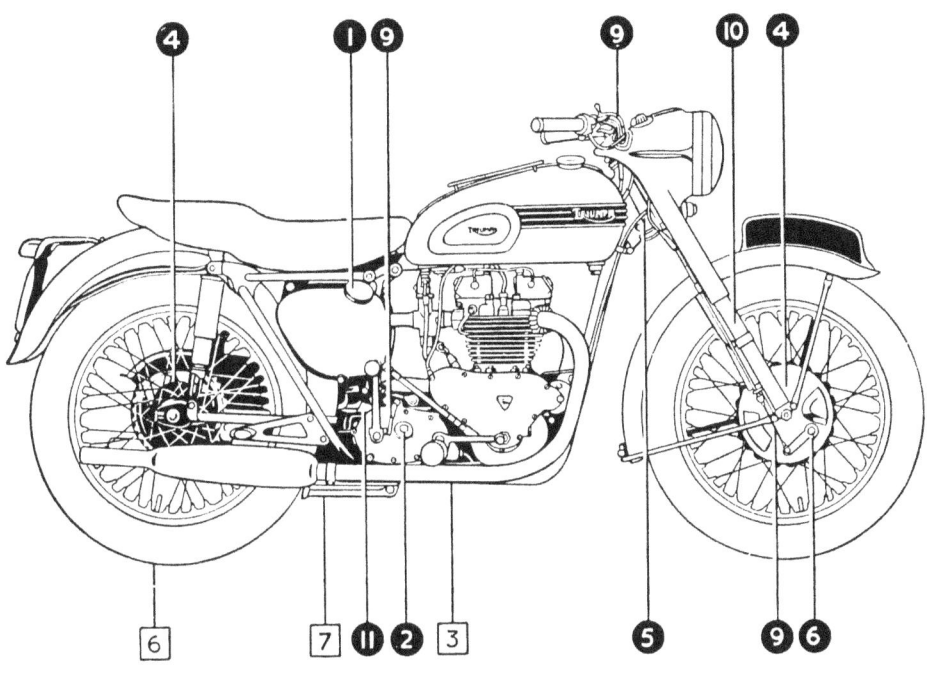

Fig. 76. LUBRICATION CHART

No.	Part.	S.A.E.	No.	Part.	S.A.E.
1	Engine Oil Tank	20 or 30	7	Footbrake Pedal Spindle	Grease
2	Gearbox	50	8	Exposed Cables	20
3	Primary Chaincase	20	9	Fork (Hydraulic)	20
4	Wheel Hubs	Grease	10	Swinging Fork Spindle	Grease
5	Steering Head	Grease		OIL-CAN LUBRICATION All Brake Rod Joints and Pins	
6	Brake Cam Spindle	Grease			

RECOMMENDED LUBRICANTS

UNITED KINGDOM

UNIT	MOBIL	B.P.	WAKEFIELD	ESSO	REGENT	SHELL
Engine—Summer	Mobiloil A	Energol SAE.30	Castrol XL	Essolube 30	Havoline SAE.30	Shell X-100 30
Winter	Mobiloil Arctic	Energol SAE.20	Castrolite	Essolube 20	Havoline SAE.20W	Shell X-100 20-20W
Gearbox	Mobiloil D	Energol SAE.50	Castrol Grand Prix	Essolube 50	Havoline SAE.50	Shell X-100 50
Primary Chaincase ...	Mobiloil Arctic	Energol SAE.20	Castrolite	Essolube 20	Havoline SAE.20W	Shell X-100 20-20W
Telescopic Fork—Summer ...	Mobiloil A	Energol SAE.30	Castrol XL	Essolube 30	Havoline SAE.30	Shell X-100 30
Winter	Mobiloil Arctic	Energol SAE.20	Castrolite	Essolube 20	Havoline SAE.20W	Shell X-100 20-20W
Wheel Bearings	Mobilgrease M.P.	Energrease L2	Castrolease L.M.	Multipurpose Grease H	Marfak Multipurpose 2	Shell Retinax A
Swinging Fork						
Easing Rusted Parts ...	Mobil Spring Oil	Energol Penetrating Oil	Castrol Penetrating Oil	Esso Penetrating Oil	Graphited Penetrating Oil	Shell Donax P

RECOMMENDED LUBRICANTS

OVERSEAS

UNIT	MOBIL	B.P.	WAKEFIELD	ESSO	CALTEX	SHELL
Engine—Above 90°F. 32°—90°F. Below 32°F.	Mobiloil AF Mobiloil A Mobiloil Arctic	Energol SAE.40 Energol SAE.30 Energol SAE.20W	Castrol XXL Castrol XL Castrolite	Essolube 40 Essolube 30 Essolube 20	Caltex SAE.40 Caltex SAE.30 Caltex SAE.20W	Shell X-100 40 Shell X-100 30 Shell X-100 20-20W
Gearbox	Mobiloil D	Energol SAE.50	Castrol Grand Prix	Essolube 50	Caltex SAE.50	Shell X-100 50
Primary Chaincase	Mobiloil Arctic	Energol SAE.20W	Castrolite	Essolube 20	Caltex SAE.20W	Shell X-100 20-20W
Telescopic Fork Above 90°F. 60°—90°F. Below 60°F.	Mobiloil D Mobiloil A Mobiloil Arctic	Energol SAE.50 Energol SAE.30 Energol SAE.20	Castrol Grand Prix Castrol XL Castrolite	Essolube 50 Essolube 30 Essolube 20	Caltex SAE.50 Caltex SAE.30 Caltex SAE.20W	Shell X-100 50 Shell X-100 30 Shell X-100 20-20W
Wheel Bearings, Swinging Forks, Steering Races	Mobilgrease M.P.	Energrease L2	Castrolease L.M.	Multipurpose Grease H	Marfak Multipurpose 2	Shell Retinax A
Easing Rusted Parts	Mobil Spring Oil	Energol Penetrating Oil	Castrol Penetrating Oil	Esso Penetrating Oil	Caltex Penetrating Oil	Shell Donax P

FAULT FINDING

The following paragraphs have been drawn up to enable the rider to diagnose trouble which may arise during normal service. For each failure, the faults and antidotes are arranged in order or probability. In each case the rider should always look for the obvious, such as no petrol, oil, controls incorrectly set, cut-out wire shorting, and, before searching for an "A.C." ignition fault, always check over all electrical connections and clean and tighten if necessary; then follow with the process of elimination.

ENGINE WILL NOT START

Lack of Fuel	Tank empty, obstruction in Petrol Pipes or Tank Filters choked.
Excessive Flooding	Dirt under Float Needle Seating (See Page 150).
Oiled up or fouled, Sparking Plug ...	Remove, clean off carbon and wash in petrol. Allow to dry.
Engine Valve stuck open	See Page 46 for Valve Removal.
Exhaust Valve seatings burned	See Page 46 for Valve Removal.
Magneto Cut-out shorting	Disconnect Terminal at Magneto and check spark at Plug.
No Spark at Plugs (Coil ignition) ...	See Page 173.
Contact Points dirty	Clean with Carborundum Stone, wash with Petrol and re-gap.
Incorrect Contact Point Gap	Re-gap to 0.012"-0.015" (Magneto) 0.014"-0.016" (Coil) (0.3-0.4 mm.) " (0.36-0.40 mm.) ,,
Contact Breaker Arm Sticking	Remove Arm and clean Pivot with fine emery, grease lightly and replace Arm. **Check gap.**
H.T. Collector shorting to body ...	Remove Pick-ups and thoroughly clean; replace if cracked or damaged.
Condensation on Sparking Plugs	Remove Plugs and heat up.

204

FAULT FINDING

ENGINE STOPS

No Petrol or Fuel obstruction	Check Fuel in Tank. Supply at Carburetter if no supply. Remove Pipes and Tank Filters if necessary.
Choked Main Jet	See Page 150.
Water on H.T. Leads, Pick-ups or Sparking Plug	Dry Ignition System.
Water in Float Chamber	Remove Carburetter and clean out.
Vent Hole in Petrol Tank Filler Cap choked ...	Clean out Vent Hole.
Battery lead off (Coil)	Re-connect.

ENGINE MISFIRES

Defective or oiled Sparking Plug	Clean and test Plugs.
Water fouling Main Jet	Clean Carburetter.
Incorrect Contact Breaker Gap	Check and adjust to 0.012"-0.015" (Magneto) 0.014"-0.016" (Coil) (0.30-0.40 mm.) ,, (0.36-0.40 mm.) ,,
Contact Points burned and arcing	Remove Points and true with a Carborundum Stone. Replace and re-gap; change Condenser if trouble persists. This fault can be caused by continuous running in the "EMG" position (Coil).
Weak or broken Valve Spring	See Page 46 for Replacement.
Partial obstruction of Petrol Supply	Clean out Carburetter and check Petrol supply at Carburetter end.
Slow Running Orifice choked	See Page 150.
H.T. Cable perished and shorting to frame ...	Replace H.T. Cable.
Sparking Plug insulation cracked	Replace Sparking Plug.
Condenser failing	See Page 173.
H.T. Cable on Coil faulty (Coil ignition) ...	Replace.

FAULT FINDING

LOSS OF POWER

Faulty Sparking Plugs	Change.
Incorrect Tappet adjustment	See Page 36.
Lack of Lubrication	See that Oil Indicator Button is working (See Page 28). Check Supply in Oil Tank.
Weak or broken Valve Spring	Remove Cylinder Head (See Page 38).
Sticky Valve	Remove Cylinder Head (See Page 38).
Valves not seating	See Page 38.
Broken or gummed up Piston Ring	See Page 46.
Brakes binding	Place Machine on the Stands and re-adjust Brakes.
Engine requires Decarbonising	See Page 37.
Head Gasket blowing	Change Gasket.
Air Filter choked	Remove, wash in Petrol, re-oil and replace (See Page 153).
Dirty Carburetter	Remove and Clean.

ENGINE OVERHEATS

Lack of Lubrication	Check supply of Oil, see that the Indicator Button is operating when the engine is running; if not, refer to Page 28. Ensure that the correct Oil is used.
Faulty Sparking Plugs	Can cause pre-ignition; change and test.
Engine requires Decarbonising	See Page 37.
Ignition Timing too late	Check Timing (See Pages 67 and 68).
Exhaust Valve burned, or pitted Valve Seats	See Page 38.
Silencer choked	Remove and clean in a solution of caustic soda.
Piston Ring worn or seized in Piston Groove	Dismantle Engine, See Page 42.
Weak Mixture	Partly choked Jet, worn Throttle Slide, check by closing Air Lever.

ENGINE REVOLUTIONS PER MINUTE

M.P.H.	4.4	4.57	4.78	5.0	5.24	5.5	5.7	5.8	6.0	6.25	6.5	6.9	7.06	7.14	7.5	8.0	8.85	9.8	10.6	11.58	12.2	13.9	14.3	15.25	16.0	17.8	18.85
20	1144	1188	1244	1300	1364	1428	1480	1508	1560	1624	1688	1796	1836	1856	1948	2080	2300	2548	2756	3012	3172	3612	3720	3964	4160	4628	4900
25	1430	1485	1555	1625	1705	1785	1850	1885	1950	2030	2110	2245	2295	2320	2435	2600	2875	3185	3445	3765	3965	4515	4650	4955	5200	5785	6125
30	1716	1782	1866	1950	2046	2142	2220	2262	2340	2435	2532	2694	2754	2784	2922	3120	3450	3822	4134	4518	4758	5418	5605	5946	6240	6942	—
35	2002	2079	2177	2275	2387	2499	2590	2639	2730	2842	2954	3143	3213	3248	3409	3640	4025	4459	4823	4271	5551	6321	6510	6937	—	—	—
40	2288	2376	2488	2600	2728	2856	2960	3016	3120	3248	3376	3592	3672	3712	3896	4160	4600	5096	5512	6024	6344						
45	2574	2673	2799	2925	3069	3213	3330	3393	3510	3554	3798	4041	4131	4176	4383	4680	5175	5733	6201	6777	7137						
50	2860	2970	3110	3250	3410	3570	3700	3770	3900	4060	4220	4490	4590	4640	4870	5200	5750	6370	6890								
55	3146	3267	3421	3575	3751	3927	4070	4147	4290	4466	4642	4939	5049	5104	5357	5720	6325	7007									
60	3432	3564	3732	3900	4092	4284	4440	4524	4680	4872	5064	5388	5508	5568	5844	6240	6900										
70	4004	4158	4354	4550	4774	4998	5180	5278	5460	5684	5908	6286	6426	6496	6331	6760											
80	4576	4752	4976	5200	5456	5712	5920	6032	6240	6496	6752	7184	7344	7424													
90	5148	5346	5598	5850	6138	6426	6660	6786	7020	7308																	
100	5720	5940	6220	6500	6820	7140	7400	7540																			
110	6292	6534	6842	7150	7502	7854																					

NOTE.—Engine R-P-M are calculated in conjunction with 3.50 × 19 Rear tyre equipment—780 R-P-Mile—and will deviate slightly from above figures for models not so equipped
4.00 × 18 Rear Tyre 785 R-P-Mile.   3.25 × 19 Rear Tyre 793 R-P-Mile.   4.00 × 19 Rear Tyre 756 R-P-Mile

GEAR RATIOS

GEARS	STANDARD RATIO				WIDE RATIO				CLOSE RATIO			
Engine Sprocket	Top	3rd	2nd	1st	Top	3rd	2nd	1st	Top	3rd	2nd	1st
17	6.46	7.7	10.94	15.8	6.46	9.22	14.30	18.85	6.46	7.06	8.42	11.00
18	6.10	7.28	10.32	14.9	6.10	8.70	13.50	17.80	6.10	6.66	7.95	10.40
19	5.80	6.9	9.8	14.15	5.80	8.25	12.80	16.85	5.80	6.32	7.54	9.84
20	5.50	6.55	9.3	13.4	5.50	7.84	12.18	16.0	5.50	6.00	7.15	9.35
21	5.24	6.24	8.85	12.8	5.24	7.46	11.58	15.25	5.24	5.72	6.81	8.90
22	5.00	5.95	8.45	12.2	5.00	7.13	11.05	14.55	5.00	5.45	6.50	8.50
23	4.78	5.69	8.09	11.69	4.78	6.82	10.60	13.90	4.78	5.23	6.23	8.12
24	4.57	5.45	7.75	11.2	4.57	6.54	10.14	13.35	4.57	5.00	5.96	7.78
25	4.40	5.24	7.45	10.75	4.40	6.26	9.73	12.80	4.40	4.80	5.73	7.46
Gearbox Reduction	1.0	1.19	1.69	2.44	1.00	1.425	2.21	2.915	1.00	1.09	1.30	1.695

ILLUSTRATION INDEX

Fig.		Page
1	Control layout	16
2	Petrol tap positions	21
3	Lubrication diagram	26
4	Oil pump	27
5	Oil release valve and indicator	28
6	Crankcase assembly	34
7	Crankshaft assembly	34
8	Adjusting the tappets	36
9	Engine in vice	42
10	Camwheel removal and replacement tool (Z89)	43
11	Removing the camwheel	44
12	Removing the crankshaft pinion	45
13	Crankshaft pinion removal tool (Z60)	45
14	Assembling the tappet block	48
15/16	Taper faced ring position	50
17	Checking connecting rod bolt stretch	54
18	Replacing the camwheel	56
19	Position of timing pinion in relation to camwheels and crankshaft pinion	57
20	Timing diagrams	58
21	Fitting the cylinder barrel	59
22	Magneto in timing position	67
23	Distributor, in timing position	69
24	Gearbox (Component parts)	72
25	Kickstarter return spring and spindle	77
26	Gearbox casing in vice	79
27	Clutch and shock absorber	84
28	Removal of clutch nuts	85
29	Method of removing shock absorber rubbers	86
30	View of clutch showing rubber inserts in position	87
31	Use of clutch extractor and locking tool	88
32	Drive shaft adaptor (Z90)	89
33	Clutch locking tool	89
34	Gearbox in position (5T & 6T)	93
35	Gearbox in position (T100 & T110)	94
36	Chains	96
37/38	Rivet Extractors	97
39	Testing the adjustment of the steering head races	99
40	Telescopic fork	100

ILLUSTRATION INDEX

Fig.		Page
41	Aligning the front fork	104
42	Adjusting the brakes	108
43	Front wheel (5T, 6T, TR5)	110
44	Front wheel (T100 & T110)	112
45	Correct alignment of front wheel in forks	115
46	Rear wheel (5T, 6T, TR5)	117
47	Stud on rear brake anchor plate which must be located in rear fork channel	120
48	Rear wheel (T100 & T110)	122
49	Removing wheel from S/A frame	124
50	Quickly detachable rear wheel (T100 & T110)	127
51	Rear mudguard section removed for tyre repair or wheel removed	131
52	Rear spring wheel (Component parts)	132
53	Spring wheel end plate removal	134
54	Rear spring wheel (Sectioned)	135
55	Jig for compressing plunger guide box springs	136
56	Illustration showing the position of the valve if the tyre has crept round the rim	140
57	Girling hydraulic damper unit	143
58	Twistgrip (5T, 6T, T100, T110)	146
59	Twistgrip (TR5)	147
60	Amal carburetter	151
61	Air filter (5T, 6T, T100, T110)	153
62	Air filter (TR5)	154
63	S.U. Carburetter (Component parts)	156
64	S.U. Carburetter (Diagram)	158
65	Dynamo model E3L	162
66	Wiring diagram (T100 & T110)	164
67	Primary chaincase cover removed to show Rotor and Stator	168
68	Wiring diagram (5T & 6T)	169
69	Alternator model RM14	170
70	Distributor model DKX2A with cover removed	171
71	Model 525 stop and tail lamp	175
72	Taking hydrometer readings	178
73	Battery model PU7E/9	179
74	Toolkit	182
75	5T & 6T Lubrication chart	200
76	T100 & T110 Lubrication chart	201

INDEX OF CONTENTS

		Page
A.	A/C Lighting and ignition equipment	167
	Adjusting the brakes	108
	Adjusting the steering head races	98
	Air filter	153
	Aligning the front fork	105
	Alternator	170
	Assembling and installing the front fork (5T, 6T, T100 & T110)	105
	Assembling and installing the front fork (TR5)	106
	Assembling the brake drum and sprocket assembly (Q.D. rear wheel)	129
	Assembling the clutch	90
	Assembling the engine	55
	Assembling the fork pressure tube	103
	Assembling the front brake anchor plate	113
	Assembling the front wheel	114
	Assembling the gearbox	80
	Assembling the Q.D. rear wheel	130
	Assembling the rear brake anchor plate (5T, 6T, TR5)	119
	Assembling the rear brake anchor plate (T100, T110)	125
	Assembling the rear brake anchor plate (Q.D. rear wheel)	129
	Assembling the rear wheel (5T, 6T, TR5)	119
	Assembling the rear wheel (T100, T110)	125
	Assembling the spring wheel	137
B.	Battery	177
C.	Carburetter (Amal)	150
	Carburetter (S.U.)	155
	Chain alterations and repairs	96
	Chain maintenance	95
	Chain rivet extractor	97
	Chains	92
	Changing the fork springs	107
	Changing the oil	30
	Charts (Engine revolutions and Gear ratio)	207
	Cleaning the motorcycle	149
	Clutch and shock absorber unit	83
	Coil	171
	Controls	17
D.	Decarbonising	37
	Dismantling, preparation and assembly of the engine units	46
	Dismantling, preparation and assembly of fork units	103
	Dismantling, preparation and assembly of gearbox units	77
	Dismantling the anchor plate assembly (Q.D. rear wheel)	128
	Dismantling the brake drum assembly (Q.D. rear wheel)	128
	Dismantling the clutch	83
	Dismantling the engine	42
	Dismantling the fork pressure tube assembly	102
	Dismantling the front brake anchor plate	111
	Dismantling the front wheel	109
	Dismantling the gearbox	76
	Dismantling the Q.D. rear wheel	128

INDEX OF CONTENTS

		Page
	Dismantling the rear brake anchor plate (5T, 6T, TR5)	118
	Dismantling the rear brake anchor plate (T100 & T110)	123
	Dismantling the rear wheel (5T, 6T, TR5)	118
	Dismantling the rear wheel (T100 & T110)	123
	Dismantling the spring wheel	134
	Distributor	171
	Dynamo	163
E.	Electrical equipment	163
	Engine (Description)	33
	Exhaust camshaft timing	64
F.	Fault finding (A/C ignition)	173
	Fault finding (General)	204
	Fitting a sidecar	148
	Fitting the front wheel to the fork	114
	Fitting the Q.D. rear wheel to the frame	130
	Fitting the rear wheel to the frame (5T, 6T, TR5)	120
	Fitting the rear wheel to the frame (T100, T110)	126
	Fitting the spring wheel to the frame	138
	Frame	142
	Front wheel	109
G.	Gearbox	71
	Girling suspension damper units	142
H.	Headlamp and top nacelle unit	176
	Horns	179
I.	Ignition timing (Coil)	68
	Ignition timing (Magneto)	67
	Inlet camshaft timing	65
	Inspection and replacement of worn parts (Front wheel)	111
	Inspection and replacement of worn parts (Q.D. rear wheel)	128
	Inspection and replacement of worn parts (Rear wheel 5T, 6T, TR5)	118
	Inspection and replacement of worn parts (Rear wheel T100, T110)	124
	Installing the engine (5T, 6T, TR5)	61
	Installing the engine (T100, T110)	62
	Installing the gearbox (5T, 6T, TR5)	81
	Installing the gearbox (T100, T110)	82
J.	Joint gaskets	152
L.	Lamps	174
	Lubrication maintenance	25
	Lubrication system	25
M.	Magneto	165
O.	Oil pump	27
	Oil release valve and indicator	28
P.	Petrol tap adjustment	148
	Primary chain adjustment (5T, 6T, TR5)	92
	Primary chain adjustment (T100, T110)	94
	Proprietary fittings (Addresses)	5
R.	Racing carburetter settings	152
	Racing ignition timing	66
	Racing valve timing	64

INDEX OF CONTENTS

		Page
	Rear chain adjustment (5T, 6T, TR5)	93
	Rear chain adjustment (T100, T110)	95
	Rear wheel (Quickly Detachable)	126
	Rear wheel (Rigid frame)	116
	Rear wheel (Swinging fork frame)	121
	Recommended lubricants	202
	Removing the brake drum and sprocket (Q.D. rear wheel)	128
	Removing the engine from the frame (5T, 6T, TR5)	40
	Removing the engine from the frame (T100, T110)	41
	Removing the front fork from the frame	99
	Removing the front wheel from the forks	109
	Removing the gearbox from the frame (5T, 6T)	74
	Removing the gearbox from the frame (TR5)	75
	Removing the gearbox from the frame (T100 & T110)	75
	Removing the Q.D. rear wheel from the frame	126
	Removing the rear wheel from the frame (5T, 6T)	116
	Removing the rear wheel from the frame (T100 & T110)	121
	Removing the spring wheel from the frame	131
	Replacing the brake drum and sprocket in the frame (Q.D. rear wheel)	129
	Routine maintenance	31
	Running-in	23
S.	Service arrangements	4
	Sparking plugs	180
	Speedometer drive	92
	Spring wheel Mk. 2	131
	Starting the engine (Amal)	20
	Starting the engine (S.U.)	22
	Swinging fork	142
	SUPPLEMENTARY INSTRUCTIONS	184
	Fitting a sidecar	185
	Monobloc carburetter	186
	T.110 instructions	187
	3T de luxe	188
	Spring wheel Mk. 1	194
T.	Tachometer drive	92
	Taking over the machine	20
	Tappet adjustment	36
	Technical data 5T	6
	Technical data 6T	8
	Technical data TR5	10
	Technical data T100	12
	Technical data T110	14
	Telescopic fork	98
	Timing the engine	64
	Toolkit	183
	Twistgrip control	145
	Tyres	139
V.	Valve timing record table	66
W.	Wheels	108

Interesting British Tables

TYRE PRESSURES

18-lb. sq. in.	1.26 Kg. sq. c.m.
20-lb. ,,	1.40 ,,
22-lb. ,,	1.54 ,,
24-lb. ,,	1.68 ,,
26-lb. ,,	1.82 ,,
28-lb. ,,	1.96 ,,
30-lb. ,,	2.10 ,,
32-lb. ,,	2.25 ,,
36-lb. ,,	2.53 ,,

SQUARE AND CUBIC MEASURES

1 sq. cm.	.155 sq. in.
1 sq. metre	10.76 sq. ft.
1 hectare	2.47 acres
259 hectares	1 sq. mile
1 cu. c.m.	.061 cu. in.
16 387 c.c.	1 cu. in.

VOLUME

.56 Litre	1 pint
1 Litre	1.76 pints
4.45 Litres	1 gallon
5 Litres	1.1 gallon
20 Litres	4½ gallons
50 Litres	11 gallons
200 Litres	44 gallons

TEMPERATURE

0 deg. C.	32 deg. F.
10 ,,	50 ,,
15.6 ,,	60 ,,
21 ,,	70 ,,
26.7 ,,	80 ,,
32 ,,	90 ,,
37.8 ,,	100 ,,
49 ,,	120 ,,
100 ,,	212 ,,

TIME — SPEED TABLE — OVER ONE MILE

Time per Mile (m. s.)	Speed m.p.h.	Speed k.p.h.	Time per Mile (m. s.)	Speed m.p.h.	Speed k.p.h.	Time per Mile (m. s.)	Speed m.p.h.	Speed k.p.h.
0 24	150.00	241.40	1 6	54.54	87.77	1 46	33.96	54.65
0 26	138.46	222.82	1 8	52.94	85.20	1 48	33.33	53.64
0 28	128.57	206.91	1 10	51.43	82.77	1 50	32.72	42.65
0 30	120.00	193.12	1 12	50.00	80.46	1 52	32.14	41.72
0 32	112.50	181.05	1 14	48.65	78.29	1 54	31.58	50.82
0 34	105.88	170.39	1 16	47.37	76.23	1 56	31.03	49.93
0 36	100.00	160.93	1 18	46.15	74.27	1 58	30.50	49.08
0 38	94.74	152.45	1 20	45.00	72.42	2 0	30.00	48.28
0 40	90.00	144.84	1 22	43.90	70.65	2 5	28.80	46.35
0 42	85.71	137.93	1 24	42.86	68.96	2 10	27.69	44.56
0 44	81.81	131.66	1 26	41.86	67.36	2 15	26.66	42.90
0 46	78.26	125.94	1 28	40.91	65.84	2 20	25.71	41.37
0 48	75.00	120.70	1 30	40.00	64.37	2 25	24.83	39.96
0 50	72.00	115.87	1 32	39.13	62.97	2 30	24.00	38.62
0 52	69.23	111.41	1 34	38.29	61.62	2 35	23.32	37.37
0 54	66.66	107.28	1 36	37.54	60.35	2 40	22.50	36.21
0 56	64.28	103.45	1 38	36.73	59.11	2 45	21.81	35.10
0 58	62.07	99.89	1 40	36.00	57.93	2 50	21.17	34.07
1 0	60.00	96.56	1 42	35.29	56.79	2 55	20.57	33.10
1 2	58.06	93.44	1 44	34.61	55.70	3 0	20.00	32.18
1 4	56.25	90.52						

Note.—Comparative Distances in Miles and Kilometres may also be found by this table, *e.g.* 60.00 miles equal 96.56 kilometres.

VELOCEPRESS MANUALS – MOTORCYCLE BY MAKE

AJS 1932-1948 SINGLES & TWINS 250cc THRU 1000cc (BOOK OF)
AJS 1945-1960 SINGLES 350cc & 500cc MODELS 16 & 18 (BOOK OF)
AJS 1955-1965 SINGLES 350cc & 500cc (BOOK OF)
AJS 1957-1966 FACTORY WSM - ALL SINGLES & TWINS
ARIEL UP TO 1932 (BOOK OF)
ARIEL 1932-1939 PREWAR MODELS (BOOK OF)
ARIEL 1933-1951 (WORKSHOP MANUAL)
ARIEL 1939-1960 4 STROKE SINGLES (BOOK OF)
ARIEL 1958-1964 LEADER & ARROW FACTORY WSM & PARTS LIST
ARIEL 1958-1964 LEADER & ARROW (BOOK OF)
BMW R26 R27 (1956-1967) FACTORY WORKSHOP MANUAL
BMW R50 R50S R60 R69S (1955-1969) FACTORY WORKSHOP MANUAL
BRIDGESTONE 90 SERIES FACTORY WSM & PARTS CATALOGUE
BRIDGESTONE 175 SERIES FACTORY WSM & PARTS CATALOGUE
BRIDGESTONE 350 SERIES FACTORY WSM & PARTS CATALOGUES
BSA SERVICE SHEETS MASTER CATALOGUE ALL MODELS 1945-1967
BSA BANTAM D1 TO D7 1948-1966 FACTORY SERVICE SHEETS MANUAL
BSA BANTAM ALL MODELS FROM 1948 ONWARDS (BOOK OF)
BSA BANTAM D14 FACTORY SERVICE MANUAL
BSA DANDY FACTORY WORKSHOP MANUAL (COMPILATION)
BSA SINGLES & V-TWINS UP TO 1926 inc. 1927 SUPPLEMENT (BOOK OF)
BSA SINGLES & V-TWINS UP TO 1930 (BOOK OF)
BSA SINGLES & V-TWINS UP TO 1935 (BOOK OF)
BSA SINGLES & V-TWINS 1936-1939 (BOOK OF)
BSA C10, C11 & C12 1945-1958 FACTORY SERVICE SHEETS MANUAL
BSA OHV & SV SINGLES 250-600cc 1945-1959 (BOOK OF)
BSA C15 & B40 1958-1967 FACTORY SERVICE SHEETS MANUAL
BSA OHV & SV SINGLES 250cc (ONLY) 1954-1970 (BOOK OF)
BSA B31, B32, B33 & B34 1945-60 FACTORY SERVICE SHEETS MANUAL
BSA OHV SINGLES 350 & 500cc 1955-1967 (BOOK OF)
BSA M20, M21 & M33 1945-1963 FACTORY SERVICE SHEETS MANUAL
BSA TWINS A7 & A10 1948-1962 FACTORY SERVICE SHEETS MANUAL
BSA TWINS A7 & A10 1948-1962 (BOOK OF)
BSA TWINS A50 & A65 1962-1965 FACTORY WORKSHOP MANUAL
BSA TWINS A50 & A65 1962-1969 (SECOND BOOK OF)
DOUGLAS 1929-1939 PREWAR ALL MODELS (BOOK OF)
DOUGLAS 1948-1957 POSTWAR ALL MODELS FACTORY SHOP MANUAL
DUCATI 160cc, 250cc & 350cc OHC SINGLES FACTORY SHOP MANUAL
HONDA 50cc ALL MODELS UP TO 1970 INC MONKEY & TRAIL (BOOK OF)
HONDA 90cc ALL MODELS UP TO 1966 (BOOK OF)
HONDA TWINS & SINGLES 50cc THRU 305cc 1960-1966 (BOOK OF)
HONDA TWINS ALL MODELS 125cc THRU 450cc UP TO 1968 (BOOK OF)
HONDA C100 50cc SUPER CUB O.H.C. 1959-1962 FACTORY WSM
HONDA C110 50cc SPORT CUB O.H.C. 1960-1962 FACTORY WSM
HONDA 50-65-70-90cc O.H.C. SINGLES 1959-1983 FACTORY WSM
HONDA 100-125cc SINGLES CB/CD/CL/SL/TL 1970-1984 FACTORY WSM
HONDA 125-150cc TWINS C/CS/CB/CA 1959-1966 FACTORY WSM
HONDA 125-160-175-200cc TWINS 1965-1978 WORKSHOP MANUAL
HONDA 250-305cc TWINS C/CS/CB 1961-1968 FACTORY WSM
HOHDA 250-350cc TWINS CB/CL/SL 1968-1973 FACTORY WSM
HONDA 250-360cc TWINS CB/CL/CJ 1974-1977 FACTORY WSM
HONDA 350F & 400F 4-CYLINDER 1972-1977 FACTORY WSM
HONDA 450cc TWINS CB/CL 1965-1974 K0 TO K7 WORKSHOP MANUAL
HONDA 500cc & 550cc 4-CYL 1971-1978 FACTORY WORKSHOP MANUAL
HONDA 750cc SHOC 4-CYL 1969-1978 K0~K8 WORKSHOP MANUAL
INDIAN PONYBIKE, BOY RACER & PAPOOSE ILL PARTS LIST & SALES LIT
J.A.P. ENGINES 1927-1952 & MOTORCYCLES 1934-1952 (BOOK OF)
MATCHLESS 1931-1939 ALL MODELS 250cc THRU 990cc (BOOK OF)
MATCHLESS 1945-1956 350 & 500cc SINGLES (BOOK OF)
MATCHLESS 1955-1966 350 & 500cc SINGLES (BOOK OF)
MATCHLESS 1957-1966 FACTORY WSM - ALL SINGLES & TWINS
NEW IMPERIAL ALL SV & OHV FROM 1935 ONWARDS (BOOK OF)
NORTON 1932-1939 PREWAR MODELS (BOOK OF)
NORTON 1932-1947 (BOOK OF)
NORTON 1938-1956 (BOOK OF)
NORTON 1945-1963 MODELS 16H, Big4, ES2, 19 & 50 WSM'S & PARTS
NORTON 1955-1963 MODELS 19, 50 & ES2 (BOOK OF)
NORTON 1948-1970 DOMINATOR TWINS FACTORY WSM'S & PARTS
NORTON 1955-1965 DOMINATOR TWINS (BOOK OF)
NORTON 1960-1970 TWIN CYLINDER FACTORY WORKSHOP MANUAL
NORTON 1970-1975 COMMANDO 850 & 750cc FACTORY WSM
NORTON 1975-1978 MK 3 COMMANDO 850 cc FACTORY WSM
PANTHER 1932-1958 LIGHTWEIGHT MODELS 250 & 350cc (BOOK OF)
PANTHER 1938-1966 HEAVYWEIGHT MODELS 600 & 650cc (BOOK OF)
RALEIGH MOTORCYCLES 1919-1933 (BOOK OF)
ROYAL ENFIELD 1934-1946 SINGLES & V TWINS (BOOK OF)
ROYAL ENFIELD 1937-1953 SINGLES & V TWINS (BOOK OF)
ROYAL ENFIELD 1946-1962 SINGLES (BOOK OF)
ROYAL ENFIELD 1952-1963 700cc TWINS FACTORY WORKSHOP MANUAL
ROYAL ENFIELD 1958-1966 250cc & 350cc SINGLES (SECOND BOOK OF)
ROYAL ENFIELD 1962-1970 INTERCEPTOR WSM'S & PARTS (Compilation)
RUDGE 1933-1939 (BOOK OF)
SACHS 1968-1975 100cc & 125cc ENGINES WSM & M/CYCLE PARTS LIST
SUNBEAM 1928-1939 (BOOK OF)
SUNBEAM 1946-1957 S7 & S8 (BOOK OF)
SUZUKI 50cc & 80cc UP TO 1966 (BOOK OF)
SUZUKI T10 1963-1967 FACTORY WORKSHOP MANUAL
SUZUKI T20 & T200 1965-1969 FACTORY WORKSHOP MANUAL
SUZUKI TWINS 1962 ONWARDS 125-500cc WORKSHOP MANUAL
TRIUMPH 1935-1949 SINGLES & TWINS (BOOK OF)
TRIUMPH 1937-1951 SINGLES & TWINS WORKSHOP MANUAL
TRIUMPH 1945-1955 PRE-UNIT 350cc, 500cc & 650cc TWINS WSM No.1
TRIUMPH 1945-1959 TWINS (BOOK OF)
TRIUMPH 1956-1969 TWINS (BOOK OF)
TRIUMPH 1957-1963 UNIT CONSTRUCTION 350-500cc WSM No.4
TRIUMPH 1963-1974 UNIT CONSTRUCTION 350-500cc FACTORY WSM
TRIUMPH 1956-1962 PRE-UNIT 500cc & 650cc TWINS WSM No.17
TRIUMPH 1963-1970 UNIT CONSTRUCTION 650cc FACTORY WSM
TRIUMPH 1968-1974 TRIDENT T150 & T150V FACTORY WSM
VELOCETTE 1925-1970 ALL SINGLES & TWINS (BOOK OF)
VELOCETTE 1933-1952 MOV-MAC-MSS RIGID FRAME FACTORY WSM
VELOCETTE 1954-1971 MSS-VENOM-THRUXTON-VIPER FACTORY WSM
VILLIERS ENGINE UP TO 1959 INC. 3 WHEELERS (BOOK OF)
VILLIERS ENGINE UP TO 1969 (BOOK OF)
VINCENT 1935-1955 (WORKSHOP MANUAL)
YAMAHA 1961-1967 YA5 & YA6 (WORKSHOP MANUAL & ILL PARTS LIST)
YAMAHA 1971-1972 JT1& JT2 (WORKSHOP MANUAL & ILL PARTS LIST)

VELOCEPRESS TECHNICAL BOOKS – MOTORCYCLE

1930'S BRITISH MOTORCYCLE CARBS & ELEC COMPONENTS (BOOK OF)
1930'S BRITISH MOTORCYCLE ENGINES (OVERHAUL & MAINTENANCE)
1930'S BRITISH MOTORCYCLE GEARBOXES & CLUTCHES (BOOK OF)
CATALOG OF BRITISH MOTORCYCLES (1951 MODELS)
LUCAS ELECTRONICS BRITISH M/CYCLES REPAIR & PARTS (1950-1977)
MOTORCYCLE ENGINEERING (P.E. Irving)
MOTORCYCLE ROAD TESTS 1949-1953 (Motor Cycle Magazine UK)
SPEED AND HOW TO OBTAIN IT (Motor Cycle Magazine UK)
TUNING FOR SPEED (P.E. Irving)
WIPAC (COMBO) MANUAL NUMBER 3 + M/CYCLE & SCOOTER MANUAL

VELOCEPRESS MANUALS – SCOOTERS BY MAKE

BSA SUNBEAM SCOOTER WORKSHOP MANUAL 1959-1965
BSA SUNBEAM SCOOTER 1959-1965 (BOOK OF)
LAMBRETTA 1947-1957 ALL 125 & 150cc MODELS (BOOK OF)
LAMBRETTA 1957-1970 LI & TV MODELS (SECOND BOOK OF)
NSU PRIMA 1956-1964 ALL MODELS (BOOK OF)
TRIUMPH TIGRESS SCOOTER WORKSHOP MANUAL 1959-1965
TRIUMPH TIGRESS SCOOTER (BOOK OF)
VESPA 1951-1961 (BOOK OF)
VESPA 1955-1963 125 & 150cc & GS MODELS (SECOND BOOK OF)
VESPA 1955-1968 GS & SS (BOOK OF)
VESPA 1963-1972 90, 125 & 150cc (THIRD BOOK OF)

VELOCEPRESS MANUALS – MOPEDS & MOTORIZED BICYCLES

CYCLEMOTOR (BOOK OF)
NSU QUICKLY 1953-1963 ALL MODELS (BOOK OF)
PUCH MAXI N & S MAINTENANCE & REPAIR (3 MANUAL COMPILATION)
RALEIGH MOPEDS 1960-1969 (BOOK OF)

VELOCEPRESS MANUALS - THREE WHEELER'S

BOND MINICAR THREE WHEELER 1948-1967 (BOOK OF)
BMW ISETTA FACTORY WORKSHOP MANUAL
BSA THREE WHEELER (BOOK OF)
RELIANT REGAL THREE WHEELER 1952-1973 (BOOK OF)
VINTAGE MORGAN THREE WHEELER (BOOK OF)

VELOCEPRESS MANUALS – AUTOMOBILE BY MAKE

ALFA ROMEO GIULIA WORKSHOP MANUAL 1300 TO 2000cc 1962-1975
ALFA ROMEO GIULIA TECH MANUAL CARBURETED CARS FROM 1962
ALFA ROMEO GIULIA TECH MANUAL FUEL INJECTED CARS FROM 1969
ALFA ROMEO GIULIETTA & GIULIA 750 & 101 SERIES 1955-1965 WSM
AUSTIN-HEALEY SPRITE & MG MIDGET WORKSHOP MANUAL 1958-1971
BMW 600 LIMOUSINE FACTORY WORKSHOP MANUAL
BMW 600 LIMOUSINE OWNERS HAND BOOK & SERVICE MANUAL
BMW 2000 & 2002 1966-1976 WORKSHOP MANUAL
CORVAIR 1960-1969 WORKSHOP MANUAL
CORVETTE V8 1955-1962 WORKSHOP MANUAL
FERRARI HANDBOOK ROAD & RACE CARS (SERVICE/SPECS) 1948-1958
FERRARI 250/GT SERVICE & MAINTENANCE MANUAL 1956-1965
FIAT 500 FACTORY WORKSHOP MANUAL 1957-1973
FIAT 600, 600D & MULTIPLA FACTORY WORKSHOP MANUAL 1955-1969
JAGUAR E-TYPE 3.8 & 4.2 SERIES 1 & 2 WORKSHOP MANUAL
JAGUAR MK 7, 8, 9 & XK120, 140, 150 WORKSHOP MANUAL 1948-1961
METROPOLITAN FACTORY WORKSHOP MANUAL
MGA & MGB OWNERS HANDBOOK & WORKSHOP MANUAL
MG MIDGET TC, TD, TF & TF1500 WORKSHOP MANUAL
PORSCHE 356 1948-1965 WORKSHOP MANUAL
PORSCHE 911 2.0, 2.2, 2.4 LITRE 1964-1973 WORKSHOP MANUAL
PORSCHE 911 2.7, 3.0, 3.2 LITRE 1973-1989 WORKSHOP MANUAL
PORSCHE 912 WORKSHOP MANUAL
PORSCHE 914/4 & 914/6 1.7, 1.8, 2.0 LITRE 1970-1976 WSM
TRIUMPH TR2, TR3, TR4 1953-1965 WORKSHOP MANUAL
VOLKSWAGEN TRANSPORTER, TRUCKS & WAGONS 1950-1979 WSM
VOLVO 1944-1968 ALL MODELS WORKSHOP MANUAL

VELOCEPRESS TECHNICAL BOOKS - AUTOMOBILE

HOW TO BUILD A FIBERGLASS CAR
HOW TO BUILD A RACING CAR
HOW TO RESTORE THE MODEL 'A' FORD
MASERATI OWNER'S HANDBOOK
PERFORMANCE TUNING THE SUNBEAM TIGER
SOUPING THE VOLKSWAGEN
SOLEX CARBURETORS (EMPHASIS ON UK & EU AUTOMOBILES)
SU CARBURETORS (EMPHASIS ON UK AUTOMOBILES)
WEBER CARBURETORS (EMPHASIS ON ALFA & FIAT)

VELOCEPRESS BOOKS & GUIDES - AUTOMOBILE

COMPLETE CATALOG OF JAPANESE MOTOR VEHICLES
FERRARI 308 SERIES BUYER'S AND OWNER'S GUIDE
FERRARI BROCHURES AND SALES LITERATURE 1968-1989
FERRARI SERIAL NUMBERS PART I - ODD NUMBERS TO 21399
FERRARI SERIAL NUMBERS PART II - EVEN NUMBERS TO 1050
HENRY'S FABULOUS MODEL "A" FORD
MASERATI BROCHURES AND SALES LITERATURE

VELOCEPRESS BOOKS – RACING

CARRERA PANAMERICANA - MEXICAN ROAD RACE (BOOK OF)
DIALED IN - THE JAN OPPERMAN STORY
VEDA ORR'S NEW REVISED HOT ROD PICTORIAL

www.ingramcontent.com/pod-product-compliance
Lightning Source LLC
Chambersburg PA
CBHW081419230426
43668CB00016B/2288